Making the Special Schools Ordinary?
Volume 2

This book is in memory of Dale Flynn,
Director of Special Education, Ferndale, Michigan

A practitioner dedicated to the education and well-being
of all children

Making the
Special Schools Ordinary?
Volume 2

Practitioners Changing Special Education

Edited by
Derek Baker
and Keith Bovair

 The Falmer Press

(A member of the Taylor & Francis Group)
New York • Philadelphia • London

UK   The Falmer Press, Rankine Road, Basingstoke, Hants RG24 0PR

USA   The Falmer Press, Taylor & Francis Inc., 1900 Frost Road, Suite 101, Bristol, PA 19007

First published 1990

British Library Cataloguing in Publication Data
Making the special schools ordinary?
   Vol. 2, Practitioners changing special education
   1. Great Britain. Special schools
   I. Baker, Derek   II. Bovair, Keith
   371.90941

   ISBN 1-85000-438-2
   ISBN 1-85000-439-0 pbk

Library of Congress Cataloging-in-Publication Data
(Revised for vol. 2)

Making the special schools ordinary?

   Includes bibliographical references.
   Contents: Vol. 1. Models for the developing special
   schools — v. 2. Practitioners changing special education.
   1. Special education — Great Britain. 2. Special
   education — Great Britain — Curricula. 3. Special
   education — Great Britain — Case studies. I. Baker,
   Derek. II. Bovair, Keith, 1949–
   LC3986.G7M35 1989   371.9′ 0941   89–203179
   ISBN 1–85000–436–6 (v. 1)
   ISBN 1–85000–437–4 (v. 1: pbk.)
   ISBN 1–85000–438–2 (v. 2)
   ISBN 1–85000–439–0 (v. 2: pbk.)

Jacket design by Caroline Archer

Typeset in 11/13 Bembo by
Chapterhouse, The Cloisters, Formby L37 3PX
Printed and Bound in Great Britain by
Redwood Press Limited, Melksham, Wiltshire

Contents

Acknowledgments

We would like to recognize the inspiration given to us by two specific educators. Derek would like to acknowledge Dr Ted Holdaway of the University of Alberta and Keith would like to recognize the influence of Professor William C. Morse of the University of Michigan.

We also would like to thank Neville Hallmark, who organized DES courses that gave us the opportunity to discuss our project with colleagues and to encourage several of them to be contributors to these two volumes.

And last, but not least, our families.

Introduction

Derek Baker

The first volume *Making the Special Schools Ordinary?: Models for Developing Special Schools*, largely explored theory as to how special schools could respond to the many challenges with which they are currently faced. After all, since the Warnock Report and the 1981 Education Act there has been a view that special schools were bound to close, that there would be no place for them in the system. Whilst not setting out to be controversial the theme of the book was that far from disappearing special schools were here to stay, although possibly not in the current form, and that their ideas and strategies were models for developments in many 'ordinary' schools. Indeed, the developments described in volume 1 show how any special school, not merely those in favoured locations or blessed with abundant resources, could continue to develop in order to better meet the needs of the students.

This volume, *Practitioners Changing Special Education*, carries forward the theme of the first volume by presenting case studies of real schools, real developments, not theory, that might be replicated or serve as a model in other settings. No solution can obviously be ideally suited to another school, all situations are unique, but these examples of innovatory practice by fellow professionals show just what can be done. What we demonstrated in volume 1 was that professionals in special schools were not concerned about the rhetoric of 'integration' or theories of 'mainstreaming', their goal was simple, to provide the very best experiences and learning environment for the children with whom they work.

We have attempted to provide readers with a selection of new ideas or new perspectives without the type of in-depth analysis of issues that was a feature of the first volume. If we have succeeded we should have opened a window on what is happening out in the real world, in real schools that are like all the others coping with enormous pressures for change whilst seeking to maintain the quality of educational environment they offer.

I have been involved for many years in exploring the potential of computers as a tool when working with students who experience difficulties in having access to the curriculum, whether they have a physical or learning disability. Many of the issues are essentially the same. Like curricula computers are not generally designed with the disabled in mind. Much time and energy is often spent adapting hardware and software to enable someone with even a minor disability to use it. Even worse though is the attitude that people with disabilities should have different equipment altogether, or 'special education' software. Such attitudes only serve to emphasize differences and create an artificial gap between 'ordinary' and 'special', to add labels that only in fact make the situation worse.

The problem with the education system is that it was not designed with everyone in mind. Just throwing all children into the same school is no solution if the curriculum is not accessible to them all. The authors represented in both volume 1 and 2 are not educational luddites, they do not argue that special schools are the best solution to children's needs and should remain forever. They do not wish to see a segregated system. The issue is the way in which we move from the current system to a better one for the children and in the meantime continue to improve their educational experience.

My experiences outside of the education system, in the 'real world' have only served to strengthen my belief in the value and relevance of what many special schools are now doing. It seems incredible to those not involved just what it is that professionals in special education are faced with. Governments that continually 'move the goalposts' by signalling new directions that are eventually never acted upon, legislation that requires fundamental changes but brings with it no more resources, cuts in staff, a reduction of in-service training, links with 'ordinary' schools, a changing population . . . the list goes on. Managers in business are astonished by what is expected of headteachers in special schools. It is to the eternal credit of all professionals in special education that despite all the changes and pressures the quality and breadth of the curriculum has probably never been greater.

Practitioners Changing Special Education is a resource book of current good practice which examines curriculum and management trends, highlights issues and provides an insight into individual responses. It is deliberately non-theoretical in nature encouraging its use as a reader for practitioners. The authors include classroom teachers, support teachers, advisers, and headteachers from a number of special educational settings.

First Keith Bovair examines the current climate of change in special education. In Section 1, Jim Crawley recounts the experience of a staff anticipating and then experiencing school closure. This is contrasted by Aileen Webber's description of moving a special school to become part of a local comprehensive.

Section 2 concerns curricular issues; Deirdre Leach on teaching in a psychiatric unit, Mike Conquest, Graham Pirt and Mike Wright on recording achievements of pupils, Dr Robert Ashdown and Kathleen Devereux on teaching mathematics to pupils with severe learning difficulties, Mike Swift on designing a teaching machine and Sean McCavera on music therapy.

Section 3 on integration and support, includes David Smith and Patricia Keogh on a decade of support in one school, Dr Peter Avis and Mike Wright on developing a regional resource, Diane Wilson on the integration of a special school, Leslie Rowsell on the development of a special needs support centre, Stan Forster on a unified approach in a multi-disciplinary setting, Andy Redpath and Brian Steedman on classroom support, John V. d'Abbro describing EBD work in Somerset, Dave Stewart on integration through physical education, and Norman Butt describing integration in Cheshire.

In the final section we explore comparative issues, Helen King gives a view of integration from the USA, and Sharon Crean compares outreach projects in the USA and UK.

Despite the focus on what has and is happening in special schools this volume is for all professionals working with children who have special needs, whether they happen to attend a special school or not. The issues raised are universal, the solutions described are not but should provide useful pointers to those seeking to effect change.

It is important to stress that the authors represented in this volume are not, with all due respect, extraordinary. They do not possess unusually large levels either of skills or resources. We do not suggest that other schools merely attempt to import their programmes in total; that would probably be the prelude to failure. Rather these 'case studies' should serve as examples of what is possible, what can go wrong, how that was dealt with, and what are the issues that were faced.

We are not concerned with the relative value of individual solutions, each has its relevance to a particular situation, that is why we present a number of different approaches to common issues. What matters is whether as a result of any changes in organization or focus the quality and relevance of the educational experience has improved or not.

Chapter 1

Special Educators — Special Education: THIS ISN'T KANSAS TOTO!

Keith Bovair

In the film of the Wizard of Oz, we see Dorothy and her pet dog Toto being swept away in their home by the full force of a Mid-Western tornado. When all has settled down, she opens her door and looks upon a world she has never seen before and proclaims, 'This isn't Kansas, Toto!' This may be a feeling that many practitioners in education in Great Britain are feeling at this time. With all the educational initiatives of the 1980s, the end of this educational decade has landed somewhere completely different from where it began.

In the field of special education, the practitioner was heading towards fuller integration of children with the full range of special educational needs (SEN). This has been the current trend encouraged by the Warnock Report on 'Special Educational Needs: Report of the Committee of Enquiry into the Education of Handicapped Children and Young People' (1978) and the Fish Report, 'Equal Opportunities for All?' (1985), and the 1981 Education Act which eliminated the ten categories of handicap, replacing them with the term 'special educational needs'. It also encouraged greater involvement of children with SEN with the ordinary system of education with possible integration of children with SEN into the mainstream. Unfortunately there were several ingredients missing: at a higher level, the planning, the will and most important, the resources, to make it all a reality.

This lack of resourcing has led many practitioners to see the 1981 Act as mere window dressing; a facade. These same practitioners have carried on improving the opportunities for those with SEN, often, not with the help of educational acts, but in spite of them. LEAs and Central Government have allowed the 1981 Act to either be loosely interpreted or ignored.

Unlike the movements in other countries such as Norway, Italy, Denmark and the United States where integration was not only taken on as a philosophy, but something worthy of resourcing, practitioners in Great Britain have instead worked towards the concept in a piecemeal fashion and often in the isolation of their specialist settings, maximizing the minimum resources that have been to hand. This is not to say that all is perfect in the countries mentioned; I personally know many of the initiatives in the United States where individual educational programming had to be bargained for under the weight of possible and sometimes actual litigation.

The 'least restrictive environment' concept which has been part of special educational thinking in the United States for the past twenty years, has just recently been developing in Great Britain. This has been delayed due to many influences which have determined the readiness of ordinary education systems to mesh with special educational systems: industrial action, lack of resourcing, lack of policy, a sense of being overwhelmed by educational initiatives other than special education etc. All of which has led to a slow moving process of obtaining greater access for children with SEN to a wider education and social community.

This slow moving process can be identified by the practitioner who has pointed to the need, the type of resourcing required to remediate a difficulty, the desired setting or changes within a setting for education to take place. All the paperwork gets pushed through and six months later they find themselves not working with the individual child, but chasing the decision makers and the finite resources they possess and protect. This has happened on a large scale. The Warnock Report and the Fish Report identified, to use Fish's phrase, the Way Ahead. I wonder though, if the committees, professionals and colleagues who contributed to these documents are asking, 'Is anybody there?' because the responses to these sources of information have been left to individual LEAs, as stated earlier, to either interpret or ignore and the latter is more prevalent. An unfortunate event, because the practitioners in the field of special education nationwide have been making radical leaps through their inventiveness and flexibility, to provide a 'least restrictive environment' for those children with SEN.

Somewhere, Over the Rainbow

There is now concern over the future outcome of specialist settings and the gains that have been made in areas of curriculum development in SEN in light of the Education Reform Act of 1988, the National Curriculum and the new financial measures such as Local Management of Schools (LMS) and the restrictive funding allocated to local education authorities.

Terminology has appeared in these initiatives which makes the practitioner in special education cautious; the initiatives speak of the ability of each school to offer a modified curriculum and the ability to exempt anyone unable to partake in the National Curriculum. Modifying a curriculum is nothing new to special education or education in general. Every time an educator approaches a subject matter, they try to ensure it is accessible to the pupils in their care. The term that created a cause for concern was the term disapplication which has now been changed to 'exception'.

It appears that the field of special education and education in general has made a major stride — backwards! It has moved from the 'statemented child', to the 'disapplied child', and now to the 'exceptional child'. (Somehow, I do not believe this is what Samuel Kirk has in mind in his book, *Educating Exceptional Children.*)

The assurances from the bodies having oversight of this initiative have stated that this would be the exception rather than the norm and if it does occur, it will be, as implied, in the 'best interest' of the child, and should be sensitively and positively applied according to Section 2.2., paragraph 58 of the DES Circular 6/89. But is it? and will it?

Once doors are created people use them. A door is a two way route (and this will be pointed out to those contesting any exclusion) by which a child can leave or return to the ordinary education system. This will be fine, as long as no one drops the latch.

Doubting Thomas?

Special educators have recently been put in the position of questioning their role in the field of education. They have been involved in reassessing their positions in light of arguments being presented by those who deal theoretically with the field, investigating, researching and reporting on the sociological and psychological influence of the field of special needs and the impact of segregating a population of children identified as having SEN. Grounded by the realism and acknowledging, but not agreeing with, the lack of resources from LEAs and Central Government for children with SEN, special educators still have been managing to take on the role as resource for ordinary school colleagues, offering advice on assessment, intervention, materials, support and teaching. This has not only been passive; special educators have been active in team teaching, course planning, identifying changes in curriculum etc. in ordinary settings, ensuring that children having SEN, remain in the mainstream. Because this process is not an all or nothing process, it allows for the specialist setting to still exist. This creates what I described in the first volume of this book as an affiliation with ordinary education. It can be seen as slow movement for those lobbyists of non-segregation, but it is movement, hopefully towards the same end, without the loss of too many finite resources along the way and the assurance that when a child is integrated, they are truly active, not just an object, in their educational community.

The link work, the shared in-service initiatives, the resource exchanges, the teacher exchanges that have been developing are a credit to the practice of education. Practitioners have worked hard to help realize the aspirations of the children in their care. They must now try to weather a situation brought on by legislation which may encourage exclusion of a population of children with SEN due to the restrictive nature of the 'market force' approach to the 1988 Education Act. Philipa Russell points out:

> The temptation may be very great for schools to take the easy option of modifying a child's curriculum, when with support, he or she could manage to keep up. Referrals to special schools may grow, not only from mainstream schools which may find special needs an expensive option, but from parents who fear that the only reliable resources will be in a special school.
>
> Inevitably the new testing arrangements will introduce an element of competition into classes. Formal teaching will become more significant. Mixed ability teaching — the cornerstone to integration — may seem less attractive.

The opportunities for populations of children with SEN to be 'a part of the ordinary education system, not apart from it', could be at risk as Philipa Russell points out, even though there are assurances in many of the circulars from the DES and the National Curriculum Council contrary to this sentiment. In the market place of education, the continuum of services and access now will have toll booths and those in their specialist settings will need toll fees, or greater bargaining powers to ensure entry into ordinary settings, because every school will be unto themselves and everything will have a price under Local Management of Schools.

Special educators and children with SEN have just gained access to the majority of performances of current trends and developments in education. They have managed to date, to get a seat in the Gods and an occasional lower stall position and have been allowed to attend evening performances. Now, the price of the seats are going up and it may be matinees only if, at first, the practitioners do not wear themselves out in unnecessary self-doubt (they are specialists), disillusionment (they do have a vision) and see their own settings as a safe retreat (they do believe in the right of access and the least restrictive environment).

Testing, Testing, Testing...

In the 1960s and 1970s, there was a plethora of articles and books related to the concept of testing and assessment. A favourite quote of the time was Mercers, who said that testing for IQ was a form of 'institutional racism'. Now the phrasing may not be exactly correct on his part but the sentiment is very clear.

It is interesting that each decade has an ogre. In the 1970s, the antipsychiatry movement was growing (Laing, Szasz, Foucault etc.). Psychiatry was a means of oppressing the individual and anything to do with psychology was a tool to oppress. In relationship to testing (and pertinent at this point in time), this was summed up by Schostok in his observation of the psychometrician. He states:

Psychometricians are pleased to study the individual as a summation of individual differences — a bundle of deviations from population norms. In this way they ignore individuals completely, seeing IQ scores, personality scores, attitude scores — dividing the individual into shreds. Modern schooling is built upon the norm.

Testing and assessment must ensure that their intent is to build steps for children and young persons, to lead to the resources and information which will assist them in their educational travels. They must never be walls which deter, frustrate and negate the worth of the individual. A further sentiment comes from Gould's, *The Mismeasure of Man*:

> The urge to classify people, to rank them according to their supposed gifts and limits, is strong in us. It has always been so, from pre-scientific times when the tools of classification were said to be divine, to our day when numbers are king.
>
> Scientists pride themselves on their objectivity. But science is a social act like any other human activity. The numbers generated by science reflect the surrounding culture. They also reflect the unconscious and very personal prejudices of the scientists themselves.

The overseers of the Education Reform Act and the National Curriculum are looking to raise standards, implying that the previous mode of education, being the comprehensive system, was not delivering a satisfactory 'marketable' commodity. In the quote from Gould, if you replace the word 'scientists' for the word 'education reformists' and 'science' for 'education', we will see a similarity to the present developments in education. If there is over-classification by testing and assessment, which would be an abuse of the supposed ethos of the Education Reform Act, educators could bear witness to an enhancement of an elite and a demoralization of a school population that has just begun to take pride in its worth as individuals. As Jackson and Marsden pointed out in *Education and the Working Class*, 'any form of *nominally academic* selection will in effect be a form of social selection'. Children will be returned to labels (modified, excepted etc.) and statistics.

A case study that points this out is the story of Terry, who at the age of eight, was referred to a school under the old label of Educationally Sub-Normal — Mild, ESN (M). He was tested and assessed and placed 'appropriately' by IQ measurement in the special school. During the early days of observation, testing and assessment, this young man listened and bore witness to conversations that informed him he was 'backward'. Terry's self-image was distorted although he was actually a capable young boy, who fortunately, through his efforts and the advocacy of educators, could at the end of his educational career return to his local community, pass many of the exams that he was almost excluded from by being placed at the special school and he could joke about the term 'backward' when he was asked if the special school made him 'forward'. How many children have been burdened with a poor self-image and how many more to come?

There is a population of adults at this moment in time who bear witness to this concern. They were part of the 11+ examinations and the selective processes that were encouraged in that era.

Famous Amongst Ourselves

Historically, those in special education have been famous amongst themselves. They have been working in the isolation of their settings, creating materials to suit the specific needs of the specific population for whom they were responsible, developing a wealth of knowledge, skills and expertise that was only shared at the occasional conference or course they attended. They felt safe in the security of their settings or programme and because of that they have been their own worst enemies, marginalizing their input into the wider educational setting. They knew what they were about and the impact they were having on those individuals in their care, but were uncertain about the relevance of their work in the ordinary setting.

Fortunately, they may be saved by their flexible nature. They have responded positively to the challenge of opening their settings up as resources and have taken the opportunity to extend opportunities for pupils and themselves to have greater access to ordinary settings and educational initiatives.

It has not been an easy process. They have had an unhealthy identity which has allowed the existence of alienation in their own profession. As stated in volume 1 of this book, they have been seen as either Florence Nightingales or individuals incapable of meeting the rigours of an ordinary system. An early description of how special educators have perceived themselves and have been perceived by others is summed up in Deno's earlier (1970) observation of the field: 'but the Statue of Liberty philosophy still persists among too many special educators. (Give me your defective, defeated and unwanted and I will love and shelter them!)'.

O'Hanlon's (1988) research has discovered that there is an alienation for a special educator that is hard to rise above: it is the view of the watered down teacher. She points out that when pupils are marginalized into special education, so are they. She states:

> School problems experienced by SEN teachers are related to the experience
> of alienation, the restrictions of the existing examination curriculum and
> it's effects on both pupils and teachers; . . .

A personal experience gave me a sense of the view of the watered down teacher. It occurred in the early 1970s when, while on a PGCE course, I volunteered to work at an inner-city comprehensive and to spend some of my time in the remedial department. I was greeted with a curious look from the head of the department who said, 'You are either crazy to want to work in the remedial department, like myself, or, you are on your way out of the profession. Being in the early days of your career, I do hope you are crazy.'

What O'Hanlon's research has given the special educator is a focus point for discussion with their colleagues in the ordinary setting — awareness raising which needs to be invested in more, not less, if we desire integration in a true sense to occur. It must occur in the hearts and minds of all, not just in relocation of the pupils from special settings to ordinary schools.

Although ordinary schools have just gradually been developing a whole school approach to special needs time will tell if these initiatives and personnel will be marginalized because of the inbuilt demands of the Education Reform Act and the implications of the National Curriculum.

The Common Ground

As practitioners, the special educator has been discovering the 'common ground' with their colleagues in ordinary settings in subject areas, pastoral care and administrative concerns. In these, they share knowledge and expertise and create a greater access to schools and communities for those pupils who have been limited by their own learning and mobility difficulties and also limited by the ignorance and (harshly put) the values of the communities where they live. They have put special education on the agenda of the majority of educational initiatives. Therefore, I feel that their challenge for the future is to ensure that what common ground they have gained is not eroded, and that they, as special educators, are not tempted to retreat into the isolation of their settings. A role they can continue to take was described in the 1970s by Deno:

> The special education system is in a unique position to serve as develop-mental capital in an overall effort to upgrade the effectiveness of the total public education effort. It has the motivation and the justification to enter into cooperative competition with regular education, to act as advocate for those children who fall out or are squeezed out of the educational main-stream's sieve-like bottom half. From its retrieval vantage point, special education is in a position to gain unusual insight into what makes children fall out of the modal system. It has opportunity to gain insight into how all children learn as it struggles to help those children who require careful assessment and controlled conditions in order to maximize the probability that learning will occur. The special educator often must help these children structure what most 'normal' children structure for themselves.

(Note: the above does not need to occur in a specialist setting.)

The time is ripe for the special educator to show their professional ability to be creative and flexible. The common ground in the 1980s has been in national initiatives such as Technical and Vocational Educational Initiatives (TVEI) and its Related In-Service (TRIST), Records of Achievement (RA), Royal Society of the Arts (RSA) modules, General Certificate of Secondary Education Courses (GCSE), Certificate in Pre-Vocational Education (CPVE), Information-Technology (IT), etc. They have delved into the subject areas and have worked to design learning experiences that would extend the children's access to a wider curriculum, while individualizing the materials related to it. They have shared knowledge and expertise in social and personal skill courses, behaviour management, testing and assessment (with purpose and sensitivity) and, a very important area, staff interpersonal skills and personal development. In other words, they have begun and continue to collaborate.

The Writing on the Wall?

There will be a few other events they will have to weather as practitioners in special education. They may be encouraged by limited resources to take up entrenched positions, unless, they rise to the challenge that William Cruickshank, a prominent educator in the field of Mental Retardation in the United States, put forward in then late 1950s and re-emphasized recently:

1 It must be recognized that a program of normalization cannot take place overnight. It is more than an administrative decision . . .
2 We must recognize that the concept of normalization leading to an appropriate understanding of least restrictive placement is a total community decision and as such requires total community orientation . . .

> a There must be a total understanding and a positive decision regarding normalization . . . by every member of a School Board.
> b All administrators and supervisors of the school system must have a complete understanding of the program . . .
> c All teachers, school nurses, social workers, psychologists, and whatever other professional staff is utilized within the school(s) must have a thorough understanding both to the psycho-educational characteristics of all types of exceptional children, and also to the concept of normalization and integration of various exceptional children within the ordinary classroom . . .
> d All support personnel in the school system, i.e., secretaries, bus drivers, custodians, and clerks, also need a good orientation to what may be a different type of pupil to appear in the school and on school buses . . .

e   All of the so-called normal pupils in the elementary and secondary schools must have a full orientation to the exceptional child who may be joining their classrooms or their schools . . . (1986)

The question to ask is, 'Can the education system and society in Great Britain take this on: can an ethos that would support such an outline be encouraged at this time?' This will be the challenge for the future. What must be ensured is that there is an on-going dialogue with all concerned about the current issues affecting children with SEN.

Already research in the United States has shown that there has been opposition to mainstreaming by regular educators (Jamieson, 1984; Knoff, 1985). There is a growing reluctance to have children with SEN in ordinary classrooms because of resource stretch, class sizes and, as recently identified, regular educators felt that they have not taken part in the original planning for mainstreaming; previously this reform has been imposed from outside the educators realm (Myles and Simpson, 1989).

Cruickshank (1986) expressed the sentiment that:

There is in the United States at the present time, a serious and appropriate backlash toward the concept of mainstreaming. It is being brought about by parents and teachers who realize that their children are not obtaining what it will take to be as independent in adult life as it is possible to achieve. In large measure this is due to two things; first, general educators are in no way sufficiently prepared by attitude or technical professional orientation to serve the exceptional children in ordinary classrooms, and, second, when decisions have been made, they have been made wholesale in nature and total populations of exceptional children have been integrated on a given date rather than selectively over a period of time.

If this statement is not an isolated sentiment that is growing in the United States, then it is possible that it may be used as one of the many rationales for the exclusion of children with SEN in this country. There is a saying that it takes ten years for an idea to cross the Atlantic. The idea that there is a conservative groundswell against the concept of mainstreaming in the United States which may arrive in Great Britain before the 'ten year limitation' is something to prepare for: It is a ready made, researched rationale which identifies that there is not the support and resources to encourage such an ideology.

Educators in Great Britain have been in the same predicament since the mid-1970s. As special educators, they are caught in the middle of the real paradoxes of: How can the ideology/concept of integration be funded? How can children with SEN have greater access to a wider curriculum and a fuller life? On the cheap or not at all?

I thus return to my premise of ensuring that the common ground educators have gained in education must not be eroded. I reiterate that they have made major strides in opening up avenues for children with SEN to ensure greater access to ordinary educational settings and the wider community. They have delved into the world of micro-electronics and have proved that, by offering a different means of transcribing, children previously limited by their handicapping conditions can now offer insights into their worlds and observations of ours which actually enhance our world (I think of Christopher Nolan's book, *Under the Eye of the Clock*, an autobiography that describes his experiences as a young boy growing up with a disability).

As identified in the current literature on SEN, special educators are establishing their roles as special educators for the future. This role development has often been under a climate of redundancy for their settings and pressure coming from the non-segregationist movement which has been underpinned by various bodies and educational courses. The concepts and principles underlying the non-segregationist movement are correct; they are not unfounded, they are underfunded. Also, unfortunately, there is an intonation that by being a special educator they are the new ogres of the 80s, oppressing a minority of children, acting in their own self-interest. This has created an unnecessary tension in the field of education and a confusion of purpose for the special educator and those whose interests lie in the non-segregationist movement. Exchanges of letters in educational publications (*Times Educational Supplement*, 2–6–89, 2–30–89, etc.) have been pointing to the good to be found on either side of the fence.

In taking all or nothing approaches to special education, we could put everything at risk. The risk is that policy makers will take advantage to simplify our intellectual debates by solid actions — the re-emergence of segregated provision or underfunded, mediocre integration programmes — thus dead-ending all our dreams of a true least restrictive environment.

Educators and those others who are concerned for children with SEN must not take defensive stances in the non-segregationist debate. We need to come to an acceptance that there will be needed for some time to come, a diversity of services that, in their common ground, share resources and ideas that will allow for a greater access to a wider education for children with SEN. There is needed a mind shift at the moment. Much gain can be achieved towards a least restrictive environment by a positive approach and new ways of thinking as many of the chapters in this book will testify. The physical shift is unlikely at the moment because of the limitation of settings and lack of financial investment.

In *Special Education for the 80's* (Gearheart, 1980), Weber has pointed to a position taken by the province of British Columbia.

> What this paper recommends as practice in the schools of British Columbia is a rational and flexible eclecticism in providing for the handicapped, accepting no single theory as a panacea for all needs.

This is a view which should be considered in the current educational climate.

Conclusion

Practitioners in special education have been forced by the realism of the existing practice of education and not by their own convictions to be marginalized along with the children in their care. As current literature in the field has shown, there is a willingness and desire to be a part of the ordinary education system, not apart from it. By working closely with colleagues in all settings (under-5s, primary, secondary, further education, training colleges and universities) educators have just begun to ensure that children who were once isolated from their peers and social and educational communities have the opportunity to take an active role. Now, the question is: What do these educators have to offer the future? In relation to the National Curriculum, special educators are able to add educational elements Pre-Level One in relationship to the expectations of the given subjects of the core curriculum. They are able to shape modules for subject areas that can include the continuum of SEN. They can help sensitize the community to be more accepting of children with SEN by workshops, seminars and, most important, by the visible acceptance of all children within the mainstream. They can continue the joint educational ventures in the numerous educational initiatives and exam programmes (TVEI, GCSE, etc.) with colleagues in the mainstream. They can experiment and research with educational materials to see how they can be accessible to all children (computer software and hardware, course work, etc.). They can clearly identify their own personal training needs and shape appropriate and effective courses. They can avoid being locked in the market place mentality by sharing and exchanging resources, whether they are persons or materials.

These are just a few things the special educator can do. One of the most important things is that they can always learn something new together with their colleagues in the ordinary sector which may offer children opportunities to enhance their well being and quality of life. What everyone can do, and this includes any professional involved with children and young people, is to recognize what Lieberman (1984) has stated in *Preventing Special Education... For Those Who Don't Need It*, that special and ordinary education are contributing to the expansion of special education beyond its presumed focus, which is handicapped children. That the financial cost and human cost, such as blaming the student and stigmatizing him, is outstripping any perceived positive result of the proliferation of special programmes for children with school-based problems. That when a student fails, the system fails. Yet the system persists in the counterproductive activity of seeking student change, while neglecting system change. That the education system is responsible for creating many of its own failures and only it holds the key to preventing these failures. And last, the most efficient, cost-effective, and potentially beneficial approach to problem solving in education is to identify and eliminate counterproductive practices, rather than trying to solve the problems caused by these practices.

Besides having a whole school approach to SEN, there is the great need for the whole authority approach (besides being solely involved in the process of special education, there must be a greater empathy for the practice of it), even a whole nation approach which would take in the above sentiments. Services for SEN would then no longer be seen as an appendage, something that is always added on in the last minute because lobbying had finally pricked a social conscience. The services would be an integral part of the education system.

Special educators must be ready for change, but change that they are in control of, Deno has capsulized Guba and Stufflebeam's observation that: 'Special education can organize and conduct itself as a tool for developing more effective instructional approaches for the hard to teach in regular as well as special education. It can function as a decision context for incremental and innovative change.' And overall, educators may take Lieberman's point that, 'Schools exist for children. Educators must obligate themselves to children, which means forever being at the razor's edge of determining positive, life enhancing practices, and excising negative, destructive ones'.

At this moment in time in Great Britain, it is definitely not Kansas. The special educators must quickly reorientate themselves and instead of lying back and or being blown away by a whirlwind, they must take positive actions to fill the gaps with their professionalism and continue to become special educators par-excellence.

SECTION 1
Choices

Chapter 2

The Integration of the Physically Disabled Pupils at Impington Village College

Aileen Webber

Impington is an 11–18 comprehensive school of around 1,000 pupils, situated in the village of Impington about 3 miles north of Cambridge. Since September 1987, the school has been given additional resources to accommodate pupils with physical disabilities. There are at present twenty-seven physically disabled pupils on roll.

Historical Resumé

The Special School for Physically Disabled Pupils

The provision for physically disabled pupils in Cambridgeshire and adjacent counties was historically predominantly at the Roger Ascham Special School in Cambridge. The school took pupils from 2½–19 years, and included the whole range of intellectual ability from pupils who needed special care, to pupils capable of taking public examinations. In 1980 I applied for the post of 'remedial teacher' — to work with any pupil who had learning difficulties. I was told that my mainstream primary remedial background was completely adequate, as the pupils were 'just like any others, except some of them are in wheelchairs'. This was, in fact, true of many of the pupils who were different only by virtue of being in special education, and by being taught separately from their peers. Others, on the other hand, had Moderate or Severe Learning Difficulties.

Working at the Special School

I was very content at the school, which had a friendly and cosy atmosphere. However, I had a vague sense that such special conditions were creating an artificial situation for many of the pupils which was lacking in stimulus and limiting academically in breadth and depth. For instance, at a special school pupils could not choose between courses, such as drama, art, crafts and humanities, as they would have been able to do at a comprehensive school. They were also only able to mix with other disabled children. I had an unarticulated feeling that the integration was backwards from the start. Subject teachers from the local secondary school would come in to teach the more academically able pupils — but I felt that these pupils were capable of being part of a normal secondary school; not as visitors on a once-a-week basis, but as full members of the college life, both educationally and socially. In 1983 I was involved in taking a group of pupils to the local secondary school for an Activities Week, which demonstrated clearly that practically, intellectually and socially the pupils could fully participate in college life. However, it also served to show that they should be able to belong to the college rather than integrated artificially from outside.

On the other hand, I also had a sense that mainstream schools had their shortcomings and that just to say that a child from a special school could be taught exactly the same curriculum as their contemporaries would not necessarily solve all the problems. I felt that mainstream schools needed to change to fully accommodate special needs pupils already present. Perhaps the presence of pupils with such apparent special needs might help to make schools more flexible. Also, even if a child were to gain 8 GCSEs, would this necessarily prepare them for life? More specifically, would it prepare a child in a wheelchair to cope in a society predominantly organized for the ambulant? However, these issues were only unformulated ideas at this time.

I enjoyed my job and working with the pupils, particularly as by this time I was involved in curriculum development with a multi-disciplinary team of physiotherapists, welfare assistants, speech therapists, school nurse, occupational therapist and teachers. We attempted to address the question:

> What do we want the pupils to be able to do by the time they leave school?
> — and how should the school organize this learning?

We produced a framework of experiences and skills which later became the basis of a course which is now offered at Impington.

At around this time, four teachers from the school attended an Open University Course — E241, entitled: 'Special Needs in Education'. This course helped to crystallize what I had suspected about the dilemmas of special education versus mainstream education and the issues of integration and change in mainstream schools.

Special School Under Threat of Closure

When the pupils, parents and staff of the Roger Ascham School learnt that the school was to be closed and units were to be built attached to separate mainstream schools, there was obviously uncertainty and anxiety.

For example, one twelve year old pupil, Sue, was quoted when she wrote to Prince Charles, as saying:

> I am very upset about the closure. I have been at the school for 7 years and I
> will carry on going there if I can help it (*Cambridge Evening News*, 1984).

It was inevitable that there would be a period of people feeling very unsettled. The closure of any school creates strong emotions, but this closure was necessarily in the absence of any concrete vision of the future in terms of building, resources, staff and especially atmosphere. How could we prepare either emotionally or practically for a future which was at best a leap of imagination?

Period of Negotiation

There began a phase of public discussions from the local authority with the parents and professionals. There were also negotiations with the architects of the two units to be built. Practical discussions about buildings and layout had to precede any definite ideas of philosophy or ideology of how the units were to be run, as no-one knew which professionals would be involved with the new venture. I was invited to attend two working parties. One of these was with the LEA. The brief was to plan for the school in the time leading up to its closure and to project which pupils might go on to the two units and then, finally, to plan based on these projections. I found it extremely interesting to watch the power play at such a high decision-making level, although it was also rather intimidating. The meetings were held in one of the huge impersonal committee rooms at Shire Hall, with high backed chairs and an awesome formal atmosphere.

The second working party I was invited to attend, was at Impington Village College. The initial task was to look at the feasibility of the unit being placed at the College. It had been decided from the beginning to build the primary unit at a school deeemed to be suitable in Cambridge. It was convenient to situate the unit at this school as it had to be rebuilt anyway due to the damage caused by fire. The secondary unit could not be built within the catchment area of this primary school, as this school was also under threat of closure. Negotiations therefore began, to build additional resources at Impington. This school was felt to be ideologically suitable and also convenient for wheelchair access as it is all on one level.

The main difficulty during this phase was that none of us had the experience of moving from a special school to a mainstream school and all suggestions therefore had to be based on imaginative guesswork. In particular, I remember being asked to prepare a paper for this influential working party, titled 'What is Integration?' and being asked to lead a discussion on it. Many practical and philosophical issues were raised in the discussion that followed. Some of the dilemmas appeared to present considerable problems — but I felt they presented a challenge that could and ought to be faced. On the other hand, at the same meeting a list was presented by one member of the working party of thirty-one reasons why it should *not* be done — this only served to increase my determination to make it possible.

Building work on the two departments began. The LEA decided to appoint the two coordinators of special needs a year in advance of the pupils transferring, to provide the schools with a focus during the preparations phase, before the arrival of the new pupils. The interviews for the two posts took place on the same day. It was then that I was appointed at Impington Village College. I had submitted my study to the Open University on how physically disabled pupils could be integrated into a large comprehensive school. My exam for the course was the next day — and I found myself writing about how integration could be done, with a positiveness and excitement based on the knowledge that I had been given the chance to attempt to turn ideology into reality!

Although my background prior to the five years I spent at Roger Ascham was working with pupils with learning difficulties in mainstream schools, I had not worked in a mainstream secondary school. I felt great apprehension about what this would be like, and in analyzing my fears I realized I had a fantasy that all the pupils would be over six feet tall and that I would never be able to feel relaxed in the classroom situation. In reality, I quickly found that I was going to enjoy working with mainstream secondary pupils enormously.

The preparation phase with staff and pupils at Impington Village College was very rewarding. I found people interested in the information I was imparting. I gave talks in assemblies and organized staff in-service (even though it was more difficult as it was at the time of the teachers' strike action), using videos, photographs, slides and anecdotes. People appeared to be looking forward to the pupils' arrival. Apprehensions were addressed, discussed and faced, rather than being ignored or avoided by pretending that they were not real issues.

The Graeae Theatre Company of disabled actors performed a workshop at the school, entitled 'Norman Normal on the Perfection Game'. My tutor group acted their own version of this consciousness-raising story, and a drama class made a video of it. A science group I was working with mounted an exhibition on disability in the main promenade of the college. However, I felt the most effective preparation of all was a visit to Roger Ascham to play wheelchair basketball — the able-bodied Impington pupils also playing in wheelchairs!

> That was great, Miss! When are they coming to Impington so we can play again?

— was the response, and also a great respect —

> They're really good at wheelchair basketball, Miss, and it's really difficult moving about in a wheelchair!

I remember very clearly the first time we took a wheelchair around the college, to work out the ideal route for adaptations. All heads turned to look through the windows at such an unusual sight — the *real* preparation work had begun.

I held lunchtime workshops and a group of pupils volunteered to work closely with me on welcoming the pupils of the future. They learnt about disability and how to use a spelling chart with pupils who had unclear or no speech. Then as new prospective pupils began to come and look around the school — these pupils became their confident and welcoming guides. They seemed to find this great fun. The good communication system set up by the new warden (who began at the college at the same time as I did), meant I could tell all staff and pupils that someone was coming to look around the college that day. Sue, after all her reservations, quoted in the *Cambridge Evening News*, bravely came to look around and her comment was:

> They treated me just like any other new pupil — not like someone in a wheelchair!

Meanwhile, the new building was gradually going up. Pupils took photographs of every stage — including the flooding, ice and snow! It was like a constant reminder that integration was to be a reality, not just a vision. I think I also acted as a focus for the plans of the future. I attended building planning meetings, curriculum development meetings and so helped to ensure that the future always included some recognition of provision for wheelchairs and pupils who might have quite diverse special needs.

My post at Impington Village College was Coordinator of Special Needs and I therefore had overall responsibility for all special needs pupils in the school. I had a support team of three teachers who were already at the school, and these staff were so supportive and welcoming that I felt a part of the college long before the disabled pupils and new staff arrived.

The Trial Run

The building programme was inevitably delayed and a decision was made to take on three physically disabled pupils a year before the additional resources were finished. So we began with the new first year pupils and a fourth year pupil, in September 1986. This meant we continued the preparations phase, whilst doing it for real.

I had a little office about the size of a small bathroom — in which the three welfare assistants and I were based. The office was used for physiotherapy (with a rubber mat completely filling the room, and children doing essential exercises) — speech therapy, occupational therapy, extra basic skills work and independence work. At times it felt as if we were trying to do all these things simultaneously! The pupils were brilliant and paved the way as no amount of preparation planning could do. For instance, David insisted on playing rugby with his classmates. Two sixth form boys would hold on to him — when he wanted to tackle someone they would just drop him in the mud! Mandy smiled and charmed her way through — no wonder she won Personality of the Year Award at the Cambridge PHAB (Physically Disabled & Able Bodied) Club last year. Claire pioneered the Pre-vocational course we were to mount the following September. Based on the curriculum development work undertaken at Roger Ascham, on 'What do we want the pupils to be able to do by the time they leave school?', she carried out the coursework on her own, with only the help and encouragement of teachers, welfare assistants and mainstream friends. For example, she rang British Rail and organized to be met by the staff on a train trip to Peterborough. She arranged to eat a meal at the Pizza Hut with a friend. She went on work experience to Unwins Seeds for a week. Then with photographs and imaginative displays of her activities, she conveyed the message of what she had done with such enthusiasm that we all believed in the course to be born the following year — and in Claire.

By the time Claire left Impington Village College she had almost learned to drive, got the choice of a job as a telephonist or to start a further education course, organized for a council flat to be adapted for her — and a friend to pay her rent, and had become an extremely self-possessed, independent young lady.

Meanwhile, pupils and parents visited Impington Village College and we talked of the vision of the Pre-vocational course and showed them the curriculum their children would be following — including CDT, home economics and art, on a scale not possible at the special school. We also crept around the unfinished building in an attempt to impart the vision of the physically disabled being full members of a large comprehensive, whilst also having their individual needs met.

The Special School Closes

It is an understatement to say that this was a difficult time for pupils, parents and staff of the Roger Ascham School. There can be no easy way to close a school. It was also necessary to re-route equipment and staff in three directions — to the primary unit, to Impington Village College and to another nearby special school (Lady Adrian). This was all happening at the same time as the pupils and staff were going through the ritual of saying goodbye to each other and their school.

The Department at Impington Opens

The new building, and most of the adaptations to the college, was ready for September 1987. We had believed we would gradually develop from the three pupils who had been at the college for a year, to nine pupils in all. In the event, we began with twenty-six physically disabled pupils at the school! One of the original welfare assistants and I worked through the summer holidays to produce twenty-six individual timetables, which organized pupils' mainstream lessons with appropriate welfare cover, and individual needs of therapy, independence work, wheelchair sport, and so on. Fifteen welfare assistants' timetables were also prepared. The master sheet of the final timetable for the welfare staff was the size of six sheets of A4 paper! Written guidelines about each pupil, including any equipment used, basic skills levels, any learning difficulties and pupils' strengths, were prepared and given to every teacher about to have a disabled child in their teaching group. We were ready to go!

Inevitably, there were some mistakes — pupils were timetabled for two lessons at once, or for lessons that did not exist; but the show was 'on the road'. My experience of this phase of the venture was simultaneously one of exhilaration and crisis management. As someone who has never been able to drive a car (despite many attempts), the analogy of my experience of this phase was as though 'I was driving a car at top speed — and we just managed to stay on the road'. But I also felt that the preparation the whole shool had done meant that we had 'good roads to travel along'. A battery operated scooter, a pedal trike, very fast electric wheelchairs, DHS electric wheelchairs, self-propelled manual wheelchairs and wheelchairs pushed by adults and pupils whizzed around the college. The school hummed with wheel-powered movement. Soon messages had to go out to tutor groups in the Daily Notices:

   ... No wheelchair users may do wheelies
   ... Do not speed in a wheelchair
   ... Never run when you are pushing a wheelchair
   ... Do not drive your wheelchair across the grass

However, the fact that children were 'misbehaving' in wheelchairs meant that they felt at home — integration had arrived.

Organization at Impington Village College

Academic Integration

When we began in September 1987, the organization was broadly similar to how it is now. Obviously the whole venture is still developing, but much of the groundwork remains the same. The physically disabled pupils belong to mainstream tutor groups, attend lessons in mainstream teaching groups and choose options like all the other pupils.

The curriculum development at Impington Village College since 1987, of integrated humanities and expressive arts work, has meant all the pupils have been able to benefit from mainstream lessons, and to have been involved at their own level. These courses have included blocks of time and an approach that utilizes child-centred work — this has been of great benefit to physically disabled pupils who might be slower at their work.

Following on from the curriculum development at Roger Ascham, I felt strongly that it is not enough to give disabled pupils just the same education as their able-bodied peers — they also require additional provision in order that their individual needs can be met. The extra areas will obviously vary according to individual needs. This might include some, or all of the following: physiotherapy, speech therapy, occupational therapy, riding, swimming all year round, wheelchair sport, extra basic skills work, typing and computer skills, and independence work.

Independence

The department takes the view that most children confined to a wheelchair lack much experience that others take for granted. They may also find some everyday tasks much harder than their able-bodied contemporaries. Consequently, the inter-disciplinary team at Impington Village College organize for all pupils in the first three years to work through RADAR (The Royal Association for Disability and Rehabilitation) Bronze, Intermediate, Silver and Gold Certificates on Independence Skills, which are adapted to meet individual needs. These activities include: pupils packing their own bags for school each day, making hot and cold drinks, snacks and packed lunches, making 'phone calls, finding out how to arrange for wheelchair repairs, etc.

The Pre-vocational Course

In the fourth and fifth years, the disabled pupils and some chosen mainstream pupils, follow a City and Guilds and BTEC Pre-vocational, 14–16 Foundation Course. This has been written by the department to fit the framework of the Examinations Board, for able-bodied and disabled to work through together. This was the course pioneered by Sue and based around the curriculum development planned at Roger Ascham.

There are fifteen fifth year pupils currently in the second year of the course and sixteen present fourth year pupils. It is organized into case studies, which include work on: First Aid, disabilities, information on Further Education Colleges for the disabled and able-bodied, travel, eating out, leisure and work. It also covers specific information and skills needed by the disabled — such as how to register as disabled and how the local DRO (Job Disablement Resettlement Officer) can help in finding employment.

Within the course Impington provides specialist careers advice in conjunction with the Special Needs Careers Service, and pupils and parents are counselled on possible career paths and, if appropriate, sheltered employment or Adult Training Centres.

The New Building

The additional resources at Impington Village College are housed in the new building, called the Pavilion, which links the two main parts of the school. It comprises of a very large, flexible central area with two class bases, an Independence Flat, a physiotherapy area, a medical room, specialist toilets and three small offices all leading off the central area. The facilities are used as a whole school resource. Mainstream lessons, lectures and assemblies all take place in the Pavilion. For example, a drama class were recently using the central area to make a video of an airport drama scene. Special needs activities include basic skills work, occupational, speech and physiotherapy groups and independence work.

As the uses of the Pavilion are so diverse, it means it is not seen as predominantly a special needs facility — pupils and staff just see it as a nice new building with a relaxed and industrious atmosphere. There are also display boards all around the central area and these are used to tell the story of the work on the Pre-vocational course, with posters and photographs designed and produced by the pupils on the courses.

Social Integration

We worked hard behind the scenes to ensure that the physically disabled pupils were welcomed into the school by the other pupils. In teaching groups and tutor groups, mainstream pupils volunteered to go around with the disabled. However, very quickly this artificial organization faded away and the children made their own friendships. Now able-bodied pupils wait for the transport to arrive outside the Pavilion and take their friends off to tutor groups.

The dining room has been adapted and wheelchairs and chairs can be placed as needed, so friends can sit together. Others share packed lunches with friends in the central area of the Pavilion.

Impington Village College hold a Sports Club on a Thursday after school, and disabled pupils can bring an able-bodied friend to play wheelchair sport, do leisure activities, and mix socially. This is run by our PE specialist teacher and has been a great help in fostering the positive social interaction that now exists at Impington Village College. Disabled pupils from other schools are invited to join and bring an able-bodied friend with them.

Staff

One of the successes of the venture is that it has been reasonably well staffed. There are the equivalent of fifteen welfare assistants — full-time — to enable pupils to have welfare cover, as it is needed in separate classes and option choices. There are six paramedical staff and eleven teachers who teach some or all of their time with special needs — this includes support teaching in classes, small group work, the Pre-vocational course, wheelchair PE, wheelchair gardening, pottery and independence work. The department is therefore one of thirty-five adults, so the coordinating role is a vast one!

The Pavilion is also well equipped. The majority of the disabled pupils need typewriters and some have portable computers that they take into lessons. British Aerospace designed and made for us some special stands for the typewriters, and this means even someone with quite a severe physical disability can use a typewriter with a keyguard and 'jellymats' to hold the machine still.

We also have a video camera. This is used by pupils doing art to film an image, for example, a tree, play it back on a monitor, choose the exact image required and print it out.

The extra equipment, which also includes computers, independence equipment, tape recorders and dictaphones, is used by all the pupils and means everyone benefits.

Preparation of New Pupils

We have Primary Day at Impington Village College, when the new junior school pupils spend a 'taster' day with us. During that day, every pupil comes to the Pavilion and looks around. This is so that there is no mystique about what goes on. They also see a Spastics Society video called 'The Land of Droog' which is of animated figures, two with cerebral palsy — one of them is in a wheelchair. The pupils respond well to this and many parents have said they mention it when they go home amongst all the new things they saw and did.

Pupils with Additional Learning Difficulties

Due to the closure of the Roger Ascham School, Impington Village College has also taken a few pupils who have additional learning difficulties. This year, with an extra input of resources, these pupils have been able to be taught on the fourth year Pre-vocational course and we have managed to provide them with an integrated timetable. In addition they join science and humanities lessons with younger year groups.

Parents

After the great anxiety created by closing the special school — it was decided to hold an additional Open Day in the Pavilion at Impington, for parents and pupils. The parents had the chance to speak to staff, have coffee, talk to each other, use the equipment and look at videos of their children in lessons. The children showed their parents around and it was a very positive occasion which I feel marked the turning point in anxiety levels.

A Vision for the Future

With the right preparation, adequate equipment and staff, I believe integration is a very positive experience. As we have the extra resources we can be very flexible and provide timetables from around 50 per cent to 100 per cent integration, with a range of support in classes as needed.

It is too early in the venture for a next phase yet, but my vision would be of further buildings being built and more staff being allocated and then it should be possible to cater for any child — including those with severe learning difficulties and it could even have a special care class attached. These pupils could benefit from the social interaction and, for instance, be taken to the shops or swimming and riding, by mainstream pupils. However, this is a leap of imagination. But then it was a leap of imagination that Impington Village College could integrate physically disabled pupils successfully, and it does seem to be working — as Claire said on a television interview recently,

> Impington has given me confidence. It's brought me out of my shell — into the big wide world . . .

Chapter 3

The Closure of the Special School

Jim Crawley

> The ideological commitment to integration can cause a state of professional myopia in which it is assumed that the needs of handicapped children can only be met in ordinary schools. Consequently, the work of special schools is frequently denigrated and devalued (Mittler, 1985, p.18).

Although the closure of special schools has been a relatively rare phenomenon, especially in the local authority sector, there are indications that amalgamation and closure of these establishments will become more commonplace in the near future. Smaller local authorities are consolidating their resources, and everyone with input into special education is watching with fascination as to how ILEA disposes of itself.

What are the implications of the long-term consequences of the 1981 Education Act for special schools in general, and schools for EBD children in particular? Can a local authority save money by closing a special school, and at what cost? To what extent does an LEA justify cost-cutting by riding the wave of 'integration'? What happens to the pupils and staff who are left behind?

Chapter Overview

'Something will come of this. I hope it mayn't be human gore.'
This chapter looks at the closure of one London borough's residential special schools: how the closure came about, the consequences for pupils, teaching and care staff, and the local authority itself. It examines the effects of enforced integration, both on pupils and the staff in the receiving establishments; the effect on morale over a long period on staff and pupils; it projects an alternative scenario and questions the wisdom of total integration.

The aim of the chapter is to look at the detrimental effects which can be consequent upon closure or indeed, upon a blind faith in integration. It will have the objective of pointing out possible pitfalls, and will succeed if it cautions any local authority, governing body, headteacher or member of staff to look before leaping!

The Threat of Closure

> If an administrator, each time he is faced with a decision, must perforce evaluate that decision in terms of whole range human values, rationality in administration is impossible (Simon, 1944).

The school, S, had been opened before World War II, as an all-age residential school for delicate children, in a small south coast resort. It had been constructed in the standard manner for such schools: dormitories facing south onto French windows, which allowed the children to be wheeled out in their beds or wheelchairs, 'weather permitting'. Classrooms were gradually added, as were kitchen and storage and recreational facilities, after 1945. The grounds were vast, and the school had its own frontage onto a private beach.

Ownership passed from a large county council to a London borough in the 1970s. Intake was from a number of London boroughs, as well as other local authorities in the Home Counties. Accommodation was for 140 children of all ages, and the school was operating at this level as recently as the early 1980s. However, as a result of the 1981 Education Act, rate capping, improvement in health care and genetic counselling, other provision was made for a majority of children previously identified as 'delicate', and the pupil intake began to drop quite dramatically.

'I expect a judgment. Shortly.'
In the mid-1980s, then, the local authority had to look quite hard at the provision that was required in special education, and the education that it was offering. The staff of S, educational, care and domestic, noted that the decreases in numbers coincided with an upsurge in visits by local authority personnel. The alarm bells began to sound and the rumours about closure began. 'Furthermore, this concentration on a limited range of values is almost essential if the administrator is to be held accountable for his decisions' (Simon, *ibid*.). The result of this renewed activity was that one significant change was followed by another (seemingly) significant change. First, the pupil intake began to take on a slightly different emphasis. Although the new intake were classed in their statements of educational needs as being 'delicate', the staff at S noticed two curious aspects: these children *all* had 'associated' behavioural difficulties (EBD), and their age range was within the secondary band, with a heavy bias towards 13–15-year-old pupils.

'Circumstances beyond my individual control.'
These shifts in emphasis had a further unsettling effect on the staff. They, particularly

the teaching and care staff, had been interviewed for, and had accepted positions in, a school for delicate children. Now they were faced with much physically stronger and larger pupils who manifested difficulties with which the staff were not equipped to cope. An emotionally and behaviourally disturbed young adult with asthma is a whole new can of worms for a teacher used to dealing with a wheelchair-bound infant with restricted growth!

The parallels throughout special education are obvious, but I shall restate them without apology for those not practising in that field. As special schools decrease in number, and face falling rolls, desperate measures are invoked to continue to justify the existence of these schools. Headteachers, and their deputies, who remain on protected salaries as long as their school remains open, might even be tempted to employ the umbrella (aka 1981 Education Act) term of 'multiplicity of handicap' to take on pupils with whom their staff are not equipped to deal . . . result misery.

The second change, which as I said seemed to be significant at the time, was the employment of a new headteacher. Whereas before no one had actually said that the school was catering for children with EBD, the authority now advertised for someone with experience in dealing with such children, and no mention was made of the delicate children. The authority was conforming to Advertising Standard Codes . . . there were no delicate children on roll. It was now a school for EBD children.

'It came like magic in a pint bottle; it was not ecstasy but it was comfort.'
The school got its new headteacher, H, with the aforementioned qualifications, early in 1987. The staff welcomed H's appointment. Here was someone who would 'sort out' the difficult children, and here was someone, so the advert had said, who would be in charge of an 'expanding' provision within the authority. Their jobs were safe. Morale soared. Well, everyone's except H's morale soared. He was in charge of thirty-five staff, thirty-five pupils, eleven acres of grounds, and more buildings than an average comprehensive. He had to provide twenty-four hour cover for all of them, and he had no deputy for either education or care. He was provided with a small flat next to the dormitories, for himself and his family. He was never off-duty for six or seven *weeks* at a stretch, as most of the pupils stayed at weekends. Eat your hearts out, junior doctors!

The governors and the local authority rushed to his aid after two terms of this. An acting deputy headteacher was appointed from within the authority, and the numbers of children were increased. Unfortunately, the acting deputy had no experience of residential work, nor of EBD children, and unhappily he left before a permanent appointment could be made.

In its enthusiasm to give a *raison d'être* for the school, the authority increased the numbers without due regard for whether the children were (a) acting-out, aggressive EBD or (b) introverted, withdrawn EBD. The two types do not mix well, and generally the weaker, type (b), go to the wall. Further, as a rule of thumb, H found that it was better/safer to operate an authoritarian regime in order to protect the type (b) pupils when one was presented with such a mix, but that such a regime benefited no one. Type (a) pupils could not cope with the vague physical and behavioural boundaries . . . H could set them and maintain these boundaries himself, but the staff were unable, for reasons given earlier, to reinforce the boundaries set.

'If you could see my legs when I take my boots off, you'd form some idea of what unrequited affection is.'

The same staff gravitated naturally towards the type (b) pupils, in whom they recognized characteristics similar to the delicate children they had been employed to teach. They saw the type (a) pupils as 'naughty' and 'ungrateful', and could never come to terms with them. And some of the staff tried very hard to accommodate these children, but the absence of INSET, line management and senior staff meant that they would avoid any situation which involved working with this type of child.

The alternative scenario which H proposed to the authority and which they duly rejected, was to close the school *immediately following his appointment* and re-open six or eight weeks later, with a homogeneous group of EBD children: either type (a) *or* type (b). In this time, he felt, he could collect the nucleus of a staff about him who were committed to working with such children. As an idealistic addendum, he also proposed new buildings which would provide an appropriate environment for EBD children. The authority informed him that this was an idealistic addendum.

H began to despair of the situation, but then things began to happen which lifted even his morale. Another acting deputy was appointed, who had experience of both residential education and working with EBD adolescents. Other staff were appointed who had similar experience in one or both fields. Appropriate curricula began to develop, new technology entered the classrooms, and H was able to shed half of his supervisory duties. He began to function as a headteacher, rather then as a caretaker, and the regime began to relax. This was reflected in the pupils themselves, who became more self-motivating, and even began to study for exams. There were still problems, of course, but S was beginning to function as a school.

> If he need consider the decision only in the light of limited organizational aims, his task is more nearly within the range of human powers (Simon, *ibid.*).

Then came the body blow. The authority had for some time been reviewing its special educational needs policy. These reviews had been in the form of discussion groups, which then submitted reports and recommendations to the authority. A final summary document was drawn up by the AEO (Special) and published early in 1988.

'This is a London particular... a fog, miss.'
Unfortunately for H and his school, there had been no submission from school S as to the future of residential EBD provision within the borough. Nor, as far as the author is aware, was the future of S discussed by any of the groups which submitted reports. The summary document recommended the closure of S. No specific date was given, but there were ominous signs. Meetings were called, H was invited, as were the governors, and it soon came to light that the closure could be at the end of the academic year, less than two terms hence, if the paperwork could be processed quickly enough, and DES deadlines could be met. Events moved quickly. The Director of Education and his Adviser and Education Officer were accompanied by an accountant specializing in re-dundancy payments, on a flying visit to the school.

'Think! I've got enough to do, and little enough to get for it, without thinking.'
Any counselling was left to H. He, of course, would also be redundant, as would all other staff, unless he was prepared to make the daily 160 mile round trip to the borough. The staff, it would be fair to say, were panic stricken. The majority had lived all of their lives in the local community, were married to people who had jobs in the area, and were in their fifties and early sixties. Ground and kitchen staff were in an area of south coast seasonal employment. The teaching staff, including H, had been led to believe that the prospects for the school and themselves were good, and some had moved from other parts of the country quite recently, and purchased property in the area.

And what of the pupils? All of them had been excluded from their previous comprehensive schools. One or two were excluded from their own families, or were not welcome there.

A date was given. The school was to close on 31st August, 1988, and redundancy was offered to all staff except the acting deputy (who was to return to his own school within the borough). H had to act swiftly on several fronts. He had to make provision for the pupils, motivate the staff for the remainder of their employment, negotiate the best terms for himself and them, and counsel staff regarding future employment or future unemployment.

'Battledore and shuttlecock's a very good game, when you an't the shuttlecock.'
For the pupils, he handed over the responsibility for integration to his deputy, who lived and worked in the borough, and had previous experience of integrating children from special schools into the comprehensives within the borough. Work placements and college places were sought for school leavers. One or two of the comprehensives were very accommodating, but their trust in the deputy was severely tested. Case conferences were held with Schools Psychological Service, AEO, parents and schools. For those for whom any comprehensive education would be deemed inappropriate,

off-site unit places would be found. In the case of the few children for whom contact with home was inadvisable, other residential schools were found.

So far, so good. Partial integration was initiated for those children entering mainstream education, staying at the parental home overnight and/or weekends, and supported by the deputy head within the comprehensive setting. Some of these comprehensive placements were found to be unsuitable, but that possibility had been allowed for, and there was still time to find them alternative placements in off-site units. The college and work placements proved to be more complex and more difficult. The perennial problem of shortage of support resources raised itself: the deputy head who was supporting those in mainstream could not also adequately support work placements — there was insufficient time.

'United Metropolitan Improved Hot Muffin and Crumpet and Punctual Delivery Company.'
By the end of the Spring 1988 term, all of the pupils had been placed outside of the school, and H was left with the problem of how to motivate the staff, with one term left and no pupils! One of the teachers had a 1988–1989 secondment to a College of Higher Education, so his time was occupied with preparation for that course. Another teacher had gained employment with another authority and had ceased to be employed at S. Yet another teacher had been offered a job elsewhere, and spent some time visiting a pupil now boarded in a neighbouring residential school. The deputy head was now based full-time in London.

The main problem lay with the care and domestic staff. The more career-minded found employment, others took early retirement. There was still a hard core of staff who were totally disenchanted with the authority's treatment of them, and could see very little point or reward in doing anything else.

H organized magnificently. He started courses in various areas which were of interest to staff, for example, weight-training. He organized a massive Summer Fête to build up funds for pupils to help them start up their own accommodation, start their own business, go on a course. He geared the whole of the school to this end for the large part of a (long) term, and the staff responded in kind.

The school closed at the end of July, and ceased to exist on 31st August 1988. Some of the staff are still unemployed, including H. All of the officers involved have left the employ of the authority, with the exception of the Director of Education. Contact has been lost with all of the pupils, but it is known to the author that one is still attending an authority comprehensive, supported totally by the resources of that school's special needs department, and the cooperation of the whole staff. The money from the sale of the school was designated by the authority for the building of a new special school for physically handicapped.

'It's always best on these occasions to do what the mob do.' 'But suppose there are two mobs?'
suggested Mr Snodgrass. 'Shout with the largest,' replied Mr Pickwick.

SECTION 2
Curricular

Chapter 4

Teaching in a Psychiatric Unit

Deirdre Leach

Forteviot is the in-patient unit of the Department of Child and Family Psychiatry in Edinburgh. Although it comes under the umbrella of the Royal Hospital for Sick Children the unit is situated about a mile from the main building in a quiet residential area. It comprises two large Victorian villas joined by a corridor and set in beautiful garden grounds with an uninterrupted view of Blackford Hill to the south.

There are advantages to having an in-patient unit attached to the main hospital, particularly if purpose built, but much of the success of Forteviot lies in its atmosphere being homely rather than clinical. Every space is utilized to the full. The children love the nooks and crannies typical of these large Edinburgh houses. There is a small indoor swimming pool. In the garden there are tennis courts, a soft environment building and an adventure playground.

The school, run by Lothian Special Education Department, is situated in one house. There are three classes, two primary and one secondary, of no more than six children in each. There are three teachers, a part time nursery nurse and myself, a non-teaching headteacher. Art and music specialists each teach on one half day weekly.

It is impossible to describe the work of the school without defining how it fits into the department as a whole.

Forteviot is part of a treatment system including out-patient and community work. Children are admitted for a period of assessment and treatment, on average of between three and six months. They will have been experiencing emotional and/or behavioural difficulties for some time. Presenting problems are seen very much in the family context and the children will have been seen initially with their families on an out-patient basis. The age range is from three to sixteen years although it is rare to admit children at either extreme. Emotional problems range from phobic and neurotic behaviour to aggression and conduct disorder.

Forteviot provides an intensive experience in a safe, supportive environment in which individual children can work on personal growth, behaviour and relationships. An atmosphere of trust and confidence is fostered in the unit. Children learn to live and work in the therapeutic milieu which allows the development of mutual respect, interest, support and empathy. Because of the low ratio of staff to children it is possible to respond to each child in the light of the immediate situation.

An eclectic approach is adopted in the unit drawing on behavioural, cognitive and psychodynamic techniques. Family therapy accounts for a high proportion of staff input. Multi-disciplinary skills are utilized in treatment programmes.

Admission

Admissions are planned although occasionally priority admissions are brought in within a couple of days of being referred.

The normal procedure is that the child's name is placed on the waiting list. Consideration is given to the group mix in the ward, and in school, and a decision about the timing of an admission is made mainly on that basis. Enough notice is given for the out-patient therapist to prepare the child and his family and to arrange a visit to Forteviot. The visit usually takes place about one week prior to admission and again is carefully planned. The nurse who shows the family around the unit will be from the child's ward and will be the same nurse who admits him, providing continuity of care.

Families are often relieved to see that the school, although small, looks quite normal and that the children attend for a full school day. As the majority of children return to mainstream education on discharge it is important to normalize the school experience in Forteviot as far as is possible. No bells ring to signal times, and the atmosphere is calm, relaxed and friendly but classes are fairly structured and there is an expectation of appropriate classroom behaviour.

The initial visit to school can be quite daunting for parents as well as children particularly if the presenting problem is that of disruptive behaviour in class as past contact with school staff is likely to have been uncomfortable, perceived negatively and, in a few unfortunate cases, perhaps even hostile.

Although it is nursing staff who have the most frequent contact with parents during a child's stay in Forteviot, it is important that parents feel encouraged to come to school regularly and hear about progress made. It is always possible to give some positive feedback which can be a relief for them and can have a therapeutic effect on their relationship with their child. If, after a period of assessment, it is found that a child has specific learning difficulties or has a deficit in one particular area, teaching staff, having built up a good relationship with parents, can advise on ways of helping the child at home.

Many families are fortunate to have had good and helpful experiences with the child's own school staff who have perhaps supported them through difficult times. Others, where the problems are purely homebased, will not have involved the school at all and the headteacher may have been unaware that the family were attending the out-patients department and that admission to Forteviot was imminent.

Liaison with Schools

It is crucially important that good contact with schools is established from the start, even before admission if possible. When this contact is successful, there is a greater opportunity for the child to fit back into school and cope after discharge. Also, information provided by the child's own school is essential when assessing his future educational needs.

It is useful if the Forteviot teacher can visit the child's school and see him in his own classroom setting prior to admission. It reassures the child to know that both teachers have met and that information regarding curriculum and level of work has been passed on. There is an acknowledgment that children are likely to experience anxiety on a social and emotional level on changing schools but there is a tendency to underestimate the worries children have about their school work.

A six year old who visited Forteviot told the teacher, 'I can only do up to ten and I can't do sentences', indicating that he worried at this young age that too much would be expected of him and that he would fail.

Face-to-face dialogue between teachers is much more satisfactory than relying on letters or phone calls. If there has been no previous contact with Forteviot and staff are unfamiliar with our work they may have their own anxieties or feelings of resentment, particularly if they have invested heavily in helping the child overcome his difficulties in school. Some teachers talk of feelings of failure or self blame if in-patient intervention is required. It is important that these misconceptions and fears are allayed. The most effective way is for the teacher to visit Forteviot and learn at first hand about the department and what can be offered to help families.

Confidentiality is respected at all times. Permission is sought from parents regarding contact with school being more than at an administrative level. Here, a welcome change in attitudes has been observed in recent years. Whereas previously there was sometimes unwillingness and wariness shown by parents at the suggestion of liaison with the child's school now this reaction is rare. It would seem that some of the stigma attached to psychiatric units is lessening and it is hoped that with improved communications and a more open door policy this trend will continue.

An information sheet about Forteviot is sent out to schools and visiting is encouraged during school hours.

Where an educational psychologist from the Regional Psychological Services has been involved he is invited to case discussions and contact is valued. Often the child's headteacher, class teacher or guidance teacher from a secondary school attends too. This is usually mutually beneficial.

However in-patient staff must be aware when giving reports that the shared understanding enjoyed within the unit cannot be taken for granted when outside agencies are involved. Problems can occur when information is taken out of context without the day-to-day background knowledge. For example, in-patient staff may talk of progress being made meaning, in some small steps. A visitor may understand from that that giant strides have been made and consequently expectations are raised too high. In-patient staff may refer to a child's behaviour in comparison with the rest of the group in the ward, or in class, which is only of significance within the unit and cannot be generalized from with any validity. An awareness of the potential for mis-understanding, then, is no bad thing as reports are carefully prepared before each case discussion ensuring all relevant points are included clearly and unambiguously.

Assessment

While in Forteviot a thorough assessment of each child's individual needs is provided. A picture is built up from reports from the various disciplines about how a child interacts in, and responds to, the different settings. For example, a child may be observed in a one-to-one occupational therapy session, in a structured class, on an outing, in a family session, in the ward at bedtime, in a group of older children or a group of younger children, with the oposite sex or with the same sex. Behaviour can vary greatly according to different factors. Often differing again may be reports from parents about weekends at home.

Occasionally the reasons for referral are not evident during admissions. Some-times it is enough that a negative pattern at home has been broken and parents and child have been given some breathing space. The child is relieved of the responsibility of fulfilling, say, a scapegoat role in the family and settles quickly into what should for him be a rewarding, positive experience on which to build up self-esteem. However after an initial 'honeymoon' period the problems usually become apparent.

There is always an awareness by teaching staff that children find it much easier to cope in a small, intimate school group and that the difficult behaviour described by the child's own school may not manifest itself. It is particularly important, then, to involve his own teacher.

Forteviot teachers contribute to the overall assessment and provide important information on classroom behaviour and peer relationships but obviously their parti-cular expertise is in educational assessment. Standardized classroom tests are admin-istered for reading and spelling, and clinical psychologists or visiting educational psychologists provide psychometric test results if requested, but most valuable is the day-to-day intensive observation.

The teachers check for specific learning difficulties such as auditory or visual discrimination problems, or problems to do with spatial awareness or directionality. It is these problems which can be so easily overlooked in large mainstream classes. A child can be seen to be coping but underachieving, or worse to be lazy, when in fact he is having to compensate for difficulties such as these. Many children successfully complete their school years by using such compensatory strategies that their difficulties are not noticeable but for some more vulnerable children it can mean added pressure.

Specific learning difficulties are frequently maturational in nature and, given appropriate exercises and games, can be overcome. It is often helpful for parents and mainstream staff to be advised of specific learning difficulties and of ways of helping the child provided it is put in such a way that there is no likelihood of the child being handicapped by a label. The pros and cons have to be balanced in relation to each child's individual needs.

The educational assessment encompasses areas such as work attack, concentration, self-esteem, independence, maturational level, motor control, creativity and problem solving. It looks at how the child responds to new situations, to praise or chastisement, to explanations and new information, to different teaching strategies and so on.

The teacher elicits information about how best to ensure enough success and enjoyment with which to motivate the child.

The most important area to work on from the beginning is in raising self-esteem. This can be done in many small ways but praise must be genuine and well earned. Children are very suspicious and wary of adults who go overboard with praise, particularly if this is quite a new experience. Praise should be given only in relation to a child's past efforts and not used in comparison or competition with the rest of the group. Some children's school problems may be that of overstretching themselves or putting too much pressure on themselves. This is often the case with children suffering from anorexia and striving for control and perfection. As part of the overall treatment they are helped to take part in activities for the sake of enjoyment and not in a competitive way.

Sometimes there are no educational problems at all.

When a child has been experiencing great difficulties in school prior to admission, whether behaviourally or educationally, and when the recommendation from the assessment in the unit is that he needs to be taught in a school which could provide for his own special needs, teaching staff, along with the educational psychologist, talk to parents about the options available. Forteviot school is a useful stepping stone in such a case as parents can see how the child has coped in the small class and come to realize that he would benefit from a similar educational setting in the longer term.

Very occasionally it is felt that in order for a child to reach his potential he needs residential schooling which could provide him with consistency of care and management. Family work continues and the aim is to return the child to the family network, to mainstream education and to his own community. Many families have been saved from break up by this option and children have benefited from the warm, caring environment and specialized teaching provided.

There is a move now in many parts of Britain to reject the idea of residential schooling on the grounds that it is better to provide for the child in his own community. Whilst the underlying philosophy cannot be argued with the many extra resources needed to give these children the best opportunities are not always available. Also the experience of placing a child with an alternative family, which seems to be the preferred option, can sometimes be more damaging to the parent/child relationship in the long-term than a period in residential school with weekends and holidays at home and support for the family. It would be sad if certain children were denied the opportunity to benefit from such an educational and social experience because of a political ideal.

When residential school is an available option it is of great advantage if the child and family can be prepared for the transition while the child is still an in-patient and ideal if he can actually make the move directly from Forteviot instead of experiencing further failure by returning to mainstream until the administrative procedure is carried out and a place found.

On discharge, an objective educational report is sent to the child's own school, highlighting any changes observed in the child's behaviour during the admission and stating any teaching strategies which were found to be useful in the small group setting. Information of a clinical nature is not included.

The School and the Curriculum

Although the children do not have to leave the building to go to school, the very fact that they have to walk the length of the corridor puts a healthy distance between the wards and school. This may seem like an anomaly as a major factor in the management of Forteviot is that staff work closely together, as a team, sharing information and communicating openly about the children. However, it lends to normalizing the school experience during a child's stay.

Some small rituals are observed such as lining-up in classes before school starts. The teachers make a point of being ready and waiting to greet the children when the nurses hand them over. Any unhappy incident in the ward is left behind with the reassurance that a fresh start will be made on returning after school, and vice versa. Although children are aware that staff will be informed of any such incident, in order to understand or allow for any mood disturbance, no form of chastisement or sanction is carried over from one area to another.

During the school day nursing staff are occupied elsewhere in the unit, writing reports, attending workshops, team meetings, ward meetings and preparing group activities for the evening. They do not work in the classroom along with the teacher.

They do, however, take an interest in the children's school work and 'visit', as parents would, to admire some particular project and boost self-esteem.

Good communication amongst in-patient staff helps keep manipulation and splitting to a minimum. Teachers and other disciplines attend the nursing Kardex meetings in the morning and hear about the previous evening or weekend and any family issues which may have arisen.

There is very frequently overlap of work carried out wich children in different areas. For example, the occupational therapist may provide a clumsy child with a sensory integration programme. Teaching and nursing staff would give the child practice through play activities to consolidate the work. A child found in school to have sequencing or memory problems may be encouraged in the ward to learn appropriate remediating nursery rhymes and play counting games.

Certain areas of the curriculum are supplemented by nursing staff and occupational therapists. The policy about sex education in the unit is that it is undertaken by nursing staff. There are several reasons for this. It is much more acceptable to the children to have a cosy chat in the ward group with their own nurse who looks after their intimate, physical needs than to have a formal lesson in school. The nurse can deal with the subject at an appropriate time. Also, their medical knowledge is valuable! Sex education has to be treated with great sensitivity in a unit such as ours where one or two children in any group may have been subjected to some form of sexual abuse. As with any subject, each child's individual needs are catered for.

Occupational therapists see children individually, or in twos or threes, depending on the aim. Children are helped to plan projects and follow them through to the end. Motor skills, self-control, confidence, problem solving and practical skills are all enhanced in occupational therapy sessions. Children are encouraged in cooperative play, turn taking, sharing and communicating. Eating disordered children are helped as part of their overall treatment programme to plan menus, shop and cook meals. They learn about healthy eating and nutrition.

There is usually an on-going mixed adolescent social skills group.

In school, education is made as enjoyable and rewarding as possible. Teaching is challenging and interesting as not only is there a wide age range within each of the three classes but also there is a huge divergence of backgrounds, intellectual abilities and emotional problems. Each child who comes through Forteviot has very different individual needs and new innovative ways of stimulating and motivating have to be found. Flexibility, creativity, enthusiasm and a good sense of humour are all important qualities in this kind of work.

Teachers aim to provide continuity of curriculum where possible. A letter is sent out to the child's own school on admission requesting information about level of work, textbooks used and so on. Headteachers kindly lend the appropriate books from any reading or maths scheme being followed in their school. We have a good and varied selection of textbooks in school but the expense of buying whole schemes could not be justified when only a few children would use them. Also, to have books supplied by their own school reassures children that they are expected to return.

The guidance teacher in secondary schools collects information from each subject teacher and liaises with Forteviot, sometimes providing worksheets. The teacher of the secondary group has a particularly challenging job. Many children at this stage are in need of remedial help for basic skills and their work is more at top primary level. Others, however, have no educational problems and use the time in Forteviot profitably. Where there is a lack in some subjects, in particular sciences, there is a development in other areas such as independent study skills and fact finding, discussion techniques, creative writing, expressive arts, problem solving, craft work, cooking, knowledge of current affairs, experience with the computer and, of course, social skills. Moral and health education by the nature of the place is on-going. Children benefit so much from these subjects that confidence is greatly increased and able children manage with support to cope with catching up in other areas on return to school. Languages to second year standard can be catered for with guidance from mainstream staff.

The basic skills — reading, maths and language — are mainly taught on a one-to-one basis throughout the school but group work is important and children are brought together whenever possible. This is often an area which children find difficult and skills such as cooperation, turn taking, sharing and listening are all encouraged.

Good use is made of the tape recorder in the primary classes with teachers compiling individual tapes for children to work at independently with ear phones. Children have to listen, follow instructions and write the answers in their workbooks, or they may listen to, and follow, stories from books. Not only is independence encouraged in this way but also children have to concentrate hard in order to keep the place. Children who find a one-to-one relationship with the teacher rather too threatening in the first few days respond well to this medium and to using the computer.

There are two full computer systems in the school. The second was bought from school funds when the first proved to be so useful. The secondary class has one permanently in the classroom and the two primary classes have one on alternate weeks. The educational games provide enjoyment and children do not think of them as work. They give immediate feedback and reward success. There is also a sense of mastery and being in control which all goes to raising self-esteem and motivating. As with the tape recorder independence and concentration is promoted. The word processor and printer enables children who find writing difficult and unrewarding to produce beautiful work. Creativity can come through in their story writing when they do not have the added effort and frustration of pencil control. Mistakes can easily be deleted and no mess is left on the page. The stories can then be kept in a folder with pride. Adventure and problem-solving games provide opportunities for cooperative work and promote abstract thinking and discussion among the children.

A recent development in Forteviot is the use of cross age tutoring where the secondary pupils work with the youngest age group. They use the paired-reading technique or play games chosen by the teacher to consolidate particular skills being taught in the classroom. Sometimes they are involved in explaining new concepts. Preparation is given to the older children by their teacher and they themselves benefit from this kind of revision, often without realizing it.

This is how one 15-year-old girl has described the benefits of cross tutoring:

> Cross tutoring helps me in many ways. It helps to know the boys in the ward before you can start teaching. I found it helped me when I broke the ice by making a joke. Neil kept calling me Lesley instead of Lindsey and I used to tease him and asked him to tell me what my name was. If he said Lindsey I was really pleased but if he said Lesley I wouldn't speak to him. I got to know him that way. Of course there is an element of 'skive' in it but that it is not really why I want to do it because I like work and anyway we still have to work to teach them. We have to know how to put it across so that it is interesting and they won't become bored. We have to be patient for naturally they take some time for it is new to them. I always look forward to my teaching during the school day. It helps me because I make friends with the children, it gives me confidence, it shows me how good I am at putting things across. I feel very proud of them if they get things right and I enjoy it and really want to help them.

There is no pressure on the older children to participate in the scheme but so far surprisingly no one has opted out and it has proved successful even with those normally less than cooperative. Both teachers watch over the proceedings closely and find it interesting to compare notes of their observations of the opposite class.

Some informal drama mainly in the form of role play, and movement to music is practised in the ward, in occupational therapy sessions and in school. Art and craft work, and music, are important media and are used by all in-patient staff in the therapeutic process but we are fortunate in having specialist teachers for these subjects.

Through art emotion can be expressed nonverbally although often verbal interation is facilitated when children are immersed in a creative task. The class is informal and nonthreatening and as in occupational therapy, children often choose to make presents for parents. They are encouraged to make a project last over several sessions taking time to perfect it instead of rushing their work. Sometimes children make glove puppets or finger puppets later used in role play at their own instigation. Clay models of figures reflect feelings in a fascinating and revealing way as do paintings. Without looking too deeply or attempting to analyze it is possible to get information about a child's mood state from use of colour, content and form. Intricate enamelled jewellery and beadwork require patience, self control and good fine motor skills. The finished result of such work ensures satisfaction and pride. So many children have hidden artistic talent which can be realized by the right kind of teaching, guidance and encouragement. Success in this area, particularly as it is visible and tangible, is an effective way of raising self-esteem.

The music specialist is employed as a music teacher but it is her extra qualification as a therapist which is of enormous importance. Her work has opened up a whole new dimension in the unit. Music is a valuable mode of expression and can reflect the emotional life of the individual. The components of music — tone, rhythm, harmony, tempo, dynamics, tonal quality and pitch — form a non verbal language that encompasses every mood and is richly expressive. The form and structure inherent in music can bring a meaningful sense of order and security to the emotionally disturbed child.

Although music is free from social ritual the music therapist, through group work, encourages the very same skills needed in social situations, that is, listening, sharing, cooperating, turn taking, alertness for cues, controlled responses, the ability to accept the focus of attention or to allow others to have attention. Musical instruments, both tuned and untuned, are used and a large proportion of each session is non-verbal. Communication happens!

One musical game used with great enjoyment involves the teacher using a tambourine and singing a lively tune as she beats the rhythm. The children sit in a semi-circle and every so often, usually at the last note or penultimate note of a melodic line, she thrusts the tambourine in front of one of the children to beat. The children have to concentrate and to be alert in order to keep the rhythm going. Another exercise involves the teacher improvizing on the piano in response to a child's improvized rhythm on a drum. They sit back-to-back and the child changes the mood by altering the tempo and the volume. In this way child and teacher interact. Singing can liberate and relax, or stimulate, through the musical shape and dramatic quality of the song. As with art, children are often self conscious and lacking in the confidence to sing at first. With the therapist's gentle encouragement many children have discovered the delights of this form of self expression and have even felt safe enough to sing for others gaining from the experience of giving pleasure.

Music therapy has been recognized for some time as a valuable aid for slow learning children and for those with physical disability but less publicity has been given to its enormous benefits with the emotionally disturbed.

Social Skills

Education in social skills is an on-going part of the overall treatment process in the unit and has been referred to throughout the chapter.

At a basic level in the ward guidance is given on hygiene and self care, respect of one's own and others' property and relating in an appropriate manner to peers and staff.

On outings children are given experience of using buses, telephones, going to cafes, shops, the railway stations and many other places where practice in using specific facilities is available.

An occupational therapist and a nurse run a mixed adolescent group weekly. Goals change according to the group mix as, unlike a closed out-patient group, the group does not remain stable for many weeks. There is usually a child preparing to leave or another newly admitted. Leaving and joining the group are issues which often come up in the group work. Children prepare for return to their own school by role playing situations which are likely to occur such as being questioned about their absence from school and where they have been, avoiding conflict or asking for help in class.

General aims of social skills group work include simple communication skills in the form of listening, responding, initiating conversation and noting and using non-verbal cues. More complex skills are those of tact, diplomacy, persuasion, dissuasion, and assertion. Insight and awareness of others' feelings are promoted through mime, role play, trust exercises and games. A group session often ends with guided relaxation to music.

Training

In a multi-disciplinary setting it is essential that there is a shared and common understanding. Roles overlap considerably although each discipline contributes its own particular skills and retains its own identity.

Opportunity for learning is boundless. There are regular workshops, open to all disciplines in family therapy, behaviour therapy, play therapy, cognitive therapy, sexual abuse and working with groups. Workers meet to present cases and discuss problems, review literature, observe and practise skills through role play, and update themselves on research. *Ad hoc* lectures are set up at short notice to deal with any topic causing concern in the unit at any particular time, for example, anorexia, epilepsy, encopresis.

In-patient staff all have the opportunity at some point to participate in an in-service training programme which runs for one half day fortnightly over the course of a year. The morning is divided into two parts, theory and practice. A wide range of subjects is offered such as language development, moral development, aggression, impulse control, child rearing practices, sex differences and sex role, and assessment and interviewing in family therapy. The lecturers are multi-disciplinary and are recognized within the department as having particular expertise in these areas. At present the course is only available to staff and students on placement but it might prove useful in the future for other professionals in the community such as teachers in special education.

An understanding of the different forms of therapy and of the psychological theories underlying the practice is useful for all staff as it lends to continuity and consistency in management and treatment.

In a wide sense, education itself can be seen as therapy in that self-esteem is raised through increased success in academic and practical skills, improved communications and problem-solving abilities. However teachers do not practise within the classroom setting any form of individual therapy which might result in the exposure of a child's inner self and leave him vulnerable to his peers. There are times when a child chooses to confide in the teacher either at a one-to-one level or by writing. Where the information is of a private nature the teacher responds supportively and with the child's permission passes it on to his therapist.

If there is good communication between teacher and therapist skills being promoted in individual therapy sessions such as assertiveness, impulse control, non-verbal communication, can be consolidated in class. One form of therapy which is proving useful in the classroom situation to work on general behavioural issues is cognitive therapy.

Cognitive Therapy

Cognitive therapy as defined by Beck (1976) has been mainly used with adults in the treatment of depression and anxiety. This approach emphasizes the role of cognitions in determining a person's feelings and behaviour. In brief, distorted perceptions of reality and the subsequent evaluation of these perceptions lead to emotional disturbance. Although it is not possible to use Beck's approach directly, cognitive therapy can be applied, with modification, to the emotional problems of children.

The cognitive therapy approach with children is still in its infancy. Most writers on the subject refer in Piagetian terms to child development which is helpful in deciding which aspects of the therapy would be appropriate.

Thinking about one's thinking is an abstract conceptual activity which is quite sophisticated developmentally and would probably require that a child had reached the stage of formal operations. However certain techniques, such as self-instructional training and role play, can be used with younger children. There are various commercial cognitive behavioural programmes for children bearing a resemblance to adult cognitive therapy. One such programme used in Forteviot School is an inter-personal problem-solving approach for children geared towards helping them to cope with transition from primary to secondary school.

Children need to accept that life is full of problems. Adults as well as children experience them and it is quite possible to deal with them most of the time. Some problems are greater than others and everyone needs help from time-to-time to overcome them.

Problem solving is a learned skill which has a wide relevance within education. Teaching children to formulate hypotheses and to generate alternative solutions is educational and promotes independence which can be generalized from into other areas of life. Children who learn problem-solving skills can come to believe they can avoid or cope with troublesome events.

Cognitive therapy with adults is a straightforward, down-to-earth approach. Therapists are encouraged to demystify the therapy process and the client is an active participant from the start. He is in control and chooses which behaviour to keep and which to discard. An advantage of this approach is that it does not lead to any great dependency by the client on the therapist. The aim is to help him help himself.

Children are not self-referred and are often understandably unwilling to cooperate and resistant to the behavioural change process. The therapist has to establish two beliefs before the child will decide to collaborate. These are, that change is possible and that it is desirable. Therefore, in Forteviot cognitive therapy does not occur in isolation but as part of an overall treatment plan usually involving behavioural, family and milieu aspects.

In the classroom situation it is possible to work in a general way using a cognitive approach. One of the enormous advantages of having classes of no more than six children is that once a group is settled and the children have developed a trusting relationship with their teacher it is possible for her to deal with issues as they come up. Once children accept that events are a consequence of their own action they can learn that they are therefore in control and have the potential to change.

Beck's idea is that an automatic thought causes a feeling which results in a certain behaviour. So, for example, a child faced with a tricky maths problem may think to himself, 'I'm no good at this. I'll never get it right', causing him to feel hopeless, angry and frustrated, perhaps resulting in some form of overt behaviour such as destroying his page.

Teachers aim in a non-judgmental way to help the child trace back to his automatic thought and replace it with a more realistic and positive one leading to the generation of an alternative solution. From a child's automatic thoughts the teacher or therapist can discover much about his basic beliefs and assumptions about life. The aim in cognitive therapy is to shake these beliefs and eventually challenge them in order that the client comes to change his distorted cognitions.

To reach this stage in therapy requires skill and training. More harm than good is caused by challenging erroneous assumptions too early. The therapist must accept that the child's belief is presently genuine for him. Direct challenges are likely to be construed as personal attacks and result in a hostile reaction. Doubts about the reality of the child's beliefs have to be introduced gradually and over time. The obvious way to do this in class is by raising self-esteem so that where a child once felt worthless he now has evidence to support the idea that in certain areas he manages well and has the potential to improve further.

When a teacher knows a child well she can note any change of behaviour or even physiological changes such as flushing or hyperventilating and can intervene using cognitive techniques to preempt any overt action. With younger children skilled teachers note these cues and use diverting strategies in order to avoid, for example, a temper tantrum. More effective with the more mature child is for the teacher to draw his attention to the cues with the ultimate aim of the child recognizing them for himself and counter-acting a distorted cognition with an alternative, more helpful one.

Cognitive therapy is a here-and-now technique which works well in the classroom setting. In many ways it is more valuable in class than in an individual therapy session when it is often difficult for the child to recapture the feelings he has experienced in the past.

A major difficulty when using the cognitive approach with children is that of language. Most children have few words for emotions and are therefore limited in their ability to conceptualize situations. By developing their vocabulary children are able to think in terms of a continuum of feelings and to understand variability of mood.

Games such as 'What's my Mime?' and 'In the Manner of the Word' are useful and fun. These games are aimed at the detection of facial and postural cues and, at the same time, increase vocabulary. Another game children enjoy involves taking a phrase such as 'Fish and Chips' and varying the manner in which it is spoken, for example, angrily, sweetly, persuasively.

Children need the words to describe intensity of emotion. Role play can show responses to the same event varying in intensity. Children of course enjoy exaggerating tremendously but the teacher must give some thought to realism in order for such an exercise to have the desired effect. A 'feelings' dictionary can be compiled by the class. Photographs of different facial expressions can be cut from magazines and labelled on a poster with the addition, perhaps, of the likely thought behind the expression.

Work on the development of language is not only beneficial psychologically and socially but also dramatic benefits are shown on creative writing.

To summarize, the cognitive approach can be usefully employed in the classroom. It is an educational model aimed at helping children help themselves. There are problems in translating the techniques to use with children and considerable thought must be given to developmental stages and ability.

The decision to remove a child from his home and his school for a period of in-patient treatment and assessment is not one that is ever taken lightly. It is very important therefore that everything possible is done to provide the child with an en-riching, happy and worthwhile experience during his admission. It is equally important to ensure that the experience is not too far removed from the reality of his own life.

Chapter 5

Recording the Achievements of Pupils

Mike Conquest, Graham Pirt and Mike Wright

Foreword

Assessment should be an integral part of the learning process and relate directly to the aims and purposes of learning.

Aims and objectives should be known and expressed in schemes of work, which set out the content, concepts, skills and attitudes to be acquired and the teaching approaches and learning recources to be used. It follows that pupils need to be given tasks, which allow them to demonstrate competence across the range of performance expected of them. In this sense the assessment process is an integral part of the curriculum.

However, experience demonstrates that it is not enough for pupils to be 'given tasks', but that greater effectiveness and improved motivation are achieved when the pupils are involved in planning their own learning programmes.

Objectives can also be given to children as guides for their own learning, to inform them, to stimulate them and, one hopes, to motivate them. Children can use objectives as advance organizers, a framework on which they can hang present and subsequent knowledge, as well as a series of targets for which to strive.

Providing children with objectives enhances achievement, regardless of the level of learning involved.

It follows that once the learning objectives have been discussed teachers need to give pupils the opportunities to demonstrate those qualities on which the record is intended to throw light. This clearly has implications for the curriculum.

Because a record of achievement is clearly designed to give an individual profile of the pupil, comparative assessment, which sets the pupil within the context of others' achievements, is inappropriate. Descriptive assessment establishes individual pupil's achievements within the context of themselves only.

In the process of assessment — this will include self-assessment — a record of achievement is created, which is more likely to be valued by the pupils and by employers or others, who need to know what the pupil's experience has been and where the strengths lie.

The Background of Change

The close relationship which has developed between education, industry and commerce has enhanced the opportunity for joint developments which have changed practice in this area of the curriculum over many years.

For example, certain aspects of special educational practice developed over the past two decades have been eventually formalized through the legislative process and in turn have become acceptable practice for all pupils. Special education has had the opportunity of being able to develop unfettered by the often restrictive restraints of examination syllabi, and as a consequence, many innovative, pupil-centred curriculum developments have been nurtured.

Work experience, work sampling, work shadowing and the whole concept of the 'leavers programme', the design for living course, etc., were developed in many special schools during the 1960s. Whilst many of these projects have since become refined with the advent of the 1974 legislation, many examples of new initiatives can be found to have begun in the special school sector of our service. Practical training or work placement links, with Pye of Cambridge, Greens of Thurcroft and Viners of Sheffield, to name but a few, illustrate exciting projects and enterprise schemes which extended the learning environment for many special schools' pupils during the 1970s.

Some of the most significant developments were the links which evolved in many special schools between these generalizing experiences and the range of skills taught with the closed curriculum to mastery level in the schools. The concept of the open and the closed curriculum developed during the 70s and was widely reported by Ainscow and Tweddle and others who focused the attention of the schools onto the record-keeping essential to the process. At the same time came the recognition of the need to plan the learning process in a more structured manner than hitherto, with clearly stated goals, objectives and sequences of recordable progress.

Historically one of the standard methods of keeping records was for the class teacher to maintain a weekly record book and to contribute to a cumulative record and termly or yearly report for the parents. This was quite a feasible approach for a teacher who used a class-based teaching approach. The teacher was able to control the progress of the children in the class albeit in a limited manner. What this technique also created, however, was the belief that because the teacher had planned and taught the material the children had, by implication, learnt it. With the onset of the comprehensive principle and the development of mixed ability classes, a wider range of ability in the children being taught exposed serious limitations in the approach. The Schools

Report (1981) looking at curricular practice for slow learners found that procedures for both the assessment and recording of abilities were inadequate.

The 1981 Education Act became, as it should, the catalyst for a reappraisal of the whole of special needs provision. Although there had already been some considerable development (Ainscow & Tweddle, 1979 and 1984). With the onset of the Act teachers not only had to cope with the already more individualized curriculum, and its attendance record-keeping, but in many cases were finding themselves with pupils who had once been placed in special schools, and the extra level of curriculum planning and detailed recording necessary to cater for those children's needs. The necessity for an annual review to be undertaken for each child with special educational needs, as part of the requirements of the Act, created a powerful demand for the development of an efficient and appropriate record-keeping system. This was further exaggerated by local education authority responses to the Act and the development of re-integration and integration programmes for children with special needs. The child with special needs in a mainstream school creates many demands for the host school, not least of which is maintaining a clear idea of the position and functioning of the child in relation to the curriculum of the school, both open and closed.

It is an essential aspect of record-keeping that staff and other professionals involved in their maintenance should have a clearly defined knowledge of the rationale behind the composition and use of the records. This has not always been the case. In a research sample of teachers in a project by the Schools Council (1981) a number of typical reasons for keeping records were expressed by teachers which included expected results such as:-

1   to chart pupil progress and achievement;
2   to communicate information to other teachers;
3   to ensure continuity of education throughout the school;
4   to ensure continuity of education on transfer to other schools;
5   to guide a replacement or supply teacher;
6   for diagnostic purposes;
7   to provide information on success or failure of teaching methods and/or materials;
8   as a statement of what has happened — to inform interested parties (parents, educational psychologists);
9   to give headteachers a general picture of achievement in the school.

There were, however, some less expected responses for the existence of records which included aspects such as:-

1   a defence against accusations of falling standards;
2   as an 'insurance policy' in the face of hostile attacks;
3   for the head to gain control of areas of the curriculum;
4   to keep balance in areas of study.

Responses as wide as these obviously reflect a wide sample of experience, some good, some not so good, with just as wide a range of techniques of record-keeping.

Perhaps some of the problems in the inability to conceptualize the intrinsic nature of recording life is the development of people's conceptions of education. A general view of education may be that it is seen as a set of learning tasks which, presumably, increase in difficulty as you progress from the beginning to the end of school.

Within this pattern it may also be assumed that, with the increased acquisition of knowledge, fewer and fewer pupils will have the aptitude or skill to achieve success. Access to the higher levels of this pyramid is usually gained by examinations at various stages. There is obviously a shortfall between those that achieve the higher stages of the education system and those that leave school without any qualifications represented by a certificate. This problem was recognized as long ago as 1983 within the Newsom Report. The record of achievement movement therefore is not a new one.

Many special schools were thus moving towards a more differentiated curriculum based on pupil assessment and a prescriptive approach to learning. The information thus formulated, being recorded in the form of 'Prescriptive Schedules' (Green Arbour, 1972) which was available for every pupil. The process, however, was still experimental. Initially the recording of progress reflected pupil performance only in basic skills and motor or language development. However, the application of the process of continuous assessment continued to develop. In a number of schools it was extended by the inclusion of a process of internal annual review of the progress of every pupil. Such multi-disciplinary reviews also set targets for the forthcoming term or year (1975, in Green Arbour School it was standard procedure, albeit informal).

These recording techniques had become more refined during the 70s with the need to encompass a more proactive learning experience for the pupil with severe learning difficulties. There was also an increasing recognition of the need for a partnership with parents if the total learning environment for the pupil was to be exploited.

It was most noticeable during the mid-70s that the relationship between this ongoing recording of progress at the classroom level and the need for the pupils to leave school with some form of 'achievement record' was being formalized. Many schools such as Green Arbour School, Rotherham, produced for leavers a profile of successes, academic attainment, Project Trident work experience reports, enterprise activity records, community involvement and sporting achievements, etc. The school's 'prescriptive schedule' had become a framework of continuous assessment and achievement. The records were accumulative from five to sixteen years and covered all curriculum areas, illustrating both skills acquired and experiences explored and contained both formative and summative evidence of progress.

These processes emerging in many schools became part of the liturgy of the legislation that was to become the 1981 Education Act and yet also underpin much of the practice indicated with the ERA.

The need to set objectives and to measure progress on a regular basis was to become the foundation stone of the 1981 Education Act, first through the staged assessment process which is totally dependent upon all schools developing a structured approach to learning and recording the progress of the pupils, subsequently through the drafting of the statement of need, and finally in the mechanics of the annual review procedure.

The annual review procedure therefore should not be seen as a discreet set of test results to show the level of the pupil at a point in time. More appropriately they are to be seen as no more than a 'freeze frame' snap shot of the changes in pupil performance when measured against earlier measures in the process of continuous assessment. The assumption being that assessment is a part of the continuous learning process and that the 'freeze frame' would produce a selection of highlights of the youngsters' development at that point in time — as such it was thus unique to each pupil. A time consuming exercise for the already busy classroom teacher if handled by paper checklists alone.

In 1983 it was decided to extend this changing schools' practice further by exploring the application of the newly emerging information technology to the process of pupil monitoring. To this end in 1984, HMI, the Manager of the Newcastle SEMERC, a special needs adviser, a couple of educational psychologists and a couple of administrators were drawn together with a limited budget to explore the feasibility of such a project. Early discussions indicated that examples of computer-managed pupil profiles thus far developed fell far short of the aspirations of the group and some concerns existed about the capabilities of existing hardware or software to reach the criteria set by the group.

The programme it was felt would need:

— to be more effective than the pencil and paper exercise;
— to provide flexible content free software;
— to be supported by detailed documentation;
— to utilize hardware compatible and available to all schools;
— to have the ability to store 'cross curriculum' information;
— to record change/or lack of change and show the direction;
— to print out progress, changes or future targets;
— to allow for interaction with word processor;
— to satisfy local authority needs as specified by the Act;
— to meet school administration and teaching/recording needs;
— to present data in a format which would be acceptable to parents.

A number of meetings left the group frustrated and dissatisfied with existing forms of commercial database software which could not match the demanding criteria. It became apparent that the only solution would be found by producing a custom written programme — a formidable task. A lunchtime discussion at the penultimate meeting between Colin Richards of the SEMERC, Mike Wright, adviser, and John Ferguson, educational psychologist, produced a feasible specification based on the earlier recording procedures of Green Arbour School, Thurcroft, South Yorkshire — a last ditch stand.

With the germ of an idea John Ferguson sped hot foot to his mountain retreat back in Powys. Within a remarkably short timescale, working with his son and burning many candle hours, John returned to the group (based at MEP, Doncaster) with a viable pilot programme.

The meagre budget virtually spent, the group became indebted to Peter Avis, Director of MEP, Doncaster, who enabled them to a degree to refine and pilot the project across the region.

What emerged was far from a Rolls Royce but, nevertheless, was a developable tool. A tool which had evolved from special school practice, initially developed to assist with the administration of the 1981 Act procedures and was able to provide, to a limited degree, a profile of pupil progress on a regular basis for all statemented pupils wherever located.

Whilst the programme met many of the group's criteria, the limited budget had seriously restricted its refinement and it was regrettably released too soon. The direct consequence being that for many the documentation was too complex, and for others the programme did not deliver to the level expected. As a programme it lost favour and but for the commitment of a few devotees to continue its development, it would have vanished into the mists of time, the story of so much 'innovative software'.

However, the commitment of Derek Cooper at the Newcastle SEMERC, the Leeds LEA via Trevor Nelson and Graham Pirt of Riverside (Humberside), Mike Wright, Chairman of Resource SEN Advisory Committee, persisted and led, eventually, to the development of a much more refined user-friendly flexible product. One important lesson had been learned, the programme provided any school with a useful curriculum development tool which for many became part of the process of curriculum management, not just a recording device. To regard it as an annual review programme alone failed to do justice to a potentially powerful concept.

Developing the System in a Special School

Following the initial development of a computerized record-keeping system in Powys; subsequently distributed through 'Resource' as part of the then MEP, Riverside Special School in Humberside, a school for pupils with moderate learning difficulties, decided to implement the program. The process was not simple and there were many problems to be overcome; philosophical, curricular and practical. The fact that the school undertook this process and its evaluation proved invaluable as the school's role changed. The on-going development is now seen as a method by which mainstream school can be monitored in a larger environment. The processes involved in the school's acquisition of the record-keeping have become a process which can be extended to the mainstream schools.

Within Riverside School it was envisaged that the process of the annual review that had to be undertaken for each 'statemented' child could well be adapted to meet the further role of a record of achievement. The process at the beginning of the procedure was far from clear. It was decided to adopt the annual review program and to develop a system of review based around it.

The first part of the development involved a total reassessment of the curriculum that was in operation at the school at that time. It was fortuitous that some of the main elements of the curriculum already embodied the structure, if not the content, that was necessary. The program demanded that the curriculum was of an objectives-based format, hierarchical in structure, if not in content, and consisting of positive statements of achievement, preferably of a measurably objective nature.

The curriculum model provided by the program enabled the staff to have a very clear format for discussion and development in curriculum covered the areas of mathematics and language. The staff were given the format of the program (Figure 1) as a base around which to work. The content of the mathematics curriculum had been developed in staff groups only a short while before and it was not felt necessary to reassess that at the same time.

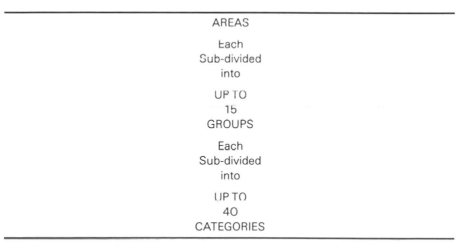

AREAS

Each
Sub-divided
into

UP TO
15
GROUPS

Each
Sub-divided
into

UP TO
40
CATEGORIES

Figure 1: Programme Format

The result of this type of analysis led to a structure which it was felt was suitable for the school and its range of pupils. An example of the application of this structure to the mathematics curriculum appears in Figure 2.

This illustrates one small section of the content and its flow.

(AREA) Maths				
(GROUP) *Computation*	*Temporal*	*Shape*	*Graphical*	*Representation* etc.
(CATEGORY) *Recognizes Circle*	*Can Draw Circle*	*Recognizes Triangle*		etc.

Figure 2. Structure as applied to Maths

The development of this aspect of record-keeping did not develop as a discrete entity within the school. It was obvious that in taking this procedure on board there was a time delay between its introduction and its efficient use. Any answer to this obviously needed to conform to the structure of the program. The key to this solution lay in the demands of the annual review format as laid down by Humberside, and also in the working of the program itself.

The Humberside document included the question, 'Changes observed in the last year?', which was the very premise upon which the program worked. The paper document was devised in the, not uncommon, pie or Gunzburg (1963) style checklist. The items on the checklist were matched with the curriculum content in the computer program so that both were interchangeable.

The checklist allowed staff to monitor, in a simple manner, any changes in achievement over a year. The baseline of achievement was found for each child and entered onto the checklist by colouring in a block for each objective achieved. Once the baseline had been found then further objectives achieved were entered in a different colour. This allowed staff to see quickly any changes. The principle was identical to the annual review except that the computer 'colours' the blocks electronically. It does however provide a much more rapid assessment of changes across the curriculum and, of course, a printout of those changes.

The decision to move ahead on the computer system came in early 1987 and since all data had been entered by that time the school committed itself to using the program. There were still some problems in that the authority did not feel that the presentation of the system was adequate for their needs. Although Leeds Authority had made some significant changes to the program, Riverside School produced a different layout which was eventually accepted as being suitable.

Staff were given in-house training in order to both understand and use the system. The system is managed by the head of the school but a self-management system is being devised. The process for undertaking annual reviews is now pursuing the following format:-

Paper records are maintained on a daily basis by the class teachers, or subject teachers.
These records are entered onto the annual review system on a half-termly basis. This takes approximately half an hour for ten pupils. Some schools achieve a daily level of interaction and revision.

At the time of the pupil's annual review the following printouts are obtained by the class teacher:

> A complete personal information printout of the pupil with spaces for comments by parents, pupil and headteacher.
> A list of recommendations concerning present and future provision.
> A list of changes that have occurred over the year in the curriculum areas.
> A sheet for the teacher to make comments upon with the relevant headings — direct interaction via a 'wordwise chip' has also been explored.
> A further list is provided for the class teacher's use which consists of a list of future objectives for each pupil. This is not distributed to parents but is used by the teacher to consider the most suitable objectives for the pupils for the following year. Some schools are currently exploring ways in which this stage of the process is negotiated with the pupil as appropriate.
> A meeting is held with parents, psychologist, medical officer, speech therapist, class teacher and headteacher at which the document is discussed and comments obtained. This is the opportunity for the school to explain what the list of changes provided mean for the pupil. Parents then receive a copy of the document.

In the initial stages of introducing the system there were doubts that arose as to whether the input of time would pay dividends at the end. The school is in no doubt now that this system provides all that is needed to undertake an efficient and accurate annual review. There are many other facets, which were not obvious at the outset, which are now coming into their own. The mundane, though necessary, administration tasks of the office are well catered for with class lists, address lists, age searches for DES returns and many other provisions, as well as extremely useful criteria searches of the curriculum objectives which allow for continuous monitoring of the validity of teaching objectives, or indeed whether they have been taught. Curriculum experiences however broad may be documented within the process.

Current thoughts about the program are in investigating where it fits into an overall aspect of a record of achievement, and there would appear to be a place for it in the formative stages. Also under review is the degree to which pupils are able to interact with the program themselves.

The National Curriculum would seem to have been custom made to fit the structure of the system and in a time when we may be looking at the provision of individualized learning within a national curriculum structure, then the structured record-keeping and reporting may prove to be a necessity for some pupils.

How does the Annual Review Process Relate to the Record of Achievement

Summary Records

Interim summary records will be produced with pupils at various stages of their school career. In most cases this has been done annually with the production of reports in the secondary school. The production of annual summary records with the involvement of pupils and parents will replace the traditional reporting procedure in secondary schools. These documents should reflect the wide range of achievements, which pupils demonstrate. They should attempt to look back and summarize progress as well as look forward towards what might be achieved and how this may be realized.

The annual summary process suggested here has many parallels with the annual review procedures required for pupils who are the subject of a Statement in mainstream and in special schools. Duplication of information is not helpful or desirable. The processes involved are described earlier as they relate to a special school. Such procedures will provide information that may be included in the documentation that must be completed as a legal requirement for statemented pupils.

The purpose of such summaries is to identify the pupil's progress for parents and pupils. They also provide a focus for agreed future learning targets or developments, which are reviewed at appropriate stages by the pupil, parent and tutor. The information for their completion will be contained in the various formative assessment and recording documents across the curriculum.

These summary records will be used as a means of reporting progress in the first three years of the secondary phase, although they may also contain information which may be included in the final summary document produced in the final two years of the secondary school.

Pupils who transfer to another school will take their record of achievement with them, in the form of an interim summary record or the annual review document, and resume the process of recording at their new school.

The summary record produced at appropriate stages in the secondary phase should include:

    (i) a statement of the curriculum followed by the pupil;

    (ii) a clear statement of the objectives for each course the pupil follows:
These will have been discussed with the pupil before the various units of work were begun. Many of these will originate from negotiated objectives arising from the various attainment targets in the profile components of the subjects of the National Curriculum;

    (iii) a statement by the pupil which describes his or her perceptions of progress against the agreed objectives in terms of knowledge, skills and understanding and the qualities he or she has expressed through subjects or cross-curricular themes of work. Some pupils may require considerable support to formulate and communicate their perceptions of progress. The process of self-evaluation is nevertheless an entitlement which all pupils should have the opportunity to experience;

(iv) a response by the teacher, which should be constructive and specific;

(v) future targets which both pupil and teacher have agreed.

Statements should also be constructed, which refer to a pupil's experiences and interests as well as the qualities, which he or she has demonstrated in and out of school. Such statements may involve parents or other adults who know the pupil well. In this way a more complete record of the pupil's progress and development will emerge.

Summary records will need to be produced for different agencies during the final two years at school. These will reflect stages in the pupil's development and may be used by the pupil as a means of negotiating entry to further education, training or employment. The contents of the first summary will have been accumulated during Year four (or before).

Reviewing and Recording

The importance of reviewing and of the self-assessment associated with this aspect of learning is made clear in the Humberside Guidelines 'Recording the Achievements of Pupils' and is also fundamental to the 1981 Education Act procedures.

Reviewing and recording progress should be a natural part of the learning process, and it may take many forms. One of these may well be tutor reviews with small groups of pupils, or in certain cases with individual pupils, as part of a tutorial or personal and social education programme. Other methods might include whole class reviews, self-assessment review sheets given in class time or as homework, or reviews in pairs or trios of pupils.

The use of computer software which enables pupils to interact with skill analysis prompt words or phrases is an interesting development which is discussed earlier.

Such reviews will lead to the identification of future targets which both teacher and pupil should agree. These should be realistic and within the capabilities of individual pupils and should identify how the pupil intends to try and meet the targets.

Reviews are generally most successful when carried out against a background of previously identified learning objectives. Normally such reviews will occur at the end of blocks of work relating to particular units of work, projects or particular topics. The 1981 Act reviews should occur *at least* annually.

Assessment

Teachers and pupils may adopt a wide range of strategies to assess progress against learning objectives. Whatever style of assessment and recording is used it should show evidence of:-

    (i) a shared summary of learning objectives or intended outcomes, which should involve reference to specific skills, knowledge and experiences. Some of these objectives will relate to the attainment levels of the subjects of the National Curriculum. Others will refer to general skills which pupils will have the opportunity to develop during the unit of work. Some of these objectives will be set for individual pupils and may have been identified as targets at the end of the last unit of work or review session;

    (ii) the assessment techniques to be used;

    (iii) opportunities for self-assessment by the pupil;

    (iv) a record of assessment by the teacher and/or pupil;

    (v) a review of progress against learning objectives;

    (vi) a record, preferably as part of the review, of the personal qualities displayed by the pupil;

    (vii) specific targets identified by pupil and teacher for future performance.

The interaction between pupil and teacher, which is part of this assessment process, should be positive and aid motivation. Negative feedback may be necessary but should:-

    (i) be specific;

    (ii) refer to behaviour or performance that the pupil is able to change;

    (iii) offer alternatives.

Personal qualities such as *RESPONSIBILITY, INITIATIVE, DETERMINATION* should be referred to only in the context of factual examples which demonstrate the ways in which the pupil has shown these qualities. The examples should be significant and indicate, where appropriate, that the quality has been shown on a number of occasions or over a significant period of time and in a particular context or series of contexts. Pupils should be encouraged to record and identify such examples although teachers should be aware that modesty may be an obstacle which prevents pupils from recognizing such qualities.

No individual can show 'determination' in everything or he or she does or indeed with the same degree of intensity for long periods of time. This should not prevent us and the pupil from recognizing that such qualities are demonstrated on many occasions.

In Conclusion

It is suggested in the DES publication —

In this brief drawing together of some of the main findings from our evaluation it has been our aim to highlight the major themes which are raised by records of achievement and the factors which appear to determine the success or otherwise of a records of achievement scheme. In particular we have pointed to the twin principles of 'ownership' and 'penetration' which are proposed as an overarching rationale for development work. Schools which are characterized by these elements are likely to be able to move easily between principles and procedures within records of achievement and to recognize the need to do so.

An important feature of the analysis is the way in which what appear at first sight to be issues which are specific to records of achievement development are revealed on closer inspection as more fundamental educational issues. Thus, for example, the existing research on 'self-esteem' and 'locus of control' have much to teach us about pupil attitudes. Learning theory and metacognition research likewise can reveal important principles in the construction of effective learning situations; interactionist and teacher effectiveness research can help us to learn what it is that leads to positive teacher–pupil relations. The extensive literature on curriculum planning and development, the management of innovation and change and on management generally has much to offer that is relevant to 'records of achievement.

At times of pressure on the teaching force it is important that together, both LEA officers and schools seek to find ways to capitalize upon good practice to use time wisely. It would seem that this is a viable option open to us in the area of recording pupil achievement.

Chapter 6

Teaching Mathematics to Pupils with Severe Learning Difficulties

Dr Robert Ashdown and Kathleen Devereux

Introduction

The Rees Thomas School is a special school for pupils with severe learning difficulties. There are forty-five pupils on roll aged between 5 and 19 years, of whom about 20 per cent have additional physical disabilities, sensory disabilities, medical problems and/or severe psychological disorders. The language development of all the pupils is markedly delayed. About 20 per cent have no apparent understanding of language at all. Forty per cent have not yet started to use single words and the utterances of a further 30 per cent are often unintelligible because of articulation problems. Of those with some comprehension skills, well over half can follow reasonably complex commands or a simple story. But most have considerable difficulties with the basic terms which are associated with a mathematics programme, that is, the vocabulary of space, size, quantity, number and time, and specific phrases and vocabulary used when talking about number operations. On the whole, the language abilities of Rees Thomas School pupils are similar to those of pupils in other special schools (cf. the surveys by Leeming *et al.*, 1979; Swann and Mittler, 1976).

It is no easy matter to teach pupils with severe learning difficulties the language and mathematics skills that most young children effortlessly acquire by the age of 5 or 6 years. Merely exposing pupils to an enriched and stimulating environment is not enough. Instead, a systematic teaching approach is necessary. This involves clearly specifying objectives and planning teaching programmes so that a number of simple steps in a logical sequence lead to the desired objectives. 'Errorless learning' may be achieved if the task analysis is adequate and if verbal cues, modelling and physical prompts are given to elicit correct responses. Positive reinforcement procedures are used and an important part of the teaching process is identifying strong reinforcers for individual pupils. Often, pupils do not spontaneously produce newly learned skills outside the original teaching setting. This problem of generalization may be minimized by using meaningful and familiar materials in natural situations as much as possible. For instance, one-to-one correspondence may be taught in the context of placing lids on jam jars, cups on saucers and cutlery next to plates at the dinner table. Pupils are usually taught individually or in small groups and repeated oportunities for learning a skill are given. Readers requiring an introductory text about the psychological reality of severe learning difficulties and appropriate teaching approaches would do well to read the book by Clements (1987).

It is most important that teachers should have a good understanding of the linguistic problems involved in teaching mathematics. Mathematics is after all a very formal type of language. It has none of the redundancy of literary or everyday language. For instance, the utterance 'Here is a girl and her dog' contains several clues about the gender of the subject ('girl' and 'her') and the number ('girl', 'is', 'a', and 'her'). If one word is not understood, there are other clues to the meaning of the utterance. In contrast, mathematics economizes on words. In the case of a statement like 'one and one is two' the whole meaning is lost if a pupil misses or does not understand just one word. As a result, there is a need to expand mathematical statements and repeat them until understanding is established. Teachers must also have a good grasp of the principles underpinning effective teaching and assessment procedures related to language development. Jones and Robson (1977) have written a review of methods used to teach language skills. Methods for teaching word production are shown in a minicourse for teachers on language development by Robson *et al.* (1982). Jones and Robson (1979) review the importance of different types of questioning strategies. Ashdown (1985) describes methods of teaching vocabulary to children who have difficulties in learning to speak. At Rees Thomas School use is made of non-vocal communication systems with pupils who have poor expressive language and inadequate auditory memory skills. We have found that signs from the Makaton Vocabulary and Signed English together with rebuses cover much of the vocabulary which is relevant to a mathematics programme. Devereux and van Oosterom (1984) describe the uses of rebuses at Rees Thomas School, and the various sign languages and symbol systems in use in the UK are described and evaluated by Kiernan, Reid and Goldbart (1987).

The Rees Thomas School curriculum emphasises teaching communication, social and independence skills and providing an indivisualised education appropriate to each pupil's particular needs. Elements of mathematics are taught only when they are functional for the individual pupil, which means that about twenty of the forty-five pupils do not yet have the prerequisite skills for learning number skills and are, therefore, at the pre-number stage. Of the remainder, 75 per cent are learning the numbers up to ten and only half a dozen are at the stage of learning numbers beyond ten. Similarly, McConkey and McEvoy (1986) report tests of fifty-one pupils in a Dublin special school who were aged 11–18 years. They found that only half of them could count by rote and recognize numerals to twenty. Even fewer, about a third of the pupils, could count up to twenty objects or hand over a specified number of objects on request. At Rees Thomas School simple addition and subtraction, mainly using counters of some sort, is appropriate for approximately ten pupils and none are doing multiplication or subtraction. Coin recognition is taught to the older pupils but all have great problems in learning their equivalent values. A few can tell the time other than by the hour but not by minutes.

Our experience shows that mathematics teaching will continue to focus on very simple skills throughout the entire school career of a pupil with severe learning difficulties. Few pupils reach the level attained by most 7 or 8 year olds in primary schools. Many will still be learning simple vocabulary and counting when they are well into their teenage years. Many leave school with major gaps in their knowledge of the simplest aspects of counting, number operations and measurement (cf. the findings of Cheseldine and Jeffree, 1982; Whelan and Speake, 1978). Therefore, we are faced by the twin problems of having to teach very basic mathematics skills for some 10–15 years and at the same time making this an interesting experience for our pupils. We have to be imaginative in the teaching activities we design and assiduous in systematically implementing them. To cap this, the group of pupils in every class shows considerable variation in ability and age. It must be appreciated that good teaching of mathematics under such conditions is an immense challenge and poses great demands upon teachers.

The Mathematics Curriculum

We have found some good sources for guidelines about goals, objectives, teaching and assessment. The books by Gillham (1987), Peterson (1973), Duncan (1978), Snell (1983) and the Rectory Paddock School Staff (1983) and a resources box by Robbins (1988) have been found to be especially useful and relevant. There is also a video course on teaching number produced by McConkey and McEvoy (1986). Of course, there are now the proposals for the National Curriculum which have to be taken into account too (DES and Welsh Office, 1988). The major aims of the mathematics curriculum for Rees Thomas School have been identified as:

> learning a meaningful vocabulary related to mathematics;
> learning to count;
> learning to use numbers;
> establishing understanding of the use of the clock, the ruler, the calendar and the
>   thermometer and those measures related to cooking;
> learning to recognize coins and notes and their equivalencies and to use money in
>   simple transactions;
> understanding and using simple number facts in 'real-life' problem-solving
>   situations.

Given that functional skills are more likely to be learned if meaningful and familiar teaching materials and activities are used, it is an aim to use real-life situations and familiar things. For instance, the skill of sorting may be reinforced in the home economics area with activities involving sorting of cutlery into trays. Workbooks and paper exercises are eschewed unless pupils actually seem to enjoy these. Most mathematics schemes are aimed at pupils of average ability and pupils with severe learning difficulties cannot easily cope with them. Usually workbooks demand reading skills which the pupils do not have. They present too much information on each page and they do not provide sufficient practice. Often, the steps leading to an objective are too few and too great. Therefore, workbooks are used for reinforcement activities only, if at all.

In this context it is worth commenting on the value of developmental data gleaned from the many studies of children without significant learning difficulties. This data, along with the goals of mathematics programmes and attainment targets for primary school pupils, can serve as a rough guide. But it must be appreciated that it is neither necessary, appropriate, nor, in many cases, possible to take pupils with severe learning difficulties through the entire sequences of skills acquired by nursery/infant pupils simply because they have a similar developmental age. Firstly, there is not enough time to teach all these skills to pupils who are learning at such a slow rate. Secondly, older pupils with a mental age of 3–5 years have very different interests and needs. Finally, developmental sequences do not necessarily mean that every skill in a sequence is prerequisite for achieving a final target. Selection of goals depends much more upon what is perceived by the teacher to be necessary as a logical next step and what is functional for the individual.

Our mathematics programme is introduced to pupils who communicate readily and have a well-established vocabulary of approximately fifty words. Pupils have to be able to use and understand some basic action words, such as, 'give', 'point', 'touch' and 'show'. They should demonstrate an ability to attend and actively participate for at least a few minutes in various games and activities. An ability to imitate is very helpful, although not essential for all activities.

A. Classification Skills

Sorting, matching and ordering activities of various kinds feature heavily at this stage with an emphasis upon simple sorting of objects and sorting of objects by size, colour and shape. Gillham (1987) provides suggestions for this kind of work which are appropriate for younger pupils. The teaching materials available through educational firms tend to emphasize the sorting and matching of arbitrarily chosen objects, usually plastic or wooden beads, counters and toys, according to their size, colour and shape. These activities are enjoyed by many pupils. However, some pupils make little progress in these sorting activities. In their case, and especially in the case of teenagers on practical independence programmes, it may be more efficient and more appropriate to teach sorting of coins, different tins of food, different sizes of spoons, and so on.

B. Vocabulary

Normally, young children learn some of the vocabulary associated with mathematics before they enter their first school and some mathematical concepts are learned before they get any real grasp of formal numbers. The ideas seem so simple that most adults might not even consider it necessary to teach them explicitly. But pupils with severe learning difficulties of all ages cannot be expected to learn these simply by listening to adults, even though, paradoxically, these are words which are used frequently by adults without any realization of the problems they may cause for pupils. It is worth giving just one example of the many quirks of adult language that may cause confusion. 'A bit' is a useful phrase which is normally used to refer to a small piece or a small amount of something. However, it is also possible to refer to 'a big bit' as opposed to 'a small bit'. Teachers must always be alert for these kinds of problems which are posed by the English language and the way it is used (see Wiig and Semel, 1980, for many examples).

An early goal is to teach some adjectives, such as, 'big' and 'small'. Like colour, the size of an object is an important aspect of its appearance and this kind of vocabulary can be introduced in early sorting and matching activities. There are also several simple spatial terms which are taught, such as, the prepositions 'in', 'on', 'up', 'down', etc. Finally, it is important to introduce the concept of similarity and the words 'same' and 'like'. At Rees Thomas School, a programme has been developed for teaching basic vocabulary associated with mathematics, particularly words relating to space, size, time, quantity and simple number (Ashdown, 1988).

C. Counting

Learning the significance of numbers does not come easily. At the outset, pupils are not used to thinking in terms of the 'numerosity' of groups. Also, there is a great deal of scope for confusion between number words and other words which occur in people's speech. For instance, there may be confusion between the pronoun 'one' and the number word 'one' as when someone points to a figure and says 'This one's three'. Then there are homophones such as 'two', 'to' and 'too' as in 'Give one to Luke too' or, worse still, 'Here's one for you too'. Again, these problems underline the need for teachers to be most careful about the language they employ.

In order to count out a set of objects correctly, pupils have to identify the items making up the set, recall the number names in the proper order, give each item in the set one number name in turn, remember the items they have counted and those which remain and, finally, realize that the last number named is the total for the set. Typical errors made when counting objects include missing out number names from the sequence, counting objects more than once or missing objects out of the count altogether. Pupils may even say a different number from the final number in a correct count. When told to hand over a specific number of items, they often count beyond the number asked for because they fail to mentally check the number counted against the number asked for. On the whole, they make mistakes more often when giving a specified number of objects than when counting the same number of items. All of these errors will be observed in young children in primary schools but they persist for much longer in the case of pupils with severe learning difficulties. Therefore, it is very important to have good diagnostic techniques and, aside from our own tests, we have found that McConkey and McEvoy (1986) provide the best guidelines.

Rigorous teaching techniques are adopted for teaching counting skills. Firstly, pupils are taught to recite numbers in the correct order starting with just a few digits and building gradually up to longer sequences. It is important to establish the habit of saying the numbers with a rhythmic pace and the teacher must regularly provide a model for good counting. This can be made enjoyable through games, rhymes and songs rather than employing repetitive drill work.

When it comes to counting objects, only a few objects are placed in a row initially. At a later stage, when counting skills are more firmly established, more items are introduced and they may be arranged in circles and haphazard patterns. The key skill to be learned is to touch each object in term and to synchronize the number recitation with the finger checking. Again, it is important for the teacher to demonstrate this and, where necessary, to use verbal and physical prompts to get each pupil to do the same. These prompts must be faded eventually. When it comes to teaching pupils to count off a number of items from a larger group, physical and verbal prompts may be necessary. Since many confuse items that have been counted off with those that have not, it has been found useful to teach pupils to separate items off onto a piece of paper or a plate as they are counted. Pupils are also encouraged to 'subitize', that is, instantly recognize how many items are in a small set without actually counting them. Subitizing numbers from one to three, and perhaps up to five, can be encouraged by revealing collections of items for increasingly shorter periods of time so that pupils do not have the time to count them.

Pupils are taught the relation between successive cardinal numbers by using wall friezes, different types of abaci and structural equipment like Multilink and Unifix Cubes. Activities include asking pupils to count off a named number of items, then to count off 'another' or 'one more' and, finally, they are asked to say how many there are.

For many pupils there is limited functional value in learning the actual numerals because their counting skills are so poor. It is quite usual for numeral recognition to lag well behind an ability to count. Teaching number-numeral association to pupils who cannot count sets containing more than five objects is of questionable value. Typically, number-numeral association has to be taught through a variety of activities involving matching numerals to sets of items and naming numerals. Most pupils have difficulty with the mechanics of writing numerals and remembering how to write them even when they can copy well and much regular copying practice is necessary.

Counting in a variety of settings is always encouraged. For instance, laying the table for a specific number of people is an activity which will foster generalization of learned number skills. In particular, shopping trips help pupils to notice numerals around them and appreciate their significance. Such activities are demanding of staff time and resources but are an essential and enjoyable part of the 'life skills' curriculum.

D. Number Games

In order to sustain interest it is vital to make or buy a variety of simple number games which give plenty of opportunities for practice and which make the task of learning to count meaningful and fun. There are a number of commercially available games which are appropriate. The ILEA 'ESN(S) Consortium' has produced some very useful activity packs and a video course by McConkey and McEvoy (1986) is a particularly good source of ideas.

As well as being fun, these number games must meet other important requirements. Every effort has to be made to simplify the process of learning to count. Therefore, to begin with, there is repeated practice with one number only and all dice, spinners and cards used bear only this number and some blanks. Teaching continues until the number is mastered and then another is substituted. Eventually, discrimination of the two numbers must be reinforced before the next number is introduced. Spots rather than numerals are used initially on dice, cards, spinners, etc., although these games are a good way of teaching number-numeral association at a later stage. Several opportunities for counting are given in every game. Adults or older more able children participate in the games so that they can act as a model for following the rules of the game and give clear examples of counting. They must demonstrate and teach methods of self-checking and self-correction. If a pupil makes a mistake he should not be told the right answer but made to check his counting.

E. Ordinal Number

Pupils are normally introduced to a few ordinal numbers. Typically, they are taught the use of 'first', 'next' and 'last' to indicate temporal and spatial position. 'Second', 'third', 'fourth', etc. are introduced only when numbers up to five or ten have been learned. Ultimately, use of a calendar may be taught when the ordinals first to thirty-first, the days of the week and the days of the month have been taught.

F. Time

It is possible to teach vocabulary like 'today', 'tomorrow', 'yesterday', 'afternoon', 'night', etc. from quite an early stage. The meanings of 'before', 'after', 'now', 'sooner' and 'later' also have to be taught in relation to regularly occurring activities and events. At a much later stage, telling the time by the hour, half-hour and quarter-hour using the clockface is introduced and there has to be much practical experience of timing familiar activities to enable pupils to estimate the passage of time and make plans.

G. Measurement of Size, Weight and Capacity

Reliable concepts relating to size are usually taught long before pupils are introduced to concepts of weight, time and capacity. Activities concerned with capacity initially take the form of structured play activities involving sand and water and a variety of containers which are either identical or obviously different in size. Through filling and pouring from one container to another and making simple comparisons, the pupils may be taught the meanings of phrases such as 'more', 'most', 'the same amount', 'as much as', and so on. Activities concerned with weight include teaching pupils to judge which is the heavier or lighter of two objects. They must learn that the weight of an object is independent of its size. Structured experiences of play with balance scales of various kinds are also important at this stage. As mentioned above, there is a specific programme of activities at Rees Thomas School for teaching this vocabulary.

H. Conservation

During these counting and measuring activities pupils may begin to learn the concept of 'conservation'. This is the dawning realization that a quantity stays the same no matter how much one moves it about, alters its shape and generally changes it around, as long as nothing is added to or subtracted from it. Unless a child can conserve, he is not going to be capable of any truly logical reasoning or performing mathematical operations, such as addition and subtraction, with proper understanding.

The ability to conserve is normally seen in ordinary primary school children between 5–8 years of age and may never be achieved by many pupils with severe learning difficulties. Nevertheless, it is possible to design activities which will foster the development of conservation. In particular, activities designed to teach the meanings of words like 'same', 'more', 'less', and so on could lay the foundations of an ability to conserve. For instance, pupils may be presented with two static quantities, such as two bottles containing different amounts of liquid. They may be asked to make comparisons of the amounts contained in the bottles and answer questions about 'same', 'more' and 'less'. Sometimes the looks of a quantity are changed but not the amount. At other times something may have been taken away from or added to the amount but the looks may or may not be different. Judging static states is much easier than judging transformations but there are a number of 'rules' which pupils should be encouraged to use to help them make correct decisions (Green and Laxon, 1978; Liebeck, 1984).

I. Number Operations

Number operations present a variety of linguistic and cognitive problems. A decision has to be made about what vocabulary and phrases to use and staff have to use this consistently. For instance, are words like 'take away', 'plus' and 'equals' to be used? Also, mention was made earlier of the special problems caused by the lack of redundancy in mathematical language. It is easier to teach addition using real-life situations and saying things like 'Here are two apples. Here are two more. Now there are four apples'. Of necessity, there must be a concerted attempt to link number operations to real-life situations as much as possible. In the case of each individual, careful consideration must be given to how desirable it is to introduce formal notation of number operations through workbook and paper exercises which involve a different style of language. Also, equipment must be chosen carefully because pupils need to count concrete items for a long time before they can be introduced to 'mental arithmetic'. In fact, because so few are capable of doing number operations in the absence of items to count, we have found it expedient to teach the use of simple calculators to enable pupils to do sums in situations where there are no items to work with (e.g., when shopping).

A major hurdle to be crossed is learning the significance of 'hundreds', 'tens' and 'units' even though these terms are not actually taught. An abacus and Cuisenaire rods or similar structural equipment are particularly useful for this work. So too, is 'home-made' equipment, e.g., bags containing sets of ten items like lollipops, marbles and beads to signify 'tens' and single items to signify 'units'. Relating bundles, bags or groups of 'tens' to the 'tens' numeral requires much careful teaching.

J. 'Life Skills'

At Rees Thomas School much emphasis is given to learning a variety of practical skills necessary for independent living. Many of these involve mathematics, e.g., learning to use money in shopping, to construct shopping lists, to follow recipes, to tell the time, to construct schedules and to use a calendar. Yet as noted above, many of our teenage pupils have very limited number and measurement skills and most cannot read printed words. This means that for the necessary 'life skills' work to proceed, we have to give careful consideration to the language which is employed and be imaginative in devising aids which will help the pupils to learn these independence skills despite their limited mathematics and reading ability.

The following description provides only a sample of the range of activities which may be undertaken. Shopping lists can be made using rebuses and the price of goods may be indicated on the shopping list by coin stamps rather than a price tag. Most pupils have not crossed the major hurdle between simple coin recognition and understanding the equivalence of coins so this presents major problems. A lot of reliance is placed upon the goodwill of the shop assistants at the local supermarket when it comes to making transactions and before they set off on their shopping pupils have to be helped to select appropriate coins or notes. Similarly, when it comes to measuring ingredients for cooking, it is easier to use standard cup and spoon measures than balance scales involving grams and kilos. Pupils have to be taught to shop for items of a particular size using visual cues since they cannot read the weights written on the goods. These few examples emphasize the need for teachers to examine curriculum content and teaching practice carefully in each individual case. A useful review of mathematics in relation to life skills in particular is given by Snell (1983) and relevant suggestions for teaching in relation to money, time and measurement are given by Robbins (1988), Peterson (1973), the Rectory Paddock School Staff (1983) and Duncan (1978).

Conclusions

One of the aims of teachers of pupils with severe learning difficulties is that their pupils should master a number of routine 'life skills'. Survival for adults with severe learning difficulties in community-based, residential settings is facilitated by learning a variety of practical mathematics skills. In addition, mathematics activities can be intrinsically interesting for pupils at school. Therefore, there is no doubt that mathematics should feature as part of the special school curriculum. However, much depends upon the imagination and skill of the teachers.

A successful mathematics programme must incorporate the following features:

1   The learning of functional skills must be the ultimate goal.
2   Learning objectives should be selected only after careful consideration of the pupil's current and future living environments.
3   Teaching must be done with realistic materials in natural situations as much as possible.
4   Careful consideration must be given to the kind of language used during instruction and in the natural environment.
5   Objectives and teaching methods should be familiar to all key workers and parents and there must be a systematic approach to assessment and recording of progress.
6   Teaching must be viewed as a long-term process which will continue beyond childhood into adult life.
7   Teaching activities must be intrinsically interesting for the pupil.

To sum up, teaching mathematics to pupils with severe learning difficulties is an immense challenge. It requires considerable skill, knowledge, a sense of fun and doggedness on the part of the teacher. But a good teacher can make mathematics rewarding and enjoyable for the pupils and at the same time derive considerable satisfaction from the intellectual stimulation involved in the whole affair of designing and implementing suitable activities.

Chapter 7

A Teaching Machine for Active Learning

Mike Swift

This chapter describes the use of a language teaching machine invented by teachers working at the Southall Special School in Telford. The school caters for children with moderate learning difficulties within an age range of five to sixteen. Over the past four years the school has developed its own symbol-word system for the teaching of early reading skills.

Most children entering Southall whether at 5, 8 or 11, have one thing in common. They have little or no reading skill, and have quite often been exposed to several years of failure. The initial approach at Southall usually depends on an assessment which will hopefully indicate a child's strength e.g., a child with strong auditory skills might be placed on a phonic programme, while a visual learner will be channelled towards the schools symbol-word system. Whatever method is adopted the overriding principle remains the same. Namely that a child will always be involved in his or her learning by being asked to carry out an action or give a verbal response within a teaching objective.

The Machine

The Action Reading Machine (Figure 1) has been developed by teachers over a number of years as a classroom aid for the development of language skills. The machine itself is a box-like apparatus with an open back and a long viewing window at its front. Each machine can take up to eight information wheels at a time that can be simply lifted out or rearranged to meet any particular teaching objective (Figure 2). When placed in the machine the wheels revolve on small rollers so that information presented in the viewing window can be changed in seconds to present a different structure to the child. The wheels are controlled by the teacher who usually sits to the side of the machine.

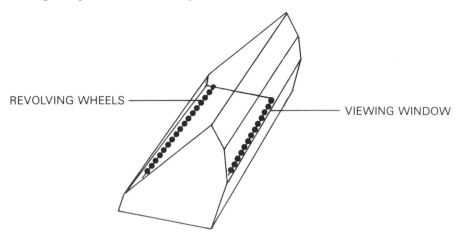

REVOLVING WHEELS ————————— VIEWING WINDOW

Figure 1: The Machine

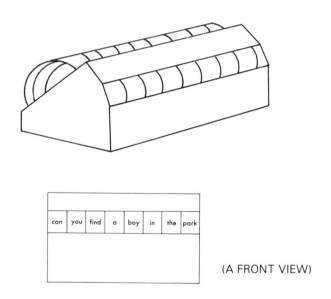

can	you	find	a	boy	in	the	park

(A FRONT VIEW)

Figure 2: The Machine Loaded with Information Wheels

The ability of the machine to work in a teaching situation rests firmly on the principle that much of our language is ordered and follows grammatical rules. This is perhaps best illustrated by looking at two teaching situations using the machine.

Example 1

Teaching situation — group of four children.

Equipment — Dolls house size — teddy, doll, cat, dog, big chair, little chair, big bed, little bed, big table, little table, big red box, little yellow box.

Teaching Objective — To teach in action way prepositions on/under/in. (Other words to be used in lesson — put, the, teddy, doll, cat, dog, big, little, red, yellow, box, chair, bed, table — already taught).

1   The equipment is placed on the table.
2   The information wheels are placed in the machine.

put	the	teddy	on	the	big	box	
		doll	under		little	chair	
		cat	in		red	bed	
		dog			yellow	table	

This particular teaching situation requires seven wheels that have words and one blank wheel.

3   A child reads the first sentence —

put   the   teddy   on   the   big   box

— and then carries out the action using the equipment (i.e., the teddy is placed on the big box).

4   Instructions to the second child might be —

put   the   doll   under   the   little   bed

This requires the teacher to change four words. With the machine this is carried out in seconds. By rotating just the four wheels indicated no less than eighty-one different sentences can be offered to the children.

Example 2

Teaching situation — group of six children.

Equipment — Dice, shaker, counters, board game (to win the dice each child in turn must sound and say word presented on machine).

Teaching Objective — To teach and practise final consonant blends.

1   The game is placed on the table and each child is given a counter.
2   The information wheels are placed in the machine.

b	a	nd					
s	e	nt					
h	i	ng					
d	o	nk					
m	u	st					
n		sk					
p		mp					
r		ld					
t		lt					

This particular teaching situation requires three wheels that have sounds and five blank wheels.

3   A child 'sounds' and reads the first word — band. If correct the child gains the dice and starts the game. The word for the second child might be sand — third child hand, and so on.

By rotating just the three wheels in the machine more than a hundred different words can be offered to the children.

Action Reading

Action Reading in simple terms means exactly what it says — the reading of a sentence is always followed by the carrying out of an action or verbal response. Let us suppose that as a starting point to teaching a young child to read we intend to use the following twenty-one words - a, big, boy, by, cat, cup, dog, draw, girl, happy, has, house, in, is, little, monster, on, put, sad, the, tree. Firstly if we intend to use the Action Reading Machine we must place these words under their grammatical heading hence — Grammatical Analysis.

Verb/ Questions	Articles	Adjectives	Nouns (Animate)	Nouns (Inanimate)	Prepositions
put is draw has	the a	big little happy sad	boy girl dog monster cat	house cup tree	in on by

Already the order of the words on the information wheels are taking shape —

1	2	3	4	5	6	7	8	9
put is draw has	the a	big little happy sad	boy girl dog monster cat	house cup tree	in on by	boy girl dog monster cat	the a	big little happy sad

Numbering is important. It allows the teacher to quickly find the required wheels and also helps in the planning of the lesson.

The first six wheels are copied straight from the grammatical analysis of the words to be taught — wheels 2, 3, 4 are repeated as wheels 7, 8, 9 to allow more flexibility with sentence structuring.

Example of Lesson

An early lesson might be to introduce and practise the following words — happy, sad, dog, monster, cat.

Equipment — happy dog, happy monster, happy cat, sad dog, sad cat, sad monster.
(Even the most unartistic teacher can soon become adept at making simple cut out figures as above. Use of manufactured equipment such as play people, doll's house furniture etc. is widely used in this teaching method.)

1 The equipment is placed on the table.
2 The information wheels are placed in the machine.

happy	monster						
sad	dog cat						

3 Teacher requests child — 'Find' — child and teacher read — 'happy monster' — child finds monster. Second instructions might be to find — sad cat. (The machine allows sentences to be changed in seconds) — third instruction — happy dog, etc.

A later lesson for the twenty-one words using the six figures might involve the following language structure.

put	the	happy	monster	by	the	little	tree
		sad	cat	on		big	cup
			dog	in			house

(Equipment needed for this lesson — happy monster, happy cat, happy dog, sad monster, sad cat, sad dog, big tree, big cup, big house, little tree, little cup, little house.)

Examples of language structures using the twenty-one words are given below. The shaded words are those to be changed for each structure. Remember action reading always requires the child to carry out a response or action.

Left structure grid:

	3 happy	4 dog				
2 a	3 big	4 boy				
2 a	3 big	5 tree				
1 draw	2 a	3 big	5 tree			
1 draw	2 a	3 little	4 girl			
1 is	2 the	3 big	4 boy	9 happy		
1 has	2 the	4 girl	7 a	5 cup		
2 the	4 cat	1 is	6 by	7 the	5 house	

Right structure grid:

1 put	2 a	4 boy	6 by	7 the	5 house		
1 has	2 the	4 monster	2 a	3 little	8 boy		
1 is	2 the	4 boy	6 by	7 the	5 tree		
2 a	4 dog	6 by	7 a	3 little	5 house		
1 put	7 a	8 dog	6 by	2 the	9 little	5 house	
1 is	2 the	3 little	4 boy	6 by	7 the	5 house	
1 put	7 a	3 little	8 cat	6 by	2 a	9 little	5 house
6 by	7 the	9 little	5 house	1 is	2 a	3 happy	4 monster

As the child gradually becomes proficient in the use and knowledge of the words the vocabulary can be extended. Obviously as more words become available the range and potential of language structures becomes far greater.

The use of action reading can and has been adapted to several different reading schemes. If it is the intention of the teacher to place the child on a published reading scheme it is important to use the vocabulary that is used by that scheme. This is not to say that extra words cannot be used — indeed practice has shown that inclusion of some additional action words adds to the variety of sentence structures available.

A Symbol-Word Method

In recent years there has been an increase in the use of picture cue symbols in the teaching of reading. This approach has been found particularly successful with lower ability children and youngsters who have not been able to gain early reading skills through conventional teaching programmes.

At Southall School in Telford, teachers have developed a symbol-word reading scheme for some of their youngest children using the Action Reading Machine. The aim of the Southall programme is to introduce the children to 118 words. This vocabulary is divided into four stages and the selection of the words took into consideration both common early reading words and developmental language structures. Many of the children placed on the Southall programme had failed to acquire any reading skills whatsoever in their previous infant and junior schools.

Most symbol-word reading methods are based on the principle that although some children find the abstract symbols of the printed word difficult to interpret and remember, they have no difficulty when the word is linked to pictorial representation.

The Southall vocabulary uses three different types of symbol-words:

(i)   (ii)   (iii)

(i) Symbol words where the symbol reproduces the salient features of the object.
(ii) Symbol-words where the symbol indicates a simple idea.
(iii) Symbol-words where the symbol gives a kinesthetic cue.

Observation of the children using the Southall symbol-word method shows clearly that all the children immediately recognize and remember the first category of symbol-words. Those words that represent a simple idea or give a kinesthetic cue require teaching, but are usually mastered very quickly by most children.

The vocabulary used in the Southall programme is as follows:

Level 1 (Black Words)

a, and, baby, ball, bed, big, blue, box, boy, castle, cat, chair, colour, count, cup, dad, dog, door, draw, flower, girl, green, happy, house, in, is, lady, little, make, man, more, mum, on, put, red, roof, sad, table, teddy, the, window, write, yellow.

Level 2 (Red Words)

at, bus, by, can, car, chimney, driver, find, go, got, has, here, hill, I, look, lorry, milk, monster, park, play, police, policelady, policeman, school, stop, to, tree, we, with, you.

Level 3 (Blue Words)

bad, behind, bike, down, get, good, have, he, into, me, name, paper, reading, river, run, she, shop, street, they, this, today, up, was, your.

Level 4 (Green Words)

Catch, climb, cook, crocodile, cut, drink, eat, elephant, hide, hippo, hit, jump, lion, met, monkey, penguin, sing, sit, slide, swing, zoo.

(The use of different colours is for the easy identification of the word level by the teacher.)

Following Grammatical Analysis the words and symbols were placed on the information wheels. The whole programme uses twenty wheels.

Because children almost immediately have knowledge of a usable vocabulary of symbol-words reading activities can begin at once using the Action Reading Machine. At every level of the Southall programme the emphasis is on action reading. The child responds to a sentence by carrying out an action or verbal response. Wide use is made of playboards (homemade) and attractive play materials — at level 1 — put / a / boy / on / the / castle / — the child finds the boy in the model village and puts him on the castle. At level 2 — make / the / policelady / stop / the / yellow / car / — the child will move the policelady in front of the yellow car in the village street.

At first the children rely heavily on use of the symbol rather than the word. The transfer to use of word only is gradual and involves a process known as fading. Practice has shown that many children exposed to action reading on a daily basis transfer naturally to use of word-only strategies. Other children though require activities such as word bingo and matching games to bring them to this level of understanding. At Southall the children are often given a bingo card containing symbol-words. The teacher shows the word — after a few seconds says the word and then exposes the symbol above the word. The Action Reading Machine is also involved in the fading process. Because of the control the teacher has over the information wheel mechanism —

ʃ	☞	🐱	⌐	☞	🏠		
is	the	cat	on	the	table		

can be changed to —

is	the	cat	on	the	table		

in a few seconds.

A child therefore can be given a sentence without symbols but if there is any hesitation on any particular word a brief glimpse of the symbol above will allow the child to complete the sentence without a lengthy break and the consequent loss of understanding.

is	☞	cat	⌐	☞	table		
	the		on	the			

A child on the Southall programme only moves to the next stage when he or she has mastered all the words on the previous level. The advantage of the machine is that at the beginning of a new level words can be shown with or without symbols. Hence at level 2 —

✏	the	🐱	🏹	a	little	boy	
has		monster	got				

— only the new words are shown with symbols. In this way knowledge of previous words is consolidated while at the same time the learning of new words takes place within the context of a meaningful sentence.

Summary of Main Educational Advantages of Action Reading Linked to Symbol-Word Method

1 Immediate Reading — immediate success so that reading is an entirely satisfactory experience. The 'chore' element is removed, and they become addicted to reading as one of the 'fun' activities of life.

2 Language structure taught same time as reading.

3 Child indicates immediately his comprehension of language/reading — 'no barking at print'.

4 Reading/language taught in a fun action way — high repetitive system put over in active way — rather than 'Here is Tom', 'Here is Mary' book form.

5 Child eventually comes to reading books at higher level of understanding and interest.

6 Child learns naturally that a word can be reproduced as meaningfully in print as in speech.

7 Teaching of new words within language context and under control of teacher.

8 No failure — child not competing to get to next book.

9 Left to right eye movement.

Phonic Work

One of the major findings of Peter Bryant and Lynette Bradley ('Children's Reading Problems', 1985) reported in *Child Language, Teaching and Therapy* (Vol 3, No 2, 1987) was that if 6-year-olds are taught phonemic segmentation this leads to an improvement in their reading and spelling. This information will come as no surprise to experienced teachers of reading. The method of their research was designed to do two things. One was to make children more aware of the sounds shared by different words, and the other to give them the idea that words with common sounds often share the same spelling patterns too — (e.g., hen, men, pen, ten etc.).

The Action Reading Machine is an ideal educational aid for the development of these kind of phonic skills. With the slightest movement of one single information wheel, hen can become pen, ten, ben, men and so on. This approach has been used with the machine in several different schools and nearly always satisfaction and success have been reported by the teachers concerned.

At Southall School in Telford the method has been adopted initially using a visual sound cue within the letter.

The teaching approach employed at Southall often centres on a board game where the child can only move an object or throw a dice after successfully sounding the word shown on the machine. As the children become more experienced with the way the machine works in changing and making words, they can take over control of the machine themselves to organize their own games or make their own words.

The Southall programme covers short vowel blending, consonant blends, vowel digraphs, final 'e' rule, doubled consonants and verb endings. The sounds are placed on twelve information wheels.

Other Uses

These short notes have been written to illustrate some of the uses of the Action Reading Machine. Experience has shown that different teachers can successfully adapt the concept of active learning using the machine to meet their own specific educational objectives.

An example of this is the way in which the machine was used to teach a language-handicapped child to talk. In this particular case the young eight-year-old boy whose only spoken language consisted of one word labels followed a programme based on developmental language structures linked to a symbol-word reading method. His labelling soon expanded to two word utterances e.g., big house, red ball, on table etc., then gradually into more complex sentences. Three years later this boy is not only able to engage in reasonable conversation, but has also acquired comparable reading skills.

At Southall School language delayed and handicapped children automatically use the Action Reading Machine linked to a Symbol-Word Method as a part of their intervention programme. At another school, children attending a Hearing Impaired Unit have successfully developed their ability in sentence formation by using the machine to make their own sentences.

The teachers who have developed the machine, believe that its diversity of uses make it a valuable teaching aid wherever the teaching of language and reading is seen as something that should be developed within the concept of understanding and pleasure. It is their belief that if this happens children will become far more skilful in unravelling the complexities of our language.

Chapter 8

More than Music:
Music Therapy in the Special School

Sean McCavera

> The music in my heart I bore
> Long after it was heard no more

Few people are not affected by the power of music. Research since Jung (*Memories, Dreams, Reflections*, 1963) first took an interest in the music therapy of Margaret Tilly in 1956 (and Jensen, 1982), shows that for children and adults with physical or emotional disabilities, work with music has been attempting to facilitate communication and unlock barriers to development. The pioneering work of Nordoff and Robbins (1975) in the use of music therapy as a progressive form of treatment in the education of severely handicapped children, was a major landmark in non-directive therapy.

In this article, I argue that the techniques used by Nordoff and Robbins and others are transferable to work with children with moderate learning difficulties, in modifying behaviour, enhancing personal communication, acquiring musical skills and making them happy. I suggest that the introduction of music therapy onto the curriculum of a school for pupils with moderate learning difficulties could yield significant benefits and I outline a programme for the content of the therapy sessions and a model timetable for implementation. The relationship between the classroom teacher and a supporting professional can be a difficult one. I identify potential problems and strategies for solving them. Finally, I attempt to draw out the parallels between the introduction of music therapy and the future development of a curriculum without constraints.

What is Music Therapy?

Music therapy uses the basic elements of music-making — rhythm, pitch and melody — to establish communication between therapist and client. The approach of music therapy owes much to the analytical psychology of Carl Jung. The client improvises with musical responses and the therapist, taking those musical responses, shares in the improvisation. The therapist uses voice/piano and simple musical instruments to reach out, through sound, to the child. An initial session might be where a child has to respond to a simple rhythm pattern. The child is encouraged to respond at will, vocally or instrumentally, and the therapist builds on that response to continue and develop the interaction. The approach is flexible, child-centred and non-directive.

> This does not require that the client be a musician or have any musical training ... the client improvises on a wide variety of percussion instruments. Having clients improvise on the percussion intruments serves two purposes: firstly, hardly anyone will say they cannot play a tambourine or beat a drum, or resist exploring the beautiful sound of one of the alto chromatic xylophones, and secondly, these instruments lend themselves readily to expressing the raw material of the unconscious. The piano the therapist plays is capable of a wide dynamic and expressive range so that music which the therapist improvises on it can encompass, move with and hold the client's sound expression (Hitchcock, 1987).

The initial sessions are constructed to provide an environment with as few constraints as possible. At the outset, the only rules are those designed to protect the personal safety of the participants. The principal aim of the therapist is to evoke an emotional response and from the pattern of the initial responses to decide on a programme of therapy which meets the specific needs of the child. This could be to modify a form of inappropriate behaviour, or to enhance communication skills. At this stage the acquisition of musical skills will be secondary to the building of a therapeutic relationship.

As the sessions continue, the therapist will aim to build on the relationship which has developed to improve the child's communication skills. The child's musical response will always be acknowledged by the therapist's musical response. The therapist sets goals (rather like curriculum objectives) for the sessions and is engaged with the child in a continuous process of working towards these goals. There is regular evaluation of the content and outcome of the sessions to assess the objectives and modify them where necessary.

For work with children with more complex learning difficulties, it is best to structure the therapy sessions on a one-to-one basis. However, there are benefits from working in groups in developing social patterns of behaviour as well as acquiring musical skills.

Why Music Therapy in the Moderate Learning Difficulties School?

All schools which cater for children with moderate learning difficulties have the common aim with mainstream education of enabling their pupils to improve educational and social attainment. However, MLD pupils have a very wide range of learning and behavioural problems. As ordinary primary and secondary schools improve provision for 'slow learners', the MLD school is left with numbers of children with particularly compex learning and behavioural difficulties. Learning difficulties are associated with various factors — physical handicap or minimal brain dysfunction, behavioural or emotional problems which may derive from familial or environmental deprivation. Not infrequently, there is also a minimal language impairment which limits verbal communication.

One group of children for whom music therapy has been shown to be particularly beneficial are those who display stereotypic movements or 'stereotypies' — repetitive rhythmic patterns of gross or fine motor movement which can be linked to mannerisms such as rocking, nodding, hand flapping, flicking (Richer, 1979). Music therapy can modify such behaviour by positive reinforcements — in clinically finding a relationship between the child's rates of rhythmicity and the particular form of stereotypy, the therapist can control these responses.

Most human beings have a replenished drive towards human activity — an 'elan vitale'. With autistic or mentally handicapped children, for example, this drive cannot take its course to fulfilment in the child's environment. The inability or inhibition to engage in a purposeful activity (learning, playing etc.) does not extinguish the energy of the initial drive towards activity, and stereotypies are a possible outlet and result (Richer, *ibid.*).

Faced with a range of children, presenting a wide variety of complex needs, it is obviously essential that the MLD school offers a flexible and responsive curriculum. Sometimes, however, special schools, with only a necessarily limited amount of resources, may fail to identify such a need, even with input from its Schools Psychological Service. A rule-of-thumb guide for identifying a child (or children) who would benefit from music therapy could be to use the same criteria as are used to identify autistic children. The child's needs and music therapy can be a starter in drawing out a line of response.

The MLD school will aim to provide access to elements of the standard curriculum, capitalizing on the possibilities of working in small groups and relatively low teacher–pupil ratios. However, it is recognized that there are many circumstances when the 'ordinary' curriculum will not be appropriate and here the purpose of the MLD school is to make available a curriculum which is modified to meet the needs of the individual child. Work with music as therapy fits very well with these curriculum aims: pupils have an opportunity to participate actively and the approach offers a definite 'hands-on' alternative to traditional classroom-based exercises!

So, music therapy is not to be restricted only to the severely handicapped child: there is much of relevance in this approach to all children falling within the broad category of 'moderate learning difficulties', and music therapy has evident potential as a method of investigating the reasons for learning difficulties.

Aims of Music Therapy: a Mirror of Good Music Teaching

Music is the medium through which therapy proceeds but we must be careful not to confuse musical change with therapeutic effectiveness (Adams, 1987).

There are many parallels between good practice in music teaching and music therapy. The difference is in approach: the educational approach is directive and the therapeutic approach is always non-directive. Both use basic musical techniques to enhance the child's skills and responses to music. However, there is an important distinction in that music therapy will aim to bring about behavioural changes and personal enhancement. The main aims of music therapy are:

— to modify behaviour
— to encourage self-expression
— to develop communication and social skills
— to facilitate pupil participation
— to contribute to the well-being of pupils within the school community
— to develop basic musical skills and to foster interest in music.

Music as therapy in the special school is much more than music.

A Programme for Introducing Music Therapy to the Moderate Learning Difficulties School

1. Implementation

The use of music therapy is relevant throughout the school, although the primary aims will differ depending upon the age range of the pupils and the length of time they have spent at the school.

Many MLD schools will cater for pupils from the age of four, up to sixteen, often including a nursery assessment/observation unit, a junior school, a middle school and a Post-14 Unit. An example of how music therapy could be structured into the nursery timetable is described by a practising music therapist:

The nine children in the nursery class come for one twenty-five minute group session per week with two or more staff, usually including their class teacher. The five more able children come for a further weekly session with one helper, and the remaining four have weekly individual sessions of twenty minutes each. This happens to be a higher proportion of individual clients than in any other class, a situation which arises from the school's policy of allowing class teachers, in consultation with myself, to refer children for individual therapy on the grounds of their special needs (Strange, 1987).

It is likely that the nursery unit will include some children who have very limited language skills or no language at all. Here it is important to combine individual work with group sessions. The therapist has a vital part to play in determining the reasons for the child's developmental problems and in structuring ways of overcoming the barriers to learning.

As the child moves up the school into the junior department, music therapy work should continue. At this stage, group work is likely to take priority, although one-to-one sessions will still be available for those children who require them. The work with music should be enjoyable, with the children learning simple songs and melodies and using percussion instruments. It might be possible to have joint sessions on music and movement. The main aims will be to improve the child's communication skills and to encourage sociability.

It is important to build upon this base in work with children in the middle school. The danger at this stage is for the music therapy to be wrongly interpreted by the school as music teaching: the head would like them to perform at a concert, for visitors, etc.

The conflict of professional interests between the educational and therapeutic, non-directive approach, particularly in the dealing of children with behavioural problems, highlights the difficulties that need to be 'talked through' by the music therapist and teachers. Teachers might suggest that the non-directive approach might be more appropriate to individual music therapy than to group sessions. This is against the spirit of social education and 'overlooks both the therapeutic role of the group in receiving the individual child's musical communication and the benefits to each child of listening as well as playing in a group' (Strange, 1987).

Rehearsing for musical performances for parents and visitors can be a serious threat to the relationships built up in music therapy sessions. It is the switching of roles from non-directive to directive teaching that is the source of conflict for child and therapist.

The teacher's contribution to music therapy is vital in supporting the music therapist. The educational and therapeutic approaches are complementary. Music therapists are anxious to demystify their specialist role and to collaborate and to support teachers across the curriculum:

Since the average special school is of under a hundred pupils, it is hardly feasible to employ both a music teacher and a therapist; there is much to be said for leaving music teaching as far as possible in the hands of other staff. In my school a few staff with musical training do put it to good use, and I try to encourage others by providing taped accompaniments of songs for PE activities and loaning musical instruments (Strange, 1987).

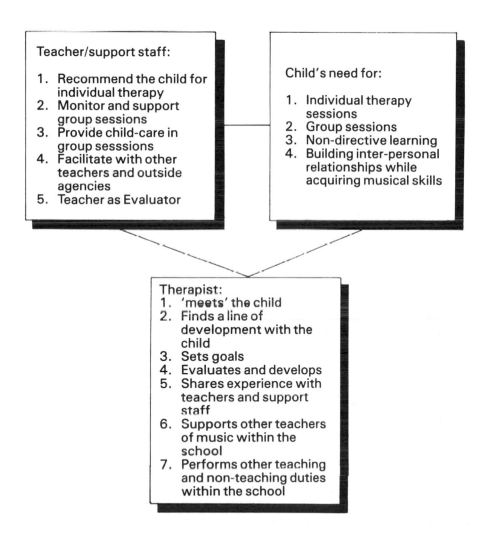

Figure 1:   Professional and Client Relationships in Music Therapy

2. Therapist and Teacher in Collaboration

Teachers in MLD schools are accustomed to drawing on the support of other professionals, such as educational psychologists, social workers and medical staff. Often the music therapist, like other professionals, will have responsibilities outside therapy sessions:

> My chief non-music therapy duty is the supervision of a nursery class in their lunchtime play period. Other duties include covering classes whose teachers are sick, on courses or attending their children's annual reviews; signing in children from their morning transport; playing for school assemblies, training a choir and helping with special school functions. Averaged out over the year, these duties occupy about ten hours of a thirty-five hour week (Strange, 1987).

The assumption of other roles not only facilitates team spirit but provides the therapist with valuable insights into the child's behaviour outside therapy sessions:

> The lunch-hour supervision of the nursery class was originally allotted to me for purely organizational reasons. [During this time] I can observe the children's spontaneous choice of activity and compare their choice of toys and mode of play — most of it solitary — with what happens in music therapy. In addition to the children's actual behaviour, I can observe with some detachment the triggering situations, some of which would not occur in music therapy (Strange, 1987).

However, it is possible that the intervention of the music therapist in the classroom may be seen as an intrusion, particularly if there is a perceived difference between the non-directive approach of the therapist and a more formal teaching style. The music therapist's child-centred, non-directive relationship relies on the child perception that the therapist is not a teacher and does not prescribe 'good' or 'bad' musical behaviour. 'Only so, it is argued, can children feel free to express themselves and reveal their true feelings.' Problems are most likely to arise in the area of discipline where the therapist does not prescribe behaviour. Therefore, it is vital that teacher and therapist work together to reach an understanding of the purpose of therapy before the therapist begins work with the children.

The relationship between child and therapist will be less formal than the teacher–pupil relationship. The therapist meeting the child as a teacher or as a member of the support staff, in the playground, outside therapy sessions can be a strain on the therapist/client relationship. Comments from music therapists suggest that 'on the whole children readily adjust to the therapist's contrasting roles inside and outside the therapy room'.

It is important that the teachers and support staff appreciate the vital contribution they can make to the process of the therapy as informed and active participants and observers. The school will need to arrange for familiarization and training sessions for staff and this might appropriately be undertaken through INSET. While it will be seen that these sessions will not and cannot prepare teaching staff to be therapists, it is unlikely that the introduction of therapy will succeed without a general understanding and commitment to its aims and an appreciation that the roles of teacher and therapist are complementary, and not competitive.

The therapist brings specialist training and input to the music therapy sessions. The classroom teacher has an important part to play in organizing and supporting the sessions and in providing the essential link between the work done in the therapy sessions and the rest of the child's experiences at school.

3. Assessing the therapy

> ...the effects of music therapy will be observed through changes in behaviour of a non-musical kind (Adams, 1987).

Levitt's (1957) review of therapy was one of the most influential studies of the major psychotherapies, because it cast doubt on the effectiveness of therapy in helping recovery from neurotic disorders. Twenty years later, the value of therapy was still doubtful: '...we still do not have sufficient information about what...therapy works best for certain children under particular circumstances' (Kovacs and Paulaskas, 1986).

Much research has been devoted to what extent, and how, music therapy actually works. Therapist observations indicate that music therapy can modify behaviour and enhance the client's well-being. In all therapy, the aim is to alleviate distress and to help the client develop coping or self-esteem strategies. 'To evaluate therapy we must have some index of distress and some measure of skill and these will not be primarily based on musical considerations' (Adams, 1987). However, as Kovacs and Paulaskas (1986) point out, that is where the major difficulty in assessing the effectiveness of any therapy lies: most research is clinical (uncontrolled), and the results of a non-directive therapy cannot be measured in a clinical setting.

Nevertheless, working in a non-clinical (controlled) setting, assessment of behaviour can be done by the teacher and therapist logging modifications in the therapist/client relationship with the therapist providing specialist information on the client's acquisition of musical skills. There are four main questions to be asked in evaluating the effect of music therapy on clients:

1 Does music therapy bring about a change in the client?
2 Given the hypothesis that a change has taken place — is this because of music therapy?

3   What part of the treatment process was a motivating force in bringing about behavioural change?

4   Will these changes be shown in other settings?

Special schools have a good track record in using computers. Music therapists can now use computers with electronic keyboards. 'It should not be viewed as a replacement for the therapist, but rather as an extension alongside more traditional instruments such as the piano or percussion' (Fitzwilliam, 1988). Computers store, retrieve and edit information and therefore can build up a picture of the client's work. This means that music therapy sessions need not be one-off sessions but can be developmental. One of the problems that faces therapists at the moment is that many of the software packages are not directly suitable for individual sessions. In the near future, music therapists with programming experience will be able to enhance the use of computers in sessions. Research into storage and retrieval of direct observation data will shortly be available for therapists. With teacher and therapist working together many music therapy sessions could use computers and synthesizers alongside the traditional piano and drums. A whole new range of sounds is now available which can be stored on disc and played back through synthesizer at a latter session. The rewards of using micro-technology in music therapy for the client are great. 'They no longer have to be constantly assisted in minor tasks, and are able to achieve results, and express themselves creatively. Rewards such as those provided by sound and graphics encourages interaction, and the private nature of the computer allows people to persist with tasks until a satisfactory level has been achieved' (Fitzwilliam, 1988).

It is difficult, as I have made clear, to quantify what makes music therapy work. However, with the use of micro-technology in measuring responses in sessions and in empirically analyzing the data, music therapists can look forward to other sources in the immediate future to interpret their own analytical observations. Observations of clients in music therapy by therapists record a significant response taking place, which offers relief, and personal enhancement:

> Whatever the degree of mental and emotional difficulties that Laura faces in life, in the realm of music — as revealed in the music therapy sessions — she has laid the foundations for communicating her needs and for incorporating her energies creatively; for exploring and playfully using her spontaneous activities within a relationship — all experiences being of immense importance to her, as they are to any growing child (Agrotou, 1988).

Music Therapy in the Future: a Model of a Curriculum Without Constraints

MLD schools will have to follow the National Curriculum from September 1989. This will have the positive effect of reducing the differentiation between 'special' schools and ordinary schools. Nevertheless, for MLD schools the introduction of National Curriculum objectives could be a distraction from the area where MLD schools can excel — that is, in tailoring a curriculum to the specific needs of the child.

The MLD school will need to retain an innovatory approach to the curriculum, incorporating approaches such as those drawn from music therapy. The Warnock Report (1978) indicated that special schools can be 'centres of excellence' in offering much more on the curriculum than ordinary schools. With the onset of the National Curriculum, this could be expansion time for special schools in offering 'specialist' resources in a wider educational setting. Music therapy offers methods of developing communication and social skills and of modifying behaviour through flexible and interactive structures which involve child, therapist and teacher as equal partners — a model for the future.

SECTION 3

Integration and support

Chapter 9

A Decade of Support —
One School's Practice

David Smith and Patricia Keogh

Much has been written during this decade about the development of the outreach support role by special schools. A variety of models has emerged as these schools have sought to redefine their place in the educational system.

The impetus for this new special school role has ranged from an underlying ethos to develop as part of the total educational community, to one of simple survival in the face of falling rolls, often accompanied by authority pressure.

Some of this material has referred, either covertly or overtly, to Heltwate School, frequently examining the ethos of the school's early development. (Dessent, 1984 and 1985; Hallmark and Dessent, 1982; Hallmark, 1983; Rider and Keogh, 1982). In the first volume of *Making the Special Schools Ordinary*, Alan Day, in his chapter, 'Reaching out: The background to outreach' sought to highlight various methods of support. It described in some detail the current level of operational staffing which goes into delivering the Heltwate Support Service.

It is not the intention of the writers, in this second volume, to repeat the documentation of the philosophies of the school's development, nor to make comparisons between the various methods of support service delivery or to analyze the cost in staffing or resource terms. Rather the purpose of the chapter is to describe the practical day-to-day, week-by-week realities of the problems and successes of delivering core curriculum support to children experiencing learning difficulties in a mainstream primary school, and consider the reasons for the continued demand for an expansion of the level of service provided.

The chapter attempts to take what might be considered a typical example (if indeed such a thing exists) outlining how the initial approach by the mainstream school is made, the response of the special school and the gradual development of a mutually satisfactory working arrangement. This arrangement, while being quite individual, also meets certain predetermined criteria.

The Situation

Mrs Keen teaches in a mainstream primary school and has a class of twenty-eight infants. She is, on the whole, very pleased with the progress they are making — except that is for two pupils. These two pupils worry Mrs Keen a great deal, she is often to be heard in the staffroom discussing their difficulties with other members of staff. Her colleagues, who are generally sympathetic, reassure her that she is doing all that is possible but Mrs Keen feels that really she could do with a bit more help and advice from somewhere. After all, these children can take up a disproportionate amount of teacher time in terms of planning, preparation and teaching. It follows therefore, that if the quality of help given to the children, covering these three aspects, is of the highest calibre then the time will be used more effectively and might even be reduced.

The Teacher's Concern

Mrs Keen describes the two pupils as being easily distracted, noisy, lacking motivation and having poor memory skills. She is particularly worried about what she considers to be their lack of progress in reading. She feels she has tried everything, both commercial and homemade, but to no avail. She is also conscious of the concern being felt by one set of parents regarding their child's reading.

Mrs Keen decides to ask the headteacher, Mr Best, if he can suggest anything which would be of assistance.

The Suggestion

Mr Best is aware that a special school, called Heltwate, in the city, has resources which are available to help mainstream teachers such as Mrs Keen. He says he will contact the headteacher there in order to gain more information.

The Response

On being contacted, the special school headteacher arranges with the support co-ordinator to visit Mr Best. The purpose of this visit being to establish what Mr Best wants and what the support service can realistically offer in order that a suitable approach can be mutually agreed. Clear statements of what is possible at this stage can avoid misunderstandings in the future.

Getting Involved with the Support Service

During the visit the following points are made and discussed:

1. What the support service offers:
    (i) Unlimited resources developed and produced for the child with special needs;
    (ii) Access to experienced special school teachers;
    (iii) Provision, if required, of teaching programmes designed to meet individual needs;
    (iv) Opportunity to meet with other mainstream special needs coordinators to exchange and share experiences, problems, common issues and to provide a forum for future progress;
    (v) Opportunity to be part of a team planning resources and influence future resource production;
    (vi) Termly meetings with educational psychologists;
    (vii) Access to INSET provided by the support team.

2. What the support teacher offers:
    The support teacher's role is to provide help for teachers who have children in their classes who give them cause for concern.

    This is done by assisting schools to identify and analyze their needs and by helping teachers to plan, develop and provide appropriate teaching responses to meet those needs.

    The ethos of the Heltwate Support Service is that the support teacher will help the class teacher to effect a change in the child's individual learning experiences throughout the week.

    Heltwate support staff are also prepared to talk to parents either as a group or individually before their children start to use the Heltwate materials. This is usually seen as very beneficial, both encouraging parental involvement and providing an opportunity for them to look at, and experiment with, materials they will not have seen before.

3. Time expectancy, i.e., amount of time a class teacher should expect to spend with a child per day following the teaching programmes.

4. Mr Best is informed of the weekly/fortnightly meetings held at Heltwate when the 'named teacher' for special needs from his school is expected to be present. This may necessitate provision for cover as the meetings begin before the end of the school day.

5. There is some commitment in terms of finance. The amount will be deducted from the schools capitation and will be in the region of £20–£60. This can, as will be seen, be little more than a token amount for the quantity and quality of resources and advice provided. The amount agreed for Mr Best's school

will probably be £30. However, this will not be confirmed until the level of need is known and until the support is working efficiently in the school.

6   It is also made clear that the school will receive unlimited resources for their money. If there are to be several classes where children are working with the Heltwate materials, then each classroom teacher will be able to have her own resources so eliminating the need for sharing, which can be very awkward and inconvenient. They will also, of course, have a weekly visit from the support teacher, who would write the teaching programmes and consult with teachers involved, she would also see the children to check the week's objectives.

Mr Best is also given the policy document which has been drawn up by the educational psychologist, support coordinator and the Assistant Area Education Officer. This document outlines the support service and details the commitment from both schools.

The policy document is regarded by the support team as the final seal of approval from the LEA as a recognition, after several years of conscientious work, of the support service's official status with the authority.

After this initial meeting it is left to Mr Best to decide, together with his staff, whether the Heltwate Support Service has anything to offer his school.

If the response from the mainstream school is positive, we would then move onto the next stage of the procedure. This would be a visit to Heltwate by Mr Best and his staff — including any ancillary staff who are to be involved.

This visit includes a tour of the school and an in-depth explanation and demonstration of the resources which cover all the basic areas of the curriculum. This meeting also provides the opportunity for repeating some of the main points previously made to the head. Past experience has shown that it should never be assumed that a head has understood and passed on all relevant information. An example of this is the understanding of the time expectancy, it is obviously vital for a class teacher to be aware of this.

This is also the time to consider in theory how a teacher might organize her class to enable her to fulfil the time expectancy, this would of course be reconsidered in more practical terms when the support teacher makes her first working visit to the school.

The mainstream staff are given ample opportunity at this meeting to study the materials and evaluate the appropriateness to their own situation. The teaching programmes are also explained in some detail, the class teacher being reassured that in the early stages, the programmes will be written, and the objectives set, by the support teacher. After this meeting the decision of whether or not to proceed is again left totally with the mainstream school. The staff know what is expected of them and they know what they are going to receive. The question is, do they wish to make a commitment to the support service and benefit accordingly?

If the mainstream school decide that they wish to receive support, arrangements are made for teachers and ancillary staff who are going to be involved to spend time in

Heltwate working alongside staff using the relevant resources. This gives them the opportunity of seeing the materials used in practice and the organization of our groups which enable individual teaching to take place.

The final stage before the support begins is to allocate a support teacher from Heltwate, who will then liaise with staff to arrange a suitable time and day for her future visits. The weekly visits take place on the same day and at the same time each week. She will liaise with as many mainstream staff as are receiving support in the school although it is normal practice to begin initially with only a few children, usually in the middle infant year. She will write the teaching programmes, set the appropriate objectives and provide the necessary resources. Discussions will take place with the teacher about the content of the following week's teaching programme and the progress being made by the child.

Mr Best, Mrs Keen and the rest of the staff decided that they would find Heltwate support most useful. Mrs Keen is hopeful that it will be just what her two special pupils need.

Meeting The Challenge

Meanwhile, back at Heltwate, at the regular Tuesday morning meeting, the support team are negotiating how Mr Best's school might be accommodated when all the team seem to have their full quota of schools to support.

The support coordinator gives the team a brief outline of the new school and indicates her expectations as to the potential level of need and involvement. She stresses the enthusiastic response made by Mr Best and his staff to the concept of support.

A member of the team suggests that one of her schools which has been receiving regular support visits for a considerable period of time and has become almost self-sufficient could be put on a monitoring basis. This means that the support teacher will visit the school on a monthly basis to liaise with staff and monitor children's progress. The 'named teacher' will continue to attend the Heltwate meetings and will disseminate information from the meetings amongst her colleagues. The mainstream staff of the school will also have the option of attending workshop sessions held by the support team.

This support teacher is willing to take on the challenge of Mr Best's school, the support coordinator agrees that this is a suitable solution and asks the teacher to make contact with Mr Best.

The Support Visits

On her first visit the support teacher spends the time in Mrs Keen's classroom talking to all the children and looking at their work, all the while keeping under observation the ones who cause Mrs Keen so much concern. Whilst seeing the accuracy of Mrs Keen's description she feels that it is the inappropriateness of the tasks that produces the resultant behaviours of the children. When the lesson is over, she talks to Mrs Keen about her observations and explains how the children's work can be more appropriately individualized. After further discussion the support teacher feels confident that the reading approach they have jointly agreed upon will be successful for both the pupils and their teacher.

On her second visit the support teacher spends time, in the classroom, with each of the two children. She tells them who she is and what she is going to be doing, she shows them some of the new reading work so making it a little easier for Mrs Keen. The support teacher writes a teaching programme for each child, their five tasks — one for each day and the week's objective.

The support visit is timed so that it runs into break providing the chance to go through the programme with Mrs Keen and a classroom assistant (who Mr Best has suggested might help) showing them which materials are for each task. It seems rather different but they very soon become familiar and confident in using them as indeed do the children. The support teacher is able to spend a few moments in the staffroom during the break so that she soon becomes a familiar figure to all the staff. On the next and subsequent visits the support teacher goes to Mrs Keen's classroom where she monitors the progress of the two children by checking whether they have achieved the prescribed objective, and programmes the following week's work. She is also delighted to see that Mrs Keen has used some of the ideas when preparing new materials for her class. Mrs Keen explains that using Heltwate resources had helped her to realize how finely broken down tasks could be and so become more appropriate for some children. After a few weeks another teacher asks the support teacher if she would see some children in her class who she feels sure could benefit from the same kind of approach as that being used in Mrs Keen's class. As for Mrs Keen, she is highly delighted with the progress being made by her pupils. Whilst accepting it is slow, she readily acknowledges that it is most definitely progress.

The Named Teacher

Mr Best asks Mrs Keen if she would be willing to take on this role and represent the school at the Heltwate meetings.

These meetings are attended by the support team and the named teachers from the supported schools. The aims of the meeting is to give teachers the opportunity to discuss progress, air problems encountered and share the successes achieved by the children. The meetings help to reduce the sense of isolation which can sometimes be experienced by these teachers in mainstream schools.

Another objective of the meetings is the planning and development of new resources. It is considered that involvement of the mainstream teachers in the creation and development of new resources will result in an appreciation of the effectiveness of the resources and consequent commitment towards their use in schools.

The meetings, although usually held in Heltwate school, are occasionally 'hosted' by one of the 'named' teachers within her own school — affording the rest of the group the opportunity to visit and see a different school, with the possibility of additional ideas and awareness being generated by such increased exposure.

These regular meetings, which are attended by all of the Heltwate support staff, provide an opportunity for them to establish the needs of the mainstream teachers and so enable them, where possible and desirable, to meet those needs.

Termly meetings are held with the 'named' teachers, support teachers, Heltwate head and the educational psychologists.

This gives the mainstream teachers the opportunity to report to the educational psychologists what is actually happening with regard to special needs in their school and to talk about any child presenting serious problems.

The educational psychologists are very positive about the support service and, as a consequence, their attitude to the 'named' teachers is one of genuine interest in their problems and acknowledgment of their efforts.

Summary

It is now time to leave the fictitious Mr Best and Mrs Keen confident and comfortable in the knowledge that the professional practical help and advice that they both sought is actually available.

It is now time to consider some of the fundamentals that originally characterized, and continue to maintain, this successful initiative:

1   Heltwate had intrinsic advantages that combined with important organizational decisions to create a framework within which it was possible to develop the service.
2   The availability of expertise within the special school and access if required to external visiting professionals.
3   Support commences with small manageable numbers of children and expands gradually.
4   The nature of the support is flexible.
5   The special school is committed to enabling the support staff to sustain regular visits and monitor progress.
6   The programmes of work jointly organized during support visits form part of the daily activities undertaken over the following week.

7   Support teachers attend mutually supportive weekly meetings.

8   As the service is voluntary, the direction and rate of growth have been self-generating — promising only what it can deliver.

9   The support team has a commitment to the ideals of supporting children within mainstream schools.

10 Support teachers are very experienced in Heltwate's methods and in using its resources, with the school's own pupil population.

What, then, are the continuing strengths?

1   Support teachers are all mainstream trained and continue to have a major teaching commitment within Heltwate, so carrying credibility as practising teachers.

2   The provision of well structured resources that have been produced to a standard equal to that of commercially produced materials.

3   Ample resources are provided which eliminates the inconveniences associated with sharing.

4   Regular visits by support teachers to mainstream schools often result in informal involvements with the schools which accumulate goodwill e.g., invitations to attend Christmas concerts and other functions.

5   The supply and on-going training of a comprehensive in-service training package in the use of Heltwate resources and methods to all primary staff involved in receipt of support.

6   Regular meetings for 'named' teachers encouraging involvement and commitment — both to the support of children with special needs and to the resources.

Conclusion

The position of the special school is an interesting one in this changing climate. Dessent (1984) writes that special schools have developed new orientations as school rolls have fallen. It should be noted though, that whilst many schools have had to consider the support role as a means to survival, this was not the case with Heltwate School as the school opened with the aim of developing some kind of liaison service to primary schools.

The service offered by Heltwate is to a large extent dependent upon resources created within the school. These packages of carefully structured learning materials are the key to enabling the support teacher to organize daily activities for up to thirty children on the basis of one afternoon visit per week. Heltwate has purposefully developed this vital resource base since the first children entered the school in 1977 and the teachers began to respond to their needs.

Indeed, there are clear lessons to be learned, but there is an overriding need for each school to look to its own local circumstances, present strengths and future potential before embarking on what might be proved to be ill-conceived or over ambitious projects.

The authors believe a good support service should fulfil certain criteria:

— Firstly, it should be available at the earliest stages of a perceived learning difficulty rather than come as a crisis intervention.

— Secondly, if it is based upon provision of practical teaching material and resources and is teamed with advice, rather than being provided by an 'expert' who is preoccupied by assessment, it is more likely to succeed.

— Thirdly, it should not be presented in a way which undermines the mainstream teacher. Support should reassure class teachers that they have the professional skills necessary to deal with the majority of special educational needs which they are likely to meet.

— Fourthly, and arguably most importantly, it needs to be firmly based upon an agreed and effective school policy which creates an internal organization to enable the school to gradually assume full responsibility for their children with special educational needs.

One must not forget the support teachers themselves: the way in which they carry out their role is essential to the success of the support service. They must earn the respect from their mainstream colleagues and this they do, not by setting themselves up as experts. They must be sensitive to the needs of individual teachers and must be non-judgmental about the capabilities and performance of the classroom teachers. Their main aim being to help teachers.

As previously stated it is most valuable for a support teacher to spend some time in the staffroom during breaks or lunchtimes. The Heltwate support team see this as a time when it is possible to be part of the whole school staff and become known to that staff in a more personal, as well as professional, capacity.

Possibly one unforeseen, but most rewarding, result of a successful support link is the way in which it can help break down barriers between the different kinds of schools. We have been able to arrange visits, in both directions, to watch concerts, plays etc. The children then play together and the staff are able to mix with each other. There is also the in-service aspect in which primary teachers spend some time in the special schools which help make progress towards the recommendations of the Fish Report (ILEA, 1985) and the 'mutually supportive arrangements to meet special educational needs and provide a focus for the development of supporting services' (3.16.22).

Through the links with primary schools we have also, more easily, been able to re-integrate some children to mainstream education, knowing that the schools will be more aware of the needs of the child. We have then been able to provide support if necessary, which in most cases it has not.

The Heltwate Support Service is a successful model and an endorsement of its success is the request from heads all over Peterborough that we should help them assume responsibility for meeting the special needs of pupils experiencing learning difficulties in their schools.

One cannot tell what the future holds, or what will happen if key staff leave. However, because of continual demand the school considered a second level of support delivery without the usual weekly Heltwate teacher input. Following an initial meeting, the response from schools to the second mode support, based on in-service training, was overwhelming. But it should be remembered that our reputation pre-ceeded the meeting, most heads and 'named' teachers having already heard of the service we offer.

It was thought, in the early days of the support service that organizing workshop sessions for large numbers of teachers would be unlikely to effect lasting change within the classroom and this is probably true. However, by including regular, mutually sup-portive meetings and some support visits together with *thorough* in-service training, it is possible that by sharing our expertise and resources (although retaining tight control) class teachers will feel better equipped to meet the needs of their pupils.

One final comment, to conclude, concerns the beneficial effects of being a member of the support team on one's own role as a classroom teacher. In many cases it is a privi-lege to be able to spend some time each week in the class of mainstream children. It keeps one's perspective in view when exposure to all levels of ability is possible and also being able to observe class teachers coping admirably with thirty children and yet still having time to devote to their group of non-readers.

The support teacher who works in the mainstream classroom and the special school classroom would undoubtedly reap the benefits of the dual role as will the pupils in both settings.

The text of this chapter is based on a decade of supporting children with special educational needs in the mainstream. The authors, the current headteacher and co-ordinator of mainstream support, along with the current support teachers and all the other Heltwate staff are still totally committed to the philosophy which first sent the school in its direction of development.

It would be an omission, however, not to pay tribute to all those others who have made such an immense contribution to that development over those years. They have moved on to new challenges, but their foresight, commitment and hard work have been rewarded in a truly unique manner.

Chapter 10

Developing a Regional Resource — An Advisory Teacher Support Network

Dr Peter Avis and Mike Wright

Within the rapidly changing field of information technology one tends to reflect on the history of change in micro-bites of time rather than decades or centuries. However, it would seem appropriate in this context to explore some significant changes that have taken place in the education scene since 1980 to the present day. It is within this particular time-frame that education has declared ownership of the computer revolution and initiated a range of innovative curriculum projects. Education has begun to harness the potential of the technology and encompass it within sound educational philosophy and practice. The true value of developing systems has been seen as a way to enhance classroom management and widen the parameters of pupil experience. Developments have been particularly stimulating through the many innovative strategies which have been seen to positively affect the lives of pupils with special needs. The concept of the entitlement curriculum has become a reality for many pupils as a result of advances in the development of hardware and software.

This rapid process of change has, to a degree, been facilitated by the activities of the regional Special Educational Microelectronics Resource Centres (SEMERCs) — almost always under-resourced and overstretched, their activities only being delivered through the intense commitment and professionalism of the various managers. The process has also been facilitated by the positive assistance provided through a variety of DTI initiatives, the early enthusiasms of CET and the driving force of Mary Hope and John Garett.

The national scene-setting attempts by the DES however, only become fruitful when LEAs become personally involved in local ownership. Then the real developments begin to take place.

The South Yorkshire and Humberside Region, for example, grasped this nettle early in the 80s with the decision to have the Regional Centre for MEP in Doncaster.

Ownership locally of this Centre developed with the appointment of Dr P. Avis as

Centre Director. It became apparent from early meetings between Dr Avis, Colin Richards (Newcastle SEMERC) and a small group of local heads and advisers that Special Educational Needs Projects would feature highly in the agenda of the Doncaster Centre and that a close working relationship would be established between Doncaster and Newcastle with obvious advantages for all. Perhaps of greatest significance was the early decision by Dr Avis to identify a significant share of the Centre budget as being specifically available for the development of curriculum projects with the special school sector of the education service.

A special education advisory group was formed and provided the framework which linked special needs advisers to the Centre's management group. This group identified appropriate projects and quickly saw the wisdom of linking together seconded teachers (with innovative educational ideas), with experienced programmers who could produce custom designed software. This practice led to the continued secondment of teachers often subsequently deployed to trial or extend the software. Software was also developed by individual teachers and headteachers who grew to appreciate the Centre and its software and hardware support facilities.

It was from these early initiatives that the concept of the advisory teacher grew in the special education field. It was invariably the enthusiasm of these teachers who led local and regional initiatives, through local user groups, MEP Regional Centre promotions and exhibitions and also jointly interacting with the SEMERC in a variety of in-service initiatives. Considerable regional cohesion was further enhanced when the group, led by Tony Ballistini, agreed to produce a regional newsletter — a project which encouraged the exchange of ideas, information and practice across the region. Throughout the period the advisory committee had continued to facilitate the activities of the special schools and units fostering networks and new developments.

One unresolved frustration throughout this period, however, was the degree of independence observed between the activities of the various advisory committees working with the Doncaster Centre. Whilst the need was recognized by the Centre management staff to provide for greater cross-fertilization between these groups and the various seconded or advisory teachers, no successful strategy was found. The principal focus was to develop programmes for primary education, secondary education, control technology or special schools and not to consider to any degree questions of coherence and continuity of experience across the curriculum or phase. For a considerable period of time insufficient attention was given to the concept of variable access to systems or software therefore, the idea of open access for all or the entitlement curriculum concept and the real possibilities which the new technology would bring to pupils with special needs was not fully exploited. 1985 saw the end of MEP funding and possibly the end of these fruitful developments and the loss of a powerful regional production and support centre. The successes of the past years were sufficient to convince a group of local authorities that within the Centre was a range of sound practice and resources which they could not afford to lose.

RESOURCE

A consortium was formed in 1986 supported by the LEAs of Barnsley, Doncaster, Humberside, Rotherham and Sheffield. Initially this was for a three year life but a five year plan has been approved for a continuation for 1989. Its aim is to support the use of IT across the curriculum. To meet this aim it produces computer software, hardware, publications and supports conferences and courses for teachers and advisory teachers. These are cross-phase and cross-curricular but there is a strong emphasis on special needs since IT has particular importance in providing access to the curriculum for children with special needs.

Software Development and Distribution

RESOURCE is set up to work with teachers and LEA organizations in order to create new computer materials to use in schools. We have already developed over 150 programs which are sold via a catalogue. They are sold nationally to provide an income to continue the service. A considerable number of these are specifically for special needs children. Many of these have come from the Special Needs Software Group. This is a group of teachers and advisory teachers who work with programmers to develop new materials.

Hardware Development and Distribution

A growing area is the development of small pieces of equipment to work with the computer. These include controllable vehicles, robot arms and interface boxes to allow models made from LEGO to be worked from the computer. RESOURCE is exploring the creation of devices specifically for special needs including input switches, controllable devices and communication devices.

Publications

RESOURCE also works with teachers and advisory teachers to develop newsletters, curriculum documents and teaching materials to support the use of IT in school. A typical example is the *Special Needs Newsletter* which is distributed twice yearly. This contains articles and advice for special needs teachers.

Conferences and Courses

During the year RESOURCE helps organize a number of conferences and courses on a regional and national basis. These enable teachers, advisory teachers and advisers to update themselves as well as providing a platform for good work in the authorities to reach a wider audience. This includes an annual conference for special needs teachers covering a whole range of topics.

Regional Advisory Teachers

RESOURCE supports a team of eight regional advisory teachers who work in schools promoting IT across the curriculum. They offer the following subject skills: art and design, business studies and economic awareness, home economics, humanities, languages, music, science and technology and special needs. However, it is important to stress the value they have found in working through cross-curricular issues.

They can operate in several ways. Firstly as individuals working alongside the classroom teacher, supporting new developments or providing subject-based inset in schools/pyramids. Secondly as a team, in part or whole, working in schools providing inset and developing IT policies on a cross-curricular basis. Thirdly in conjunction with LEA-based advisory teachers. They are all interested in and work with special needs teachers but are supported by a special needs advisory teacher who acts as a consultant to the team.

The central role of special needs in RESOURCE is reflected in the way the structure is set up through committees. There is a special needs advisory group who steer the direction of RESOURCE with reference to special needs.

RESOURCE Special Needs Steering Group

The strong SEN Steering Group has a membership which reflects primary, secondary and further education and includes expertise from advisory teachers, curriculum support teachers and special school and service representatives. Positive links have been retained with the Oxford ACE Centre, local university Medical Physics departments and NCET/MESU.

The group produces a regular newsletter, and has continued through a variety of strategies, to generate a range of software. They have developed assessment procedures to assist LEAs across the region working with profoundly disabled youngsters. They have arranged a variety of in-service days: the group has continued to evolve and has recently changed its composition.

The group now more strongly represents practising teachers than was hither to the case. It also provides a strong link between the ESG regional advisory team and the various local authority change agents. As well as including the five regional LEAs there is a wider network linking Yorkshire and Humberside and the North East in general.

The role of the advisory teachers directly working with schools across the region enables a range of information technological expertise to be brought to bear on the curriculum experience of pupils and students in all institutions across the region.

Good practice is nurtured and easily transferred to other institutions. Good working relationships are being developed between the RESOURCE based advisory teachers and those located with the local authorities.

With the demise of the SEMERCs in 1989 it was felt sensible for all of this expertise and support to be brought together as one unit — SENSU — The Special Education Needs Support Unit based at RESOURCE. It was felt important that this unit should be firmly based in a centre dealing with all aspects of education and the curriculum.

Special Educational Needs Support Unit for the RESOURCE Consortium

Since 1982 the four regional SEMERCs have made a most significant contribution to special educational needs on a variety of levels, initially under the auspices of MEP and more recently MESU.

The four regional centres at Bristol, Newcastle, Oldham and Redbridge have served their geographical areas in the following ways:

1 Providing a training resource for teachers, advisory teachers and LEA advisers.
2 Providing LEAs with information about software and hardware applications by means of newsletters, catalogues, briefing sheets and inset.
3 Advising software developers, promoting software development and encouraging in-school software and hardware development.
4 Establishing a network of contact points within LEAs to disseminate information and freely copiable software.

Through exercising these functions over the years the SEMERCs have established themselves as key focal points in an information network (both formal and informal) the continued existence of which cannot be overestimated. With the withdrawal of national funding for the SEMERCs in March 1989 it became necessary for MESU to invite established regional consortia to take on the continuing role of support for IT within the field of special educational needs.

The RESOURCE consortium of LEAs (Barnsley, Doncaster, Humberside, Rotherham and Sheffield) have responded to this situation by the establishment of SENSU.

SENSU is based at RESOURCE in Doncaster and staffed by an advisory teacher with programming and clerical support. The advisory teacher is a member of the Regional Advisory Teacher team based at RESOURCE and has a one third time commitment to that team with the remaining time available to coordinate the activities of SENSU and make input to the various services on offer. It is intended that SENSU shall continue the function of the Newcastle SEMERC within the region and, through an evolutionary process, enlarge upon current provision as follows.

Programming Support

This currently consists of the services of one full-time special needs programmer based at RESOURCE and working mainly on authoring and conversion of existing programs to meet the specific special needs of children within the region.

Curriculum Materials Development

Support available includes project management, graphic artists and desk-top publishing to work with teachers and advisory teachers to produce materials to specific needs.

In-service Training

SENSU has the staffing and facilities to run inset courses on a variety of subjects either at RESOURCE or LEA based if this is preferred. This will include collaborative work with LEAs as they refine their modular award bearing SEN courses.

Physical and Sensory Handicap Support

Involves the combined services of a support advisory teacher together with technical and programming help to work with the LEA's own special needs staff to develop simple switches, communication aids and devices interfacing to computers and appropriate software.

Library and Evaluation Service

Open access to both the software and hardware libraries. LEA loans will be feasible eventually and will be made on the basis of contributions from that LEA. The libraries will initially be based on 50 per cent of resources currently held at Newcastle SEMERC but LEA contributions will be used to enhance the provision and manufacturers will be approached to loan equipment.

Technical Support

Provision of a telephone help-line for schools and advisory services and including a call-out service for technical support.

Assessment and Equipment Modification

Access to the assistance and cooperation of the Rocky Mount Assessment Centre and Barnsley General Hospital Medical Physics Department to enhance existing LEA special educational needs assessment work or to provide inset to further the provision of such services where appropriate.

Participating LEAs have a time entitlement to all the above services proportional to their sizes although additional time may be purchased if an individual LEA deems that necessary.

It must be stressed that the establishment of such a resource is very much a collaborative venture and that the intention is to maximize expertise and facilities which already exist within the region whilst at the same time continuing the SEMERC tradition of evaluation of new technology leading to innovation within the classroom. SENSU will act as a focal point for special educational needs within the region but will also liaise outside the region with other organizations and groups as may be necessary or desirable.

It is envisaged that the services provided by SENSU will maintain and enlarge upon those previously available to education through the Newcastle SEMERC but the main beneficiaries will be the children and young adults within the region who have special educational needs for whom the quality of life can be vastly improved by sensible use of appropriate technology.

The LEA Scheme links closely with the regional consortium. Within Humberside this work is cemented by the Manager of the Humberside Microelectronics Centre who has responsibilities for the deployment of the whole range of IT advisory teachers who represent all phases and disciplines of the service. The Centre enjoys the close collaboration of both the SEN advisers and the IT adviser and consequently whilst the whole team have a responsibility for and to address special educational needs issues a number of the advisers have quite specific job descriptions; one concerned with:

— curriculum enrichment for children with SEN within mainstream education;
— access — switches, hardware, etc.;
— record-keeping — annual review development and promotion;
— the area of post compulsory education,
— the needs within the secondary special phase.

A brief description of how these roles operate is provided by the advisory teacher concerned.

A. Review of Areas of Advisory Teacher Work

1. Supporting Pupils in Mainstream Schools

A significant part of my role involves this aspect of work. First contact can come about in a variety of ways, namely:

(a) direct contact from the school:
This is increasingly the case, however another support agency has often suggested that the school makes the contact;

(c) a visit requested by an educational psychologist:
This is usually a formal request with copies of assessments forwarded;

(c) visit requested by Frederick Holmes Service:
These cases would usually be discussed in some detail with GH at one of our liaison group meetings;

(d) Learning Support Services request visits to individual pupils with whom they have contact;

(e) statementing panel including IT on the statement.

A visit will lead to appropriate action being taken, usually in the following ways:

— general advice on IT use;
— the loan of suitable software and hardware;
— reports written to formalize the liaison aspect with other agencies involved.

Probably the most difficult aspect to overcome in respect of the support mentioned above arises when the class teacher involved is not a convinced or experienced computer user.

The following strategies I have found help to increase effectiveness of support:

(a) include all staff involved, if possible, with the child in the initial discussion of support on offer (class teacher, SEN coordinator, support services/agencies involved, etc.);

(b) Highlight support from within the school, i.e., IT/SEN coordinator etc.;

(c) support from the appropriate IT advisory teacher (primary) — liaison with colleagues important here;

(d) my contact telephone number with the school.

2 Inset

Three types of inset work can be identified:

— school-based inset;
— HUMMEC courses and modular structure;
— SEN modular course.

(a) *School-based Inset*

This can take many forms, i.e., linked to individual teachers, groups of teachers, whole staff or combined staff groups. It can take place either during school time or after school (directed or non-directed time) and it can be classroom based or not in order to meet appropriate needs.

It is difficult to identify a preferred mode of working since all systems have their advantages and otherwise!

I have been involved in many sessions recently where the school has released teachers using GRIST funds in order to concentrate on a specific aspect of IT work — this is a useful way of working and this should develop further in the future.

One of the arguments which is often used against the using of 'framework' programs is the time factor when putting in the appropriate content. The use of such time to plan and input content, create overlays, etc. could see the latest range of MESU framework programs 'List Explorer' and 'Touch Explorer Plus' become widely used.

Many requests for inset revolve around two main areas of IT use, these being the development of writing skills and the use of framework programs.

Writing software recommended:

Write (ACE) — allows modelling of a sentence.
My Word (RESOURCE) — use of word lists.
Wordbank 2 (RESOURCE) — a simple word processor with individualized word banks.
Fairy Tales, Old MacDonald's Farm (RESOURCE) — use of pictures.
Folio (Tediman) — choice of fonts, size of print, concept keyboard option.

Pen Down (Logotron) — flexible word processor with dictionary facility and large range of fonts.
Popular framework software:

Intro. Tray (MESU)— prediction of text.
Matchbox (RESOURCE) — variety of uses linked to development of early skills.
Window (MESU) — use of pictures.
Click (MESU) — use of pictures.
Touch Explorer Plus (MESU) — cross curricula use.
List Explorer (MESU) — early information handling.

(b) *HUMMEC Courses and Modular Structure*

I welcome the chance to input into the HUMMEC county courses. Over the last two years we have targeted senior management in primary schools (heads and deputies) and special schools (heads).

For the primary heads I focused on general IT/SEN issues and focused on appropriate software areas (Writing, Framework, etc.). For the primary deputies I focused on Information Handling in light of the National Curriculum, stressing the differentiation of tasks which can be identified in software such as 'List Explorer', 'Touch Explorer Plus' and 'Junior Find'.

The HUMMEC structure, although very much in its developmental stage, is the one which schools refer to in order to identify the courses on offer and to match these to their needs at any particular moment, e.g., I am presently devising the 'Word Processing and Special Needs' module for use in Grimsby in May. (Requested for the first time.) We have recommended a set of modules which would be appropriate for the SEN coordinator in a school.

(c) *SEN Modular Course*

After one run-through of the IT option we are in a position of evaluating our part of the course. We felt that we catered well for the wide range of IT experience and breadth of SEN work within the course.

The course offered a variety of presentations including demonstrations, workshops, seminars, videos etc. We needed to work in two groups for much of the time in order to complete our target aims.

3. *Regional Cooperation at RESOURCE*

The opportunity to cooperate as past of a regional group is an exciting part of the role. In the last year we have:

(a) mounted a regional event — SEN Conference;
(b) produced two regional newsletters;
(c) software development work continued;
(d) MESU projects in the pipeline, i.e., video;
(e) SEN Unit to act as a focal point in the future (hardware and programmer).

Close liaison and constant communication are fundamental to efficient and effective working of our group. Our half termly meetings with the Frederick Holmes Service, FE/IT Unit together with the four staff working within the HUMMEC structure are vitally important.

B. Advisory Teacher — Role of Facilitator

The job as an advisory teacher (IT) within Humberside is one of a facilitator. My brief within the county is to work with any child who has access problems to the curriculum. This means that I can be called upon to give advice on children from the ages of three to sixteen, in any sector of the education system, who have some problems of access usually through a disability.

I work in conjunction with the Frederick Holmes Service, a PH support service as well as being in close liaison with the other members of the HUMMEC team (both primary and secondary) and also with the special needs advisory teacher at RESOURCE.

When the staff from Frederick Holmes have decided that a child needs specialist help, in the field of microcomputers then they involve me in discussion on appropriate software and input devices. Sometimes, they may put hardware or peripherals into schools for the use of the child if they think that he or she needs such equipment. When this has been done, I make a follow-up visit to the school to suggest suitable software which the child may benefit from, after consultation with the teachers involved and assessment of the child's needs.

For some children the Frederick Holmes Service may decide that the child's physical disablement is such, that he would not benefit from a rig for his sole use, and a peripheral such as a key guard is all that the child requires to use the school's computer. Some children require alternative input devices, such as switches, touch-screens, extended keyboards, etc. to obtain access to the 'normal' curriculum. I refer back to the service when I have been to see children using one of the peripherals, especially if changes have occurred and perhaps what the child is at present using is no longer meeting the child's specific needs. The software that a child is using also needs to be reviewed at regular intervals because the child's needs should change to his requirements.

Part of the role that is beginning to emerge is in the field of annual reviews of statemented children. A lot of schools are asking me to attend when the child has had a computer input so that the statement carries the information for the following year and it can then be pursued. They feel that it is necessary for the continuing input for the child to have the information recorded on the statement.

Another part that the role involves is in-service training for teachers. This would either be to give a special needs slant to a course being run by one of the other members of the team, or it could be for more specialized in-service training relating specifically to aids for access. I will also be putting an input into the modular course for the Certification/Diploma in Special Education. This will give those teachers who are only just beginning to have integrated into their classrooms children with specific disabilities, who require more specialized equipment to enable them to keep up academically with their peers, the opportunity to see what is available for the use of the child in the classroom, and how these aids can help to overcome some of the problems. Within the near future it is hoped to undertake a project on the development of 'control' for children in schools with severe learning difficulties. This project will give the children the opportunity to control a piece of equipment, to do what they want it to do, and to record in some fashion what they have found out. This will be for many schools a new innovation.

We have recently formed a group to look at the development and usage of switches and related software for children with profound handicaps, and I am trying to coordinate the use of software that the special schools find valuable.

With the policy of integration of children with a physical handicap into the mainstream of the education sector I can see more use being made of advisory teachers, such as myself, to help these children to obtain their potential using whatever aids are applicable. These aids must be reviewable though, because the children's requirements do alter for many reasons.

C.   Advisory Teacher — Recording Pupil Achievement (SEN)

As an advisory teacher I have found that the work falls into two quite distinct areas; a general role generated by team membership and a specific role defined by my own specialism of SEN; profiling.

The general role consists in the main of inset work, entailing preparing and running the HUMMEC inset modules for classroom teachers. This requires knowledge of a wide range of software ranging far outside my own special needs field and cutting core-phase, thus giving a wide overview of information technology and its classroom applications, essential for any teacher with as specific a specialism as my own.

As a bridge from the general to the specific I also have a responsibility to the Learning Support Services of Humberside and support their teachers in the use of IT for children with special educational needs.

The main part of my work is with profiling, particularly with reference to using the Annual Review System (ARS). Special schools and units within Humberside are supported by training in the implementation and use of the system. The ARS often generates curriculum development. One project which has been initiated is the adaptation of The Derbyshire Language Programme so that it can be put on disc in a form which is meaningful to structure for the people who teach it. It is hoped that an interdisciplinary approach may be adopted and that the Speech and Language Unit therapists will be involved.

The advent of the National Curriculum has also generated interest in record keeping and profiling in mainstream schools and a number have shown interest in using the ARS for this purpose. Therefore part of my work involves investigating the possibilities of putting the targets of the National Curriculum on ARS so that mainstream schools can record the progress of children with special educational needs against those targets. A project is planned for the summer term in a junior school to investigate the practicalities.

Records of achievement and how they tie in with annual reviews and the Annual Review System is also under consideration. Schools are eager not to produce two separate sets of records but are investigating the possibility of combining the records of achievements and annual reviews in one compatible process within the Humberside Guidelines.

The Humberside team for IT consists of four teachers and has close associations with other teams in further education and education for the physically handicapped so close liaison is essential. Meetings are held on a regular basis.

Attendance at SEN conferences and maintaining a programme of professional developments, leading to a higher degree, makes it possible to keep abreast of developments in the field of special needs.

D. Further Education/Information Technology Unit — Staff Support for IT in Continuing Education and Training

Background

The FE/IT Unit offers a support service to all staff in the continuing education and training sector, with emphasis on integrating IT across the curriculum.

The FE/IT Unit was established in July 1985, with Education Support Grant funding under Section 5 of the Department of Education and Science Circular 5/86. IT was awarded sub-regional status in 1987.

Staffing

The Unit has a full-time coordinator, full-time (seconded) Curriculum Development Officer (CDO), and a part time clerical assistant. ESG Staff Development Funds currently support a team of six on part-time secondment (usually one day a week for one academic year).

Accommodation

The first two years the Unit shared premises with HUMMEC. This arrangement was highly satisfactory from a professional point of view: the work of HUMMEC and the Unit supplementing each other. However, the growth of the Unit and of HUMMEC led to severe space problems and in 1987 the Unit became housed in the Curriculum and Staff Development Centre.

Special Educational Needs

The Unit has a strong interest in the use of IT in the education and training of those with special educational needs. The Unit's Special Needs Officer (seconded for two days a week) offers training, help and advice to all CET organizations and has been active in raising awareness of the uses of IT to enrich and provide access to the curriculum and to training opportunities. This has included working with staff and students in the six colleges of FE, Adult Basic Education Groups in Hull, East Yorkshire, Scunthorpe, Grimsby and Goole, the Prison Service, i.e., Hull, Full Sutton and Everthorpe and the John Leggott Sixth Form College. Links relating to IT have also been made with the County Support Services.

County Liaison

A network of contacts operates through the College's Special Needs Coordinators, the County Basic Education Group, and the CSDC Special Needs Inset Group. Formal Liaison mechanisms have been established with the Special Needs Advisory Team at HUMMEC and the Frederick Holmes School (Special Needs IT Liaison Group).

Regional Liaison

The FE/IT Unit is represented on the Special Needs Steering Group at RESOURCE and informal links have been made with the ACCESS Centre at Wakefield District

College and a regional group of staff involved in the Council for Educational Technology Project, IT for Slow Learners in FE. FE/IT also represented on the Regional Advisory Teachers Group IT/SEN.

National Liaison

Links have been made with the National Centre for IT at Trowbridge.

E. Role of Advisory Teachers, Secondary Phase, Special Educational Needs

I have been working as an advisory teacher for information technology for only a few months, and I specialize in SEN pupils in secondary schools. One question sometimes asked me is what per cent of pupils have a special educational need and one could easily argue that it really is 100 per cent. However, generally it is accepted that some figure of 20 per cent of pupils have SEN. Fortunately, only a small percentage (2 per cent) have special SEN, when they are physically or mentally handicapped, and often are still in special schools, although many are now being supported through IT in mainstream schools. Part of my role is the supervision of these pupils in the school. IT for these pupils means access to the curriculum. This is achieved by using portable computers and other special adaptations like switches. As a result these pupils can be supported in an ordinary classroom where they are fully accepted by the rest of their peer group. Indeed it often benefits the peer group to have them there.

For many of these children IT has already been realized for its true worth but, for the mainstream teachers, who are often faced with a pupil with SEN of this type for the first time, they find that they are often totally unaware of the IT and equipment. This is where I come in and explain the hardware and software and help the teachers concerned to become familiar with the equipment.

This really illustrates the biggest area of my work and this is helping teachers to be IT literate so that they themselves can realize the potential of IT as a tool for teaching and particularly for helping pupils with any learning difficulty.

There are many pupils who benefit considerably from the use of IT in everyday learning. They may lack motivation, may feel they have been labelled failures and therefore act out the part. Indeed it is impractical to mention all the various examples of pupils who constitute the category of SEN. I have had pupils who would not work in the conventional situation because they would be disloyal to their parents, who hate teachers and expect their offspring to do likewise. Some pupils feel that they are failures academically and do not wish to participate as they are at a disadvantage for some reason.

Is there any wonder that the behaviour of these pupils tends to be disruptive and they do not wish to cooperate? If school consisted of running races, which I cannot do, I would not wish to attend either and I would disrupt the race or make up an excuse not to run, or I would play truant, for the latter would at least get some respect from the peer group. However, if I was to be given a go-cart to race in, then I would at least attempt the race and might even enjoy it.

IT is like giving a child a go-cart. My job is trying to inform teachers of this fact and of the powerful tool that a computer is for teaching. It enables the pupil to have peer equality and takes away the 'chips' on their shoulders of failure. The product they produce is professional and they are never told off by a computer. To enable me to do this I have structured the type of work I do in the school. I introduce the teachers to word-processing, then data bases and other framework programs, followed later by thematic software and subject specific software.

The most powerful software, and the one most teachers are beginning to appreciate, is word processing. It is a delight to see teachers who have never word processed before, managing to produce 'wanted' posters and newspapers. They feel the enjoyment of seeing their own work in print and this they wish to pass on to their pupils. Word processing allows for draft copies to be made and it is so easy to edit the work that pupils will actually do so.

Often a boy or girl, after writing a long piece of work, refuses to treat the piece as a draft copy as recopying will possibly take hours. With a computer it is just a case of loading from the disc and editing. The teachers can discuss presentation in a new light, not just a case of making it legible but a case of 'which font would best suit that piece of writing'. The work is not graffitied by the teacher's marking in red. Equally, when the writing is on a monitor somehow the pupils do not feel that it is their work, it is not an extension of themselves as handwriting is, therefore suggestions for improvement are easily accepted and corrections are not an insult. Only when the work is printed is it considered their own property.

For the gifted child a good essay or piece of work is often requested to be written again for display purposes and the child is, in effect, being punished for doing good work, as they have another couple of hours work facing them. Not so with word processing when any number of print-outs is possible. When teachers realize that pupils can have their own discs with individual dictionaries and essay planners to assist the writing and work being done, they begin to realize to potential of the machines. Pupils with their own disc made with an individual environment of dictionaries, etc., have a degree of independence from the teacher as they can help themselves a little more. This gives confidence. However, the teachers do need a great deal of help in understanding the various word processors and especially the use of the concept keyboard and making their own overlays.

As a result it is a gradual process of learning before any results are apparent in a classroom. Nevertheless, teachers are requesting me to visit them and give them instruction in all these areas.

Belonging to a good team of advisory teachers led by a head of HUMMEC has enabled the team to produce modular foundation courses consisting of five sessions, each two hours long. In these we introduce teachers to the hardware, word processing, data bases, the versatile micro and thematic software. After this introduction they can request specific courses or more detailed help and assistance. One school has had eighteen members of staff taking part in the Modular Foundation Course that I, assisted by a colleague, have taken in to the school one evening per week. As a result of this some of these teachers have requested further information and have become quite interested in computers, to the extent of taking them home to familiarize themselves with the software.

Data bases are a wonderful teaching aid and I am just beginning to interest a few teachers in them. They enable the pupils to search for information and this process is essential for them when they leave school, as career centres have data bases like Cascade and Micro Doors as well as Taps. If you are familiar with a keyboard you stand a better chance of understanding how to get information. Data bases involve a great deal of discussion and decision making. They require a cooperative effort of the peer group and again there is peer equality. The data bases that I have used also allow for graphs to be constructed. The pupil, who would not normally be able to draw a graph, so never actually gets to the stage of evaluating the information on it, can now do so. One could ask why not use printed graphs from books but they do not contain information that the pupil has collected him or herself and they are not personal. If he or she has fed the information in to the data base, the resultant graph is important and he or she can appreciate the learning situation more. However, once again helping teachers to become familiar with the data bases and being competent enough to use them in a teaching situation, is taking a little time, but the ideas are beginning to be sewn.

Computers are also very creative. One thinks of a machine as being a lifeless tool, and so it is, but it can still be creative, just as much as a brush. As a result Paintbrush on the Nimbus is becoming a favourite of mine to show staff some of the applications of IT. One or two people have been a little nervous of the Nimbus machine, but playing on Paintbrush has soon relaxed them and I have been asked to give them more instruction.

Lots of discussion goes into a lesson when computers are used. Some software is designed for this. I once collected information from pupils regarding how many minutes in a day they spoke to an adult and it was not surprising to find that it was often only for a few minutes. Even in school they are often told to sit down and be quiet. Working on a computer in groups of two or three means that they can discuss and negotiate and make decisions.

'The Best Days of Our Lives' and 'Camping', are marvellous programmes which can be used for decision making. These programs give a print-out of the decisions made and ask suitable questions. This is beginning to interest some teachers too, as previously they have looked on the computer as being a machine that would not benefit a pupil in mixing with their peers or in preparing them for their future place in society. It is difficult not to be judgmental in making suggestions and so I try to have available different types of software and to assist the teacher in viewing, only by operating the computer if this is needed, so that they can evaluate the software for themselves.

I have also been fortunate to have my own course for secondary teachers concerned with SEN (the first one of two) during the day and held at a local Teachers' Centre. This was a huge success and I tried to cover a range of suitable approaches to teaching pupils with SEN. It was on this course, when I was being assisted by a colleague, that she remarked how surprised she was at how unaware the teachers were of the available IT. However, as they are becoming more aware there is a tremendous amount of work to be done in assisting them to become competent enough to be able to use computers in a classroom.

Unfortunately in secondary schools IT has consisted of a few pupils using the machines for computer studies and the teacher was often a mathematics teacher. As a result mathematics and computers tended to be linked together and access to the machine was very limited. Indeed, this is still the case in some establishments. People were under the impression that IT was only for those who could program the machine. I feel this is like saying you have to be a mechanic to drive a car. Also some IT teachers tended to be a little technical in their approach to answering questions about the computers. Mystique resulted and the expensive machines were often used by only a few pupils and a few teachers.

My job is to try to help change this situation and persuade teachers to let all pupils in the schools access the machines and for them to be used as a teaching tool. The computer is such a perfect medium for learning and the pupils adore it, excuse the pun.

Obviously my work has only just begun but it is proving a wonderful challenge which really is most enjoyable.

An interesting series of examples of the ways in which work in the information technology field has been fostered and allowed to develop. The advantages for the young person with special educational needs which arise from the collaborative working of a range of experienced teachers as programmers is perhaps obvious. Initiatives have developed rapidly from the time when the MEP programme began when 'special' was seen to be special school orientated and today when in the field of IT it is seen to be an integrated part of the process of learning, across the curriculum for all pupils whatever their need for support or intervention.

Chapter 11

Integration of a Special School: John Watson School

Diane Wilson

The following is offered as a personal history of events which have taken place in a small area of Oxfordshire.

The events owe much to individual and group understanding and nothing to theoretical models.

Personalities and personal insights have ensured growth and development for special education in our area and many people have been involved. Far too many to thank individually.

I offer this account as a tribute to everyone involved in this exciting venture.

John Watson School is a forty place school for children with severe learning difficulties. The geographical location is fairly typical of 1960s planning of such schools as it is built in beautiful rural surroundings but also isolated from its nearest small town of Thame and from the local village of Wheatley and its primary school which is one mile away. However by a lucky accident the school was built almost adjacent to the local girls grammar school which then developed into a lively comprehensive school. The school was built in 1966 and until 1980 was, as a direct consequence of the location, completely segregated from the local educational community. The education of the children within the school had all the benefits of a special school. Small classes with specifically trained teachers, family support, and everyone did their best to inform the community of the children and their special needs by the usual trips out, fund raising functions, etc.

The children aged from 2–16 years were taught from a detailed individual programme derived from a curriculum divided into the following six main areas: intellectual development, gross motor, fine motor, play, language, and creative development. Both teachers and parents set curricula goals for each term which were then reported on. There is no doubt that the children did develop well both educationally and socially but they were also in splendid isolation from their peers in mainstream schools.

In 1978 The Warnock Report was published. Everyone was encouraged to begin to question educational isolation and to suggest ways in which schools like John Watson could begin to join with the local educational community.

Paragraphs 8, 10 and 12 in particular were specific.

— We recommend that firm links should be established between special and ordinary schools in the same vicinity.
— There should be some sharing of educational programmes between special and ordinary schools.
— Considerable benefits to both pupils with special needs and other pupils as well as to teachers can result from shared arrangements.

Discussions began within the school as to how we could retain all that was good, in our view, within the school, and yet extend its influence in order to allow the children to benefit from social and curricular integration. We decided upon the following plan.

Familiarization of the Staff

Knowing that staffing was already a problem in mainstream schools, we decided that we should acquaint ourselves with an overview of what would be required for our staff and children to be acceptable within local schools.

Teachers began to spend some time each week at local schools. Some took classes, others helped with groups of slow learners or assisted in activity groups. By the end of the term we were able to begin sending children alongside the staff for specific periods and all were made welcome.

Establishment of an Outpost

At that time (1981) there was a group of 5-year-olds within the school. They had all started school with us at 2 and consequently were well established and socially adept. It was decided that they should spend two days in each week at the local primary school, along with a teacher and classroom assistant. A temporary classroom was allocated to them and in the beginning mixed only at break and lunchtimes. However, because of the familiarization of the staff, they were quickly invited into music, craft sessions and PE where our own staff could also assist. Gradually a team spirit developed.

From that first outpost three other schemes followed.

A Secondary School Outpost

As our own school was actually situated on the same campus as the local comprehensive school we decided to discuss with them the possibility of some of our children over 11+ joining some of their classes.

The secondary school is large (over 1,000) but with an orderly atmosphere and a large campus, although on one site.

We began to send two John Watson pupils aged 12+ along to PE, HE and art and craft lessons accompanied by the same teachers who had established the primary school scheme. This little scheme prospered and staff contact began to grow.

A Special School Outpost

Because of problems of space and access within both the primary and secondary schools it was not possible to accommodate the profoundly handicapped who were in wheelchairs. If these children were to integrate, and we did want them to, we had to discover a host school which was accessible and who had the space to accommodate some extra children.

We were fortunate to find that our local school for the physically handicapped was willing to accept our scheme for a trial. Consequently one teacher and several children attended each day during 1986–1988.

A 'Home Area' Primary School

During 1986 we discoverd that we did have four children aged 9+ who all lived in one small area. We approached the primary school in that area and were given one extra teacher for one year by the LEA for those four children to spend their last year at primary school with youngsters from their home area. Hopefully they would then progress to the comprehensive school having made friends locally.

All of these schemes have now developed over the past six or seven years and have been refined into our three present schemes. The development is interesting to trace. It reflects the progress made by children, staff and the local community towards the educational integration of children with severe learning difficulties in the Wheatley area.

Primary Children

From our original two days each week in an unused classroom, we have progressed during the past eight years to become an integral part of Wheatley Primary School.

The school changed sites to a converted secondary modern school and as the old headteacher retired, a new head was appointed who wished to develop the community aspect of the school. This event coincided with a small increase in staffing at John Watson School and so it was possible to base a teacher and classroom assistant full-time at the 'new' school.

Thus more children were able to spend time at the primary school and they were supported by our own teachers within the mainstream classrooms.

During 1988 toilet and changing facilities have been provided by the LEA and aids to access. This enabled the transfer of the scheme for the profoundly handicapped from the school for physically handicapped to the primary school.

Thus we now have two full-time teachers and one classroom assistant based at the primary school and all our children between 5–11 years spend some time there during the week.

Each child has an individual timetable both for time spent and for lessons attended. Our aim is to offer each child an appropriate balance of social and curricular integration and also to consider the best educational programme for each child. Thus children attend for varying periods of time during each week. I give two examples. Table (a) is for a child who is physically able and who can cope with support within a mainstream classroom. Table (b) is for a physically handicapped child who cannot walk unaided and who needs much individual tuition and therapy. However, he benefits from the spontaneous language and the hustle and bustle of the primary school to say nothing of the music and movement groups which he adores!

Whenever possible our teachers are alongside the children in the mainstream classroom. At all times, the teachers have appropriate, alternative work available for the children. Mainstream work, even in infant groups, is often far too difficult. However, we do try to match subjects. Teachers do not always spend all their time with the John Watson children. Often, according to expertise, roles change and small group work may well involve mainstream children with our group and vice versa.

Some of our profoundly handicapped children can be disruptive and also unpredictable and so it is possible for them to spend some time in the small base which we have but to integrate socially during breaks, play times and free play.

Relationships between the staff of the two schools have developed well. Six different primary teachers have worked with our children and indeed we have recently split our own groups so that we now have children, with support, in both infant and junior groups. I think that neither school could imagine life without the other and it is sometimes difficult to separate roles.

The children seem to accept each other as individuals now. The progression of the 'titles' given to our children has been fascinating. Firstly, we were 'the handicapped' then 'the John Watson Children' and now we all have individual names.

I suppose total acceptance will come when we have nicknames — perhaps we already have!

Timetable

	9.0	10.20	10.40	11.0	12.05	1.10	3.00	3.15	after school
Monday	Handwriting Reading		ASSEMBLY & PLAYTIME	Performance Painting Poetry		DINNER Lunch and outdoor play	Riding		Netball
Tuesday	RE Reading		ASSEMBLY & PLAYTIME	Language		DINNER Lunch and outdoor play	Project 1st & 2nd year games		Keep fit & Dance
Wednesday	Maths		ASSEMBLY & PLAYTIME	Language		DINNER Lunch and outdoor play	Singing Language Sewing & knitting		Gym
Thursday	Project		ASSEMBLY & PLAYTIME	Maths		DINNER Lunch and outdoor play	Apparatus in hall		Swimming
Friday	Language		ASSEMBLY & PLAYTIME	Project		DINNER Lunch and outdoor play	Singing in hall at John Watson		

Timetable

	9.0	10.20	10.40	11.0	12.05	1.10	3.00
Monday (Primary)	News/Discussion Individual Work in classroom		Assembly and Play Time	Topic Work		Lunch and Outdoor Play	Riding for Disabled with John Watson
Tuesday (John Watson)	Language Physiotherapy			Cooking			Hand Group Singing
Wednesday (John Watson)	**Number** Body Awareness			Art Rhymes and Music			Topic Ball Computer skills
Thursday (Primary)	News/Discussion Individual Work Choosing (shared activity)			Large apparatus			Art and Craft
Friday (Primary & J. W.)	News/Discussion Individual Work in classroom			Music T/V			Swimming with John Watson

Secondary Age Children

The development of the scheme for children aged 11 + –16 years has been steady and positive. Obviously the task of integrating our young people into such a school was one which required tact and patience. What actually did develop however was a real mutual respect between staff and some enduring friendships between children. Also the interest of families connected with the school was friendly and positive. There have been some problems — timetabling is one aspect which can prove to be trying — lunchtimes and the noise and hustle of the large dining room is difficult for our children as is the constant movement within the large campus.

However, the strong personal support from the headteacher of the school who delights in the progress of the children, and of his deputy who makes time to discuss any difficulties, have I feel been the key to the outstanding success of this scheme, combined with the enthusiasm and strength of our own staff.

In 1985 a teacher and classroom assistant were based full-time on the secondary school campus. We were given a classroom in a second year area just away from the main school. The classroom is warm and comfortable and we have sole use of it and have decorated the walls with pictures and put the timetable onto the blackboard. During the academic year 1987–1988 children from John Watson School were integrated into forty-two lessons during a ten day timetable of fifty periods. Once again, the children are assessed individually and spend differing amounts of time at the school.

Each year the timetable is renegotiated. Children attend lessons only when the subject teacher is happy for them and their support staff to join in. There has been no shortage of offers of time and space for us but high class numbers have precluded our involvement in some subjects.

There are three levels of integration:

(a) Attending classes unsupervised. This is rare, although some boys PE is very successful.

(b) Attending classes accompanied by John Watson School staff who provide suitable class work in appropriate subjects.

(c) Attending individual sessions or small group-work in our own base at the school (e.g., computer studies). Any child may be introduced to any or all of these levels. It can be seen that we do not actually integrate via the comprehensive schools own special needs unit. As staff we do link professionally and share expertise. However, we do feel that perhaps some of the young people with special needs on the role of the comprehensive school may feel that attention would be drawn to them if our children were to join them in their unit, at a later date this may well develop if they so wish.

Here I show timetables for two children who integrated into first and second year lessons.

NAME   Annabel   WHEATLEY PARK SCHOOL

FORM   John Watson Group

DAY	Period 1 9.10–10.05	Period 2 10.05–11.00	Period 3 11.20–12.20	Period 4 1.10–2.05	Period 5 2.05–3.00	HOME WORK
1 *	Base	Art (ix)		W.W. ⟵————⟶		
2 *	Music (ITR)	Base	Drama (IJF)	PE (IC)	HE (IB)	
3	John Watson ⟶					
4	John Watson ⟶					
5 *	Base	Base	HE (IB)	John Watson ⟶		
6 *	Music (ITR)	Drama (IJF)	Base	Horse riding ⟵————⟶		
7 *	Music (ITR)	HE (IB)	Base	PE (IC)	Base	
8	John Watson ⟶					
9 *	Base	Base	Art (ix)	Base	PE (IC)	
10 *	Base	Base	Art (ix)	John Watson ⟶		

* Days at WP   Parent's Signature

132

NAME   Sean   WHEATLEY PARK SCHOOL

FORM   John Watson Group

DAY	Period 1 9.10–10.05	Period 2 10.05–11.00	Period 3 11.20–12.20	Period 4 1.10–2.05	Period 5 2.05–3.00	HOME WORK
1	Base	Base	Art (iy)	Horseriding ⟷		
2	Maths (2S)	Base	Base	Base	PE	
3	City & Guilds Agriculture & ⟷ Conservation (4th yr)			CLASS OUTING ⟷		
4	Base	Base	Art (iy)	Base	Base	
5	HE (2EB) ⟷		Maths (2JS)	Swimming ⟷		
6 *	Base	Base	Base	W.W. ⟷		
7 *	Base	Base	Base	Base	Drama (2CP)	
8 *	City and Guilds Agriculture & ⟷ Conservation (4th yr)			Maths	Base	
9 *	Base	Base	Maths (2JS)	Base	PE (2EB)	
10 *	Base	Art (iy)	Drama (2CP)	Swimming ⟷		

* Days at WP   Parent's Signature

_____

The Integrated Nursery

It may seem odd that the youngest age group was the last to be integrated. However until recently the school for many years had no nursery-aged children. Although we were prepared to accept children from age 2 or 3 none were referred to the school.

During 1987–1988 we had four new children all aged under 5. The hunt for an integration base began in earnest! There was no nursery school in the immediate area and so we began to investigate the possibilities of providing an integrated nursery within our special school.

We certainly had the room. On any day up to 50 per cent of the children were out. With some reorganization (again!) we could provide the staff. Education officers and governors were very supportive as was the Adviser for Nursery Education who spent time discussing problems, suggesting equipment, etc. So in June 1987 we had a small piece in our local *Educational Newsletter* asking local mums interested in their children attending an integrated nursery to contact school. The response was overwhelming. Within one week all places were filled and we had a long waiting list.

In September 1988 the class opened. One teacher, one classroom assistant and one YTS trainee are usually involved.

Mainstream children attend for either morning session (9.15–11.45am) or afternoon (12.30–3.00pm) and special needs children for either the morning or the whole day including lunch. We operate a flexible ratio of about one third of children with special needs and two thirds of mainstream children.

At the present time all is well. The local mums approve, more families with children with special needs are interested and the rest of the school welcome the mixture of children and families involved.

However, this scheme along with all the others except one has not received any LEA finance or extra staffing. The nursery, in particular, could develop and include many more children with minimal extra staffing. We hope that this future development is possible.

Some Reflections

As this is a personal account of one school's efforts, perhaps it may be useful to add some points which have affected the schemes in both a positive and a negative way.

In the beginning we were constantly faced with the unexpected. Our first surprise came when we found parents of John Watson children reluctant to accept integration. They were worried about bullying and also about failure both social and academic. It was only when we promised each family that we would remove their child if faced with major problems that we gained their consent.

Although most children have settled and their families have accepted integration, some have withdrawn their consent. The wishes of these families have been acted upon immediately and the children withdrawn.

The Retention of the Special School Base

At the present time we are keen to preserve our special school as a base.

We would like to see it used as a resource base whereby a whole team of experts for children with SLD could be based. Our teacher counsellor is already a very regular visitor, and we would like to see special therapists and others based in the school. It is important for staff with expertise in a particular area to be able to meet together in a working environment. Isolation must be fought at all levels!

The Educational Programme

The programme for each child and the recording of progress proved to be a minor problem. Each teacher must know exactly what has been done each day. Thus a file, containing a daily diary of events, work done and messages from home, travels with the child between schools. Annual reviews and meetings with parents, etc. are always attended by teachers from John Watson and the integration base. Home/school diaries for parents are completed by the staff dealing with the child on each particular day. It seems a complicated system, but it does work. Obviously time must be given for teachers to meet to discuss individual children. Twice during each week we all meet. Once after school when details are discussed and difficulties sorted out and on Friday afternoons when everyone returns to John Watson. The children meet together for a singing session, celebrate birthdays and achievements and we are a school together. This session is, I believe, an essential part of our week and is much enjoyed.

Change of Staff

I was worried when I considered the damage that could be done to a scheme if I placed a member of staff who either did not believe in the benefits or who perhaps did not have the skills and flexibility required to continue a scheme.

We have had several changes and although the schemes may have developed differently I have been fortunate to appoint, in every case, enthusiastic hard-working staff who have ensured the progress of the schemes.

It is not my intention to try to sell integration as a philosophy. I merely point out that in our area at this time and most important with the present personalities involved that we are happy with the results of integration. I do believe that the success has been due to several major factors:

1 Staff who have been willing to sit in on other classes and of course to those who have allowed us to sit in!

2 A close relationship with parents and constant communication between school and home.

3 Excellent communication between special school class teachers and integration scheme teachers. Files travel hundreds of miles but everyone knows what has been done in each school.

4 A willingness to experiment, to try to shake off what was in our case an over-protective environment.

5 Positive consideration of the benefits of social and curricular integration for all children.

Future Plans

Each development seems to inspire others and although I keep promising the staff a quiet year it really never seems to happen.

Next years 'good idea' is for us to offer support to some children who are able to cope within their local primary school. *If requested* we could offer equipment and some time to develop programmes or assistance with particular difficulties.

We would wish to move further towards a real resource base model — perhaps offer some in-service to teachers wishing to acquire specific skills — teacher swaps are feasible, perhaps on a termly basis, or perhaps part-time role swaps? Could we introduce intensive therapy courses for children with a specific difficulty within their special need?

I feel that the possibilities are wide and far-reaching. Other schools have already developed along this road — we shall be looking to learn from them and adapt new systems to the needs in our area.

The future will no doubt change the role of schools like ours. It is for us to ensure that we capitalize these changes to ensure the maximum benefit for children, their families and for staff that support them.

Chapter 12

The Development of a Special Needs Support Centre (SNSC)

Leslie J. Rowsell

May I invite you to join me on a short journey? But before we depart we ought to make a few plans to include:

— Where are we going?
— Who is our travelling companion?
— Why are we going?
— What plans should we make for our journey? and
— What problems are we likely to encounter on the way?

The analogy of considering educational change as a journey is, I believe, a useful one. The planning stage leads to implementation into practice, or the journey, and when we reach the end we try and reach some sort of conclusion about our experience: was it useful, did we learn something, is it worth repeating and, perhaps most importantly, did we enjoy it?

Our journey is the story of a special school, Critchill School, situated in the small rural market town of Frome, in Somerset. We opened in 1977 in new buildings to cater for pupils aged 3–16 years with moderate and severe learning difficulties. We consider ourselves to be a dynamic school (I am sorry, I have no space here for false modesty), and we have strived to develop the best practice. When the idea of special schools becoming centres of expertise (incidentally, we dislike this terminology, and it is only used to preserve the historical context) became current with the Warnock Report (1978) we felt that our then present state of practice was compatable with the notion and was a route along which we would wish to develop. It is at this point our journey will begin. It is the account of the school's development as a Special Needs Support Centre (SNSC).

Your immediate travel companion is the present headteacher of the school; my name appears elsewhere. But I am perhaps only a guide, for your journey was, and is still being, created by a team of fellow professionals composed of present and past members of staff. Amongst them I not only include teaching staff, but also assistant teachers and the cleaning and catering staff for reasons that will become apparent later. For my own part I describe myself as a realistic pro-integrationalist. I am often taken to task for pro-integrationalist views and what some others see as a contradictory professional life in a special school. For me it presents no contradiction or professional dilemma. I do believe that all children have a right of access to the same educational opportunities. But to put this belief into practice is perhaps to make at least two incorrect assumptions: that all children require the same opportunities, and that the educational system is ready for integration. Hence my description of my philosophy as a pro-integrationalist is qualified by the adjective realistic. We should move toward integration at the pace that is appropriate for children and the system.

The introductions over and with a clear view of our destination, we ought to consider the circumstances that influenced us coming together and travelling together. If asked, most educationalists would identify the deliberations of the Warnock Report (1978) as the watershed in terms of reconsidering the educational provision for children with special educational needs. Most readers will be familiar with the Report's recommendations, which I do not wish to labour here. I would remind you only of the Report's analysis of integration, a simple concept, which in the context of the practicalities of everyday classroom work, I believe, we often lose sight. Warnock talked of locational, social and functional integration. It was implied that functional integration was to be the desired goal of good integrative practice but both locational and social integration were valuable in appropriate circumstances, and as stages along the way to functional integration.

The Education Act (1981) attempted to provide legislative backing for integrative practice in schools. In this aim, I suggest it failed. Little credibility can be attached to legislative intention that remain unimplemented for two years, and, while the massive resource implications have been identified, received no governmental funding.

> One thing is clear . . . the integration in ordinary schools of children currently ascertained as handicapped . . . is not a cheap alternative . . . indeed . . . the dispersal over many schools of the specialist teaching and supportive services at present concentrated in a few schools will be considerably more expensive (Warnock Report, 1978, p. 118).

> The committee concludes that the lack of specific resources has restricted implementation of the 1981 Act. A commitment of extra resources is needed if significant further progress is to be made (Education, Science and Arts Committee, 1987, p. xiii).

Furthermore, the House of Commons Select Committee's recent report is pessimistic of the legislative power of the 1981 Act to fulfil its intention. I suggest that the intention to promote the integration of children with special needs as outlined in

Section 2, paragraph 2 of the Act was devalued by Section 2, paragraph 3 which drew attention to a number of exceptions, and allowed for wide interpretation of the Act's intention at local level. A recent CSIE survey reports this view:

> The survey highlights how no local education authority is going to abandon either the concept or practice of separate special school provision — at least in the near future. This calls into question the effectiveness of Section 2 of the 1981 Act — the development of a spirit of integration as an established part of the education system (Rogers, 1986, p. 5).

On a national basis then, we might expect the intention to integrate as expressed in the Education Act (1981) to be widely interpreted and impelimented at LEA level. Further reading of the CSIE report (Rogers, 1986) would provide the evidence for this assertion. Wilf Brennan also recognized the tension that exists between the Act and practice:

> It (The Education Act, 1981) is entirely short term. It reaches nowhere and, of itself, it gives those who operate it no idea of where it is intended to lead. In practical terms this means that development beyond the Act is left to the initiative of Local Education Authorities . . .
> Experience has shown that much can slip away between legislation and practice. (Brennan, 1982, pp. 107 and 108).

During the two year period leading up to February 1988 my own LEA drafted, considered, consulted and redrafted its own policy for children with special educational needs. Somerset adopts a pragmatic view of the process that should develop good integrative practice. The provision includes developing a whole school approach to curriculum planning, support for mainstream schools with additional staffing and a positive role for special schools as providers within a structured continuum of provision. I am perhaps fortunate to work in an LEA which has carefully considered and balanced the philosophical advantages, the legislative requirements and the practical realities of providing supportive educational mechanisms for children with special educational needs.

I suggest our travelling together is not only based on common understanding of the philosophical issues that surround the integration of children with special educational needs but also the practical issues, which although partially addressed before, should, I believe, be investigated in the additional dimension as a process of educational change. In this context we should agree that the implications are massive — let us search for some evidence.

Attention has been drawn to the tension that exists between the organizational and personal dimension during the process of change, and the effect on the eventual outcome, Getzel and Guba (1957). Perhaps more usefully Fullan (1982) analyzed the dimensions of change in terms of objective and subjective realities. Objective realities relate to the planning, resourcing and organizational structures as they exist before during and after the change. Subjective realities relate to those personal perceptions with which individuals within the organization see the change effecting the context within which they work and thus effecting their own lives.

The objective realities with regard to integration may include effectiveness of the legislation to achieve its intention, resourcing problems, the interpretation of the 1981 Act at LEA level, the existing provision within LEAs, and interpretation of LEA policy at school level. As the reader will realize, these are very open ended objective realities in the movement toward integration and therefore it would be reasonable to expect numerous outcomes when implemented at school level. Some of these outcomes will be successful, others may not. We should perhaps pay some attention to the American experience:

> Because we may think mainstreaming (integration) is desirable it is no excuse for assuming that institutional realities will accommodate our hopes Sarason and Doris, 1979, p. 355, authors parenthesis).

Institutional realities at school level will also include individual teacher's perceptions of the change. It is these perceptions, coupled with the support that teachers receive during the change process that are the most powerful dynamics and which influence the eventual outcome. We should not under-estimate the magnitude of achieving good integrative practice. The following observation perhaps gives a flavour.

> Integration requires new ways of working on the part of many professionals. There is a need to collaborate with colleagues, share information, view pupils problems in a comprehensive light, disseminate skills and generally move toward interdisciplinary working (Hegarty, Pocklington and Lucas, 1981, p. 512).

Fullan (1982), in his analysis of the subjective realities of educational change introduces a concept which is particularly appropriate to integration as an innovation. He maintains there are three levels of change that teachers may adopt at a personal level:

1   The possible use of new or revised materials.
2   The possible use of new teaching approaches.
3   The possible alteration of beliefs. (Fullan, 1982, p. 30)

Fullan later indicates the increasing difficulty of encouragement of personal change within each of three levels:

> The innovation as a set of materials and resources is the most visable aspect of change, and the easiest to employ . . . Change in teaching approach or style in using new materials presents greater difficulty . . . changes in belief are yet more difficult: they challenge the care values held by individuals regarding the purposes of education (Fullan, 1982, p. 35).

Fullan's analysis is useful in recognizing a personal change process. However, it is also useful in a comparison of provision required by children with differing special needs. Hodgson, Clunies-Ross and Hegarty (1984) suggest the following typology of school curriculum organization:

1   Mainstream curriculum.
2   Mainstream curriculum with modifications.
3   Mainstream curriculum with significant modifications.
4   Special curriculum with additives.
5   Special curriculum. (Hodgson, Clunies-Ross and Hegarty, 1984, p. 171)

They further suggest that physically or sensory impaired children are most often suited to a curriculum organizational pattern described either in (1) or (2) but that children with learning or emotional or behavioural difficulties are often more suited to (3), (4) or (5). Where physical or sensory impairment is the primary handicap to educational progress, a modified environment or adoption of curriculum materials is all that is required to meet a special need. These changes can easily be accommodated within the mainstream school environment. However, for children with learning or emotional and behavioural difficulties, the curriculum needs to be significantly changed leading to a change in approach. The integration of such children will require teachers to adopt different styles of curriculum delivery across a range of children to be found in a class. The 'new ways of working' (Hegarty, Pocklington and Lucas, 1981) will necessitate teachers rethinking the philosophical values that underpin their practice, or as Fullan (1982) simply puts it, change their beliefs.

Let us then attempt to summarize the itinerary for our journey. The journeys end is good integrative practice, but we recognize at least some of the difficulties along the way. These may arise from within the organizational context of the change (additional resourcing is always an important issue), but more likely from individuals who will display resistance because of the way they perceive integration affecting their personal professional life. People then, particularly teachers, are established as central in the process of change toward integration. It is people we must work with, convince and make confident in a 'new way of working'. Our journey should commence with this thought in mind — Critchill Special Needs Support Centre, a resource for people.

To claim that people are central to our work is perhaps factuous, as all schools can equally make the same claim. Our aim is specific: the promotion of sound and realistic integrative practice working with teachers in our local educational community. We are particularly mindful of the levels of change suggested by Fullan (1982) and that depending on the primary handicapping condition, good integrative practice may be achieved at each level. As a special school whose past experience lies with children with learning difficulties we are also aware that for some handicapping conditions it is necessary for teachers to change in respect of all three levels if a claim for good practice is to be made.

Our purpose, as distinct from our aim, is to act as an agent of change. In a scenario where a whole county is moving toward radical change, support mechanisms must be established. On the one hand our institution is changing and we require support, on the other, schools around us are having to change and they also need support. Our school, and the four other Somerset special schools designated Special Needs Support Centres (SNSC), can be perceived as part of a mutually supportive change agent system.

The concept of change agent within the context of developing a county-wide approach to good integrative practice is multifacited. It is a false exercise to attempt to identify a SNSCs individual parts. However readers may find it useful to consider the four main strands that the school has identified, and help to prioritize our work:

1   To work as a partner in a continuum of provision.
2   Providers of material resources.
3   Providers of inset opportunities.
4   Community resource for advice and information.

As readers will understand our state of development is further in some of these areas than others. In particular much effort has gone into establishing a Curriculum Resource Bank and providing inset opportunities. However, I shall briefly review our state of development and future plans within each area.

I believe there is a single key word that mediates our role as a SNSC and in particular our work as a partner in a continuum of provision: this word is confidence. Our partners have to have confidence in our school and we in return need to have confidence that the work we do is valuable in the wider context outside of our school. The way to begin building that confidence, which of course is based on mutual respect, is for special schools to become less insular. They should be part of joint local initiatives, to share common training needs with their mainstream partners, undertake joint teaching programmes and welcome and be welcomed in each others schools.

Once that rapport is established, strategies for mutual support can evolve. It has been suggested that SNSC should provide short-term and part-time placements for pupils thought to need temporary specialist help or who might have a specific learning difficulty. A number of issues need to be addressed and answered before this suggestion becomes a reality.

—   The special school will need to consider its organizational arrangements to ensure these are compatable with the proposals. Arrangements of this type will cause disruption to the schools normal programmes and we must be certain the organization is robust enough to withstand the challenges.
—   Consideration may need to be given to greater flexibility within the statutory statements especially with regard to provision.
—   The establishing of a clear understanding of the reasons and purpose of individual pupils attendance at a special school between the parents,

mainstream and special school. This agreement may even need to extend to some form of contract.

— A close working relationship between all the professional agencies, e.g., medical, psychological, administrative and teaching.

Might I recall to mind Fullan's comment:

'The innovation as a set of materials and resources is the most visible aspect of change' (Fullan, 1982).

Being 'visible' and I suggest, 'concrete', the adoption of a new set of materials is the most tangible form of change and therefore the results, hopefully positive, assume relative immediacy. It seems to me that the early work of a SNSC should include a bank of materials for both the use of the school and other professionals in the educational community. Critchill was the first special school in Somerset to establish a Curriculum Resource Bank (CRB), and we like to believe that the good practice this represented was influential in persuading the LEA to extend the idea to four other centres in the county. I further suggest that such tangible efforts to be involved with our mainstream colleagues can only improve mutual respect and confidence.

There is much that could be written of the ups and downs, disappointments and successes over the past three years of the CRBs development. In the space available I suggest that the most economical way of conveying the context of our experience is to form a list. I make no attempt at providing answers, only raising some of the issues that have become apparent from practice. Answers lie only in the context of one's own organization.

— There is an ownership dilemma involved. Firstly, who does the CRB belong to: the school, the local education community, the LEA? The source of funding in the initial stages may be indicative of perceptions. At Critchill School the CRB was established by centralizing all our school materials and funding by ourselves with the help of the Schools Curriculum Development Council and sympathetic publishers during the first two-and-a-half years. Secondly, how far can all the staff be involved in establishing the CRB? Nothing encourages ownership more than having a personal stake in the initiatives development.

— Siting is also important in the ownership debate. Our CRB is centrally positioned in the school building and as such acts as a hub or focus for our classroom activities. This siting also ensures that visiting professionals also visit the school as well as the CRB, an expedient to building understanding of *all* our work and thus mutual confidence.

— Mutual confidence is increased by the professional presentation of the Resource Bank, including:

— The quality and status of the coordinator (deputy head at Critchill School).
— A clear identity — The 'bank' has its own stationery and logo based on a modification of the school's.
— Welcoming appearance.
— Effective access and retrieval facilities.
— Sympathetic times of opening. Critchill 'Resource Bank' is open two nights per week until 6pm. This raises a management question: effective use of staff time especially in the context of 1265 hrs.

Adequate resourcing is important but much can be achieved with minimal resourcing. In my opinion the personal dimension of supporting the change is far more important. In a situation where a system is being changed to include the development of a SNSC the majority of resourcing should be used to support the system through the change. Therefore, resourcing for the CRB can be perceived as either direct or indirect. Some of the latter may initially surprise you but are easily understood.

DIRECT
— Books
— Materials
— Computer — hardware
                software
— Furniture etc.

INDIRECT
— Modification to building
— Adequate car parking
— Adequate communication
  — improved telephone system
  — data base links
— inter County 'Bank' links
— Adequate electrical sockets
— Increased need for redecoration
— Improved or modified cleaning and catering arrangements.

— A Curriculum Resource Bank should be for all children with special needs of any kind. A central bank of good general materials should be supplemented by smaller sections as appropriate.
— Experience has shown us that the work of a CRB takes integration past level one in the process of change as analyzed by Fullan (1982). The use of new materials often requires a change in approach but in addition it is an encouraging sight to observe a group of visiting teachers from a number of local schools in the CRB exchanging views and ideas. I am sure these are

carried back to many schools and put into practice. Therefore an experience which might be thought of as encouraging only the adoption of new materials may be encouraging a change in practice by the adoption of new approaches.

I do not believe that a SNSC would ever profess to attempt to change people's beliefs in educative practice. It can only provide a route to this desired goal through presentation of alternative materials and introduction of new approaches through inset activities. It is to these I now turn.

The school has developed during its evolution as SNSC machinery for the development of in-service training activities for the local educational community. Upon our initiative a group of local professionals have been selected to form a management team. Representation includes: A teacher from Critchill School who has responsibility for the professional development of school staff; an educational psychologist; a member of the special needs support team; and teachers who represent schools throughout the phases found in the Frome area.

Their purpose is to provide relevant inset opportunities in the Frome area, usually at the school. A small budget was negotiated and secured from the LEA in-service training budget. The programme usually takes the form of short (one-and-a-half hour) twilight sessions on at least four occasions each term. Recently, however, we have been approached more frequently by a number of agencies within the LEA to provide a venue for longer courses. This we have welcomed and readily accommodated.

It should be emphasized that the management committee go to some considerable lengths to ensure the programmes they offer are those required by local teachers. Regular surveys are undertaken and, equally importantly, the programmes are evaluated. This process has recently shown a need for a locally provided, externally evaluated course leading to an advanced qualification in professional studies. I believe that in rural communities, where travel to centres for training is so difficult, SNSC should provide local opportunities of this kind.

The role of an SNSC is dependent upon the special school involving itself with other schools and education services in the local community in general. We can clearly define a role for the SNSC within the context of LEA policy and the perceived and expressed needs of the local education community, but it is perhaps more difficult to define the role of an SNSC within the general local community. We are primarily an educational institution, but as those who have worked with children with special educational needs will realize, it is often difficult to distinguish an educational need from all the other needs that impinge upon a child's, or person's, life. Those professionals involved with children with special educational needs will be acquainted with a multi-disciplinary style of working where roles are not clearly defined. The key to our work then is need, meeting that need is a pooling of resources. The role of the SNSC and the issue of meeting the needs of the local community may be understood in terms of specific need identification, and the means to meet that need. Therefore the

SNSC work should address specific needs when they arise. It may be helpful to consider three ways in which Critchill School has been involved with the community.

For a number of years now we have provided a summer playscheme for children with special educational needs. The school has provided a venue and a member of staff. Financing has come jointly from the Health Authority and Social Services. The facility has, I believe, been useful to youngsters with special needs by organizing constructive use of their recreation time, and to the families of these children in providing constructive relief care knowing they are in a secure and caring environment. The provision of this sort of service is clearly specific to children with special needs. It should be anticipated that community use of the SNSC would normally benefit a similar clientele.

Recently the school helped facilitate the establishment of a parent support group. The need was identified by parents of the school and the initiative also supported by the local Social Services Department and the Frome Family Centre. The group is now successfully established, holding weekly meetings, inviting visiting speakers on relevant topics and organizing occasional social outings for the whole family. The school believed that the group should ultimately be as independents as children in the area with special needs attend institutions other than our own, and that the strength in the group would be the ability to act unilaterally. The school, of course, still remains supportive to the group and is prepared to continue in its role as facilitator. It is not necessary, therefore, for the SNSC to undertake every task, but when a need is identified the community should be mobilized to meet that need.

Needs are not always necessarily identified from within the community but also from ideas within the school, interpretation of policy or as examples from good practice. An example of this is our very recent thoughts on developing a section in the CRB that is specific to community needs. This might contain reading and reference materials that are useful to parents, relief carers and others with an interest in this area. Although the idea was created within the school we believe it should be a joint effort for at least two reasons:

— For this section to be as comprehensive as possible parents and other caring agencies should be consulted.
— The resources are more likely to be used if the community has had a hand in developing them. It is an ownership/publicity question.

Nor do we believe that this resource is best housed in our CRB. There may be many reasons why it might be better placed elsewhere in the town, or duplicated in a number of places. Therefore it can be observed that joint efforts by the SNRC may be preferable and more effective in meeting the special educational needs of children within the community.

I hope the three examples of a SNRC involvement in the community is useful in extending our philosophy in this field. They also conclude our journey. However, it will be understood that it is a journey that never reaches an end; SNSCs are a long-term development. What I have outlined is our current state of practice together with a few indications of the way forward. I anticipate that the next few years will be a time of development, if we are fortunate this may be followed by a period of consolidation. But, of one thing I am certain, we shall never be static.

I consider myself fortunate to work for a local authority that has a realistic attitude to the process of change that will encourage sound integrative practice. It has recognized the enormous implications and decided upon a steady course. I recognize the part my school has to play in this process; the extending role of a Special Needs Support Centre. At the beginning of our journey, I spoke of enjoying the venture. Perhaps enjoyment is too simplistic a term to describe a time of innovation. My school welcomes the challenge and looks with some enthusiasm at the exciting times that are with us, and before us. If I have enabled any of my readers to share in our enthusiasm then I consider our journey worthwhile; if I have been helpful in any small respect, I consider that a bonus.

My final comment is to emphasize what I consider to be the overriding message of this chapter. Good integrative practice is possible, but will necessitate a complex and possibly lengthy period of change. We must be realistic about what is possible. We must be resolved that integration is not a matter of pupils being educated in one institution or another. It has a wider philosophical base that has much to do with professional educators working together, developing the available provision and ensuring that individual needs are really met.

Chapter 13

Towards an Unified Approach in a Multi-Disciplinary Setting

Stan Forster

The following is an attempt to trace the development of a multi-disciplinary team within Crowthorn, a residential special school for children with learning, social and emotional problems. No child should be admitted to a residential school for purely classroom-based problems, therefore the education/treatment of our pupils should not, by implication, end when class is out. The potential of schools such as Crowthorn to meet the needs of very damaged children is tremendous in terms of two powerful resources, those of people and time. To be effective, however, these need to be managed efficiently. This management of those resources leads us to the notion of a 24-hour curriculum.

Within our setting we define the 24-hour curriculum as being a structured attempt to meet the individual and diverse needs of our pupils, using teams of teachers, residential social workers, field social workers, as well as consultants, ancillary workers and support staff. We aim to enable staff to organize their time and team approaches so that we do not over-structure groups of children. To achieve this, clearly stated and commonly held aims and objectives, methods of implementation and evaluation have to be adopted.

This chapter follows the adoption of an objectives-based curriculum model by the educational staff at Crowthorn and the subsequent adaptation of this approach by the residential social work team. The 24-hour curriculum does stretch beyond these two disciplines in the school but the emphasis here is deliberately on the training programme formulated to increase the professional input of an often undervalued group, the residential social worker, within special education.

Differing Professional Disciplines in Residential Schools

Although the concept of maximizing the resources, people and time is essentially simplistic, there are strong factors which make this a potentially difficult task in residential schools. Within most of these there are at least two professional teams of staff, teachers and residential social workers. Field social workers, psychologists, therapists, medical specialists, invariably add to what may become a complex multi-disciplinary team. All these have differing, often apparently opposing, philosophical standpoints and training backgrounds. This, notwithstanding variances of renumeration, hours worked and holiday entitlements, can make for a minefield of conflict.

The philosophical differences can perhaps be highlighted and confirmed in the extracts of evidence submitted by Department of Social Work at the University of Bristol to the House of Commons Select Committee on Children in Care, and referred to by Sonia Jackson in her book, *The Education of Children in Care*. This stated that to be in care was 'an educational hazard', and suggested 'that the root of the problem lies in the professional division between social work and teaching'. Social workers, it purported, did not give a very high priority to the fulfilment of educational potential when faced with seemingly endless problems of emotional disturbance caused through a child being abused or abandoned. Teachers also were not always sympathetic to, or aware of, background problems when faced with an overtly acting out pupil in a busy classroom.

My own experience of coming as a teacher into a social work orientated residential establishment some years ago, was that of almost being deskilled. The expectation was that I was first and foremost a member of the residential team, that being an educator was at least secondary. At the time I accepted the devaluation of my traditional function. I began to subscribe to the conventional wisdom that children who are emotionally disturbed should not, or could not, be saddled with the burden of academic learning. The whole emphasis of the work in which I was involved was the repairing of emotional damage before painful expectations, such as classroom attainments, were addressed. Until such time as this was achieved the educational curriculum and, by implication, the function of the teachers involved in the learning process was professionally irrelevant. The result of this was that there was generally a low expectation of the children's academic attainments and the law of self-fulfilling prophecy prevailed. It was also the case that the emotional damage that many had suffered was so great that we could never make up for, or repair, their hurt.

It was much later that as a headteacher of a special school in Coventry and faced with having to formulate written curriculum documents to be used with emotionally and behaviourally disordered adolescents, I discovered providing disturbed pupils with progressive academic success was a powerful therapeutic tool in its own right. The self-esteem that they gained through planned curricula achievement not only allowed potential to be achieved, examinations to be passed and jobs to be obtained, it also had transferable positive effects into the pupils' emotional and social development. Success did, in fact, breed success! Concentrating on things which could be improved, progress in learning, was also seen to be more positive than concentrating on things that we were unable to change, such as abandonment or abuse.

This experience of an over-dominant social work model is perhaps one extreme of the taking over of one profession by another within residential education. The opposite also prevails, for the hierarchy in many schools is frequently weighted towards teachers. The headteacher, deputy headteacher and senior teacher may provide the only nominated leader roles. Teachers working extraneous duties can account for a significant amount of the care time during evenings and weekends. Residential social workers may, as a result, have little or no status within the school. This I believe can present equally serious problems. It can, amongst other things:

1 provide over-emphasis on teacher-based activities so that children may never get away from the classroom ethos or expectation;
2 provide an unreal, institutional model where teacher and carer roles are blurred and atypical;
3 seriously limit the provision of good alternative parenting/home models within the school;
4 seriously limit the input, growth and development of what should be a significant professional body, residential social work, within a multi-disciplinary team because of teacher domination.

Where one philosophy or working practice dominates within a team, there is a wastage of both people and time. If either the teaching team or the social work team is undervalued and underused in an environment which offers such a powerful potential for change as a residential school, then that establishment is not either effective in its use of the time available, or efficient in its use of its human resources. Children with special needs have a right to the best possible academic education, as they have the right to the best possible care, substitute parenting, counselling and medical help. The potential of a total living situation provided by the residential schools, the range of professions and training of the staff allows them to deliver this from the basis of a multi-disciplinary team of equal professional status. From this basis we have endeavoured to develop the notion of our 24-hour curriculum model at Crowthorn School by:

1 Encouraging the development of each professional group in its own right, but within the bounds of a common working practice. This practice is, to quote our school prospectus, 'to provide individual programmes of positive intervention on both a long- and short-term basis. Differing expectations or inconsistent handling between them, school and local environment, can often compound the child's learning difficulties. At Crowthorn we use the resi-

dential experience to create a total learning situation. We endeavour to eliminate inconsistency by careful individual planning'.

2   Acknowledging the equal status of each professional group within the multi-disciplinary team.

The School

Crowthorn is a non-maintained special school and part of the National Children's Home (NCH) a national child care charity. It is situated on the edge of the West Pennine Moors, six miles distant from Blackburn, Bolton and Bury. It forms its own village community and presently caters for up to ninety-eight pupils, who live in one of ten separate residential units spread over a large campus. Crowthorn became a special school in 1952, having previously been a large children's home/orphanage. In recent years there has been a conscious policy to improve the quality of service offered by the school by gradually decreasing the number on roll from 120, whilst increasing both staff numbers and the amount and level of training. The provision of a quality service in all its work is a stated aim of the NCH. The present staffing levels in the school reflects this, there being fifteen teachers and six classroom assistants to support the academic department, and over fifty full-time residential social workers. The field social work team, made up of a family case worker/therapist, a play therapist and an after-care/support worker was appointed to the school some eighteen months ago.

On taking up the appointment of headteacher of the school some five years ago, I inherited a strong teacher-dominated establishment. Much good work was being achieved within the classrooms but there was little continuity of approach apparent, and curriculum documentation was sparse. The effects of the 1981 Education Act with regard to the type of referral being received by the school made it, I felt, essential that we formulated a definite, agreed and written policy regarding curriculum content and delivery. The diversions in range and need increasingly being manifest by our new intake made the provision of individual treatment programmes, based on a method which could quickly feed back its efficacy, an essential component of this. Most of our pupils had failed time after time, we therefore had to arrest this cycle. Instead we needed to provide something which better ensured success. The use of an objectives approach was therefore adopted by the teaching staff and work undertaken to write our curriculum documents in objectives terms. This had the direct and required result of shifting the teacher's emphasis from class needs to individual needs. The on-going recording and monitoring systems providing immediate feedback on whether or not these individual needs were being met. The move to an objectives approach was not, initially, universally popular amongst the teaching staff, because of its apparent behavioural standpoint. The types of teaching method employed to tackle priority areas highlighted by the use of a behavioural approach, however, were subsequently seen not to be necessarily behavioural in practice. The positive results achieved by the pupils then led to teaching staff acceptance.

A long tradition of good child care, gained through more than 100 years of practice within NCH, provided the legacy of a potentially good residential social work team at Crowthorn. There were similar examples of good, if often intuitive and un-coordinated treatment programmes evident in all thirteen living units then operating. There was great emphasis on the domestic aspect of their job, however, and this caused many to have a low expectation of what they could and should be aiming to achieve. Within their own conditions of service there were anomalies between the cover expected of resident, those who lived on-site, and non-resident staff. The working week for resident staff also often exceeded seventy hours. These clearly had to be, and were, tackled immediately and morale was raised considerably.

At this point also a change in job title from housemother/father to residential social worker was made. This we felt necessary to recognize the shift away from the introverted domestic role to that of a professional worker who would be active in the treatment and reintegration of pupils back into their own home base.

Towards a Unified System of Working

A pattern of twice yearly, formal reviews of each pupil's progress was introduced during my first year at Crowthorn. This was an attempt to set definite aims and objectives in each area of a child's development. With the classroom environment we were able to judge progress against our objectives-based curriculum documents and the individual's weekly, monitored records. Residential social work teams had begun to formulate written individual programmes in terms of handling or shaping behaviour, teaching social skills, encouraging and developing interpersonal relationships of the children in their care. They then had to justify and develop these both as written reports and verbally at the child's review. This expectation of planning, implementing and monitoring of their work, was then the same as that of the teaching staff. The profile of the residential social worker was then raised within the school and respect gradually earned from their teacher colleagues because they were now being seen to have a definite contribution to the total programme for an individual. The written require-ment of the review report and the verbal presentation in a multi-disciplinary meeting also provided a recognized platform for delivering this.

Residential staff greatly welcomed the opportunity to become a more obvious, recognized and important part of the treatment plans of the children in their care. Difficulties, however, became quickly apparent. These revolved around questions of where to start, what to do, and over the accurate monitoring of progress. It was necessary, therefore, to design an in-service training programme in order to tackle these. It seemed logical that the content of such a course should bring into line the philosophy, methodology and language of the residential and teaching staffs. The aim was that, initially at least, all the work done with the damaged children in our care should be based on the provision of success, a positive intervention approach. In order to standardize and make this compatible with the work already underway in the classroom, this needed to be based on observable objectives. I therefore undertook, in consultation with the authors and publishers, to rewrite the Coventry Education Committee SNAP Small Steps Programme, to be used as a training package with all members of the residential social work team.

A Way Forward

The introductory section of the completed rewritten course, renamed 'A Way Forward', states the purpose of the exercise, namely that

> this (course) has been compiled in order to aid the process of *positive, planned intervention* for teams of workers involved in helping and teaching clients (pupils) with special needs in the areas of social, emotional, physical and educational development. It can be used in any setting where staff are working in a cooperative way towards improving the level of functioning of the individuals in their care.
>
> The compilation of this course was felt necessary because of the increasing complexity of problems being presented by the clients referred to us through education and social services departments. Without a professional and structured approach to the often multiple handicaps suffered, and behaviour manifest, by those we endeavour to help, the sheer enormity of the task can easily overwhelm and strangle progress.
>
> 'A Way Forward' therefore adopts the *optimistic* assumption that all clients can make progress as long as we start from the individual's present and known level of functioning, i.e. we begin to work from the security of a base of known achievement. Once this level has been ascertained, and areas of concern isolated, then priorities about what we are able to work on next with a client are decided, and goals are set at such a *realistic* level as to ensure their *successful* completion.
>
> *Optimism, realism* and the provision of *success* are fundamental in the methodology of this approach but to ensure that these are transferred into a practical, working situation, there must be a high degree of commitment on behalf of the staff team towards good record keeping, consensus decision-making and regular evaluation. This is emphasized and built into the course.
>
> 'A Way Forward' uses a behavioural approach in order to isolate, quantify and rank the often complex, multiple problems manifest within

those with whom we are employed to help. The same approach is then used for us to state clearly and precisely what we are expecting to achieve after our planned treatment/education/intervention has taken place. The methods used in implementing such plans, however, can and should be wide ranging, reflecting the need of the client, the individual philosophical persuasion of the groups using them and/or the area in which change is being sought. Hence individual counselling, group work techniques, therapeutic approaches as well as behavioural modification techniques, have a place in the treatment decided. The main criteria applied to the method of remediation used to achieve a stated plan should be whether or not it works!

Course Content and Delivery

'A Way Forward' divided naturally into a five unit course and was delivered through five staff contact sessions led by myself and other senior members of the school residential social work staff. Full house staff teams attended each session together and there then followed a two or three week period where practical, on-the-job, tasks were undertaken by each team cooperatively. As well as introducing a standardized way of working and a common language throughout the school, the course was also able to provide training in good residential social work practice through the emphasis on the following themes:

1   the importance of staff teams using definite procedures in order to assess accurately what pupils can already do, and simultaneously underline the variety and diversity of need which they manifest.

The original 'A Way Forward' course had within it a very simple Basic Skills Checklist. One of the tasks set through the course was for the participants to write their own checklist to fit the requirements of the working situation at the school. Within Crowthorn the residential staff decided that this should be done across the disciplines so that one document covered the whole range of developmental areas. A working party of residential social workers, teachers and senior staff therefore cooperated to produce the comprehensive Crowthorn School Basic Skills Checklist, Social and Emotional Needs. This not only provides the backbone of the 'curriculum' worked to by the residential social workers, it can also be used by teachers in classroom situations in cooperative work with the RSWs. This Basic Skills Checklist (BSC) is completed on each pupil immediately prior to their initial review, some three months after admission to the school. This is undertaken by members of the residential team cooperatively. From the completed checklist, house staff teams are able to select *areas of priority* on which to base their Individual Treatment Programmes.

The Checklist covers five main areas: in the home, health and hygiene, moving into the community, ourselves and others, and communications, and is meant to provide the cornerstone of the RSWs work. It provides an initial recorded assessment of needs in full, informed judgments regarding Individual Treatment Programmes can be made, and progress monitored on a regular basis. The compilation of this by teachers and residential workers also served to provide a platform for further co-operative practice. It also gave the school staff ownership of the completed document.

2 the importance for staff teams to provide appropriate and precise programmes to meet needs.

As children with more and more complexity of problem were referred to us, it became increasingly more important to know where to start. Within the realities of a busy working day staff must make the most effective use of their time. It is not enough to suppose that each client's skill and knowledge is being developed by experiencing a therapeutic climate. There has to be a structure of working pattern which ensures that this is so, otherwise the unpredictability of the job can mean that crisis intervention is the norm, or that the more active and extrovert of the children in our care get an unfair share of the attention. The setting of priorities and precise programmes for each pupil by the whole residential team is the beginning of a more effective use of staff skills and time.

The more precise the programme set also, the more easy it is to judge and measure its efficacy. Because many of the pupils learn slowly, progress is often extremely difficult to estimate. This can lead to children becoming frustrated and disillusioned. Job satisfaction for staff may also be difficult to achieve within an apparently continually failing situation. By breaking tasks down into logical, progressive but obtainable steps, set at the level appropriate to the individual, success can be seen to be achieved by both pupils and staff members.

3 the advantages of involving pupils in the formulation of programmes to meet their needs.

Each of our residential social work staff have a responsibility to monitor the needs and progress of individual pupils living in their house group. The course allowed for this to be developed by providing the practical reason for staff and child to meet, discuss and agree on areas where work was to be undertaken. There is little point in beginning any programme if a child is unwilling, unsure or uncooperative. Once agreement is achieved, however, and mutual success experienced, the relationship and trust between the two can only be enhanced. We have found that this has been the case and as a result the level of work being attempted has shifted from initially practically based social skills programmes into the more complex areas of interpersonal relations. This has not only increased the team work aspect of the RSW, but also focused, practised and increased their individual counselling skills.

4   the importance of planning a programme in such a way as to ensure that both staff team and the pupil are clearly aware of what is expected of each of them in its implementation.

The team work aspect of the residential worker's role is perhaps its most powerful attribute. Where this is not utilized fully and varying standards of expectations of behaviour or performance are accepted from the child then it is also its weakest link. The vital importance of regular, weekly, staff meetings at which preparation of consensus agreed planned target objectives programmes were made was, therefore, seen as fundamental to 'A Way Forward'. Areas of priority highlighted through the use of the Basic Skills Checklist are translated into target objectives. The methods and approach in the achievement of these are agreed by all staff and recorded, as in the following examples from the course material.

WEEKLY TARGET OBJECTIVE SHEET   Week beginning 18.10.87

NAME: Fred. B.

OBJECTIVE	METHOD/APPROACH	PROGRESS
Prepared own breakfast each morning for 1 week without help	Call 15 mins. before others. Make sure coffee, bread and milk are available	Mon. Refused to get up when called. Tues. Completed. Wed. Milk late – had temper tantrum. Thurs. Completed. Fri. Jackie hid the bread. Sat. Sun.

WEEKLY TARGET OBJECTIVES SHEET   Week beginning 26.10.87

NAME: Ida Down

OBJECTIVE	METHOD/APPROACH	PROGRESS
Plays table tennis with up to 3 other girls whilst adults keep score for 10 mins.	Miss Nuff to organize table tennis game with Ida, Jacky, Freda & Jane immediately after tea each time she is on duty.	Mon. Wed. Thurs.
In a group of one adult and two other children is able to wait her turn in a discussion of planning a trip to town for up to 15 mins.	Use Friday just before bedtime to organize an outing for Sat. after-noon. Ida to be told before the meeting that she will only be included if she speaks in turn.	
Puts on coat without assistance when asked to do so on 5 separate occasions.	Always give the same instructions, 'Put on your coat'. Always use same coat.	

The advantages of doing this include:

(a) it states clearly what the programme sets out to achieve;

(b) programmes are planned away from the pressures of day-to-day client group interaction, in a regular weekly staff meeting. Problems such as the availability of a tennis ball, transport, or whether or not there are sufficient staffing levels for a programme to be implemented can be addressed;

(c) consistency and continuity of approach can be achieved;

(d) progress is recorded easily and regularly so that immediate, positive re-inforcement is possible. Failure, when it occurs, can be pinpointed accurately, allowing staff to make informed decisions on when and why failure occurred. With this information, teams can intervene quickly and reappraise their methods/approaches or levels of expectation. Continued or re-inforced failure should then be avoided;

5   the importance of regular staff monitoring, evaluation and recording of an individual's progress.

In the past those working with pupils with special needs have been somewhat self-effacing with regard to their role in assessment. They were often led to believe that it was not their responsibility, instead expecting that this should be undertaken by highly trained experts, psychologists, psychiatrists, psychotherapists and the like, who would take children out of their normal environment for short sessions in order to ascertain the source of difficulty.

It is now recognized that those working with special needs pupils have a fundamental role in assessment since:

(a) It is important to have a clear, longitudinal picture of a client's behavioural pattern undertaken in his everyday, familiar environment. *A systematic observation and recording* of this behaviour will thus provide the vital information in clearly defining each individual's special needs. It will indicate clearly what a person is *normally* capable of in the whole spectrum of his daily functioning. Long term observation will addition-ally clarify the levels of *frequency* and *intensity* of his abnormal, maladaptive or inappropriate behaviour and therefore put the importance of this into time-factor perspective. Such assessment can best be achieved by those who live and work intimately with the pupil.

(b) Specialist psychological or medical assessment may only be meaningful to those carrying out such assessments. They may also only tell us of things which the pupil cannot do. The teacher or social worker needs to know what the child can do in areas where change and improvement to the quality of life is possible. This is not to negate the use of specialist assessment but to recognize its limitations without the wealth and depth of information available through the professional organization of day-to-day recorded observations.

(c) Assessments should be regular and on-going ('A Way Forward' suggests that these should be carried out through daily recordings and weekly team meetings). Assessments will be based on the observed progress, or otherwise, of the client from where he started (from an area of known achievement) on his target objective. In this way:

(i) Both the workers and the pupil can see movement, however small, and thus gain both greater job satisfaction and increased self-esteem.

(ii) Regular appraisals of both team efficiency and effectiveness is possible.

(iii) Regular assessment of the efficacy of target objectives means that these will change and grow as appropriate to meet to current unique needs of the individual.

Staff Response to the Course

This was generally positive and enthusiastic because they were able to see that through it their professional practice, credibility and esteem within the school would increase. The language and techniques were strange at first but these were quickly mastered and this resulted in a more more confident residential staff group. They wanted to learn, to progress professionally, and this is a much easier base on which to enact change than one of opposition or complacency. The programmes that have been worked through have been varied. Objectives have been set to cover areas from putting on the coat, to independent travel programmes, through to gradually getting a coloured child to undress with others for swimming and athletics. Facing is a flow chart showing the different areas worked on by one residential staff team with a pupil, Philip, over a three year period. Although not couched in pure objectives terms it does give some idea of the range of work and the development of this in terms of the sophistication of programmes.

Staff Comments

The following are quotes from the individual appraisals undertaken after the first 'A Way Forward' course in 1986.

'He is really pleased with his efforts (at learning to clean his teeth). He knows we want him to succeed and for the time he has tried hard and had a good success rate.'

FLOW CHART
FOR OBJECTIVES OF 'A WAY FORWARD' PROGRAMME

Name: Philip

Date of Birth: October '72

Year June 86	June '86	Began July '86	September '86
Change To learn to fasten own school tie **1**	To learn how to make a hot drink **2**	To develop reading ability, in conjunction with school, through 'Paired Reading' **3**	To write a letter home with 1:1 help **4**

November '86	November '86	October '86	October '86
To open a Post Office Savings Account and save regular pocket money **8**	To identify coins 1p to £1 **7**	To prepare a simple well-balanced meal **6**	To make a public telephone call home **5**

December '86	December '86	January '87	February–March '87
To make journey by public transport to local village (one mile) **9**	To purchase one item from local village shop **10**	To be escorted by staff on public transport to home locality **11**	To increase awareness of the need of care of clothing i.e., washing, ironing **12**

September '87	April–September '87	March–April '87	March '87
To increase self confidence in water i.e., group swimming water play **16**	In conjunction with school, individual tuition was given in swimming **15**	Encourage regular hair washing and bathing **14**	To develop understanding of good personal appearance **13**

September '87	Sep–October '87	Oct–December '87	Dec –Jan '88
To learn rules of a simple board game (individual) **17**	To participate in the playing of a simple board game (Group) **18**	To develop learning of more complex board games (Group) **19**	To learn simple board games (individual) **20**

May–June '88	March–May '88	February '88	Jan '87–Feb '88
By use of Adventure Play Ground develop further cooperation **24**	To encourage communication on 1:1 basis in safe environment i.e., the swings **23**	To learn to share the use of swings (Group) **22**	To learn to 'wait your turn' in games (Group) **21**

June '88	July–September '88	Sept–Oct '88	October '88
To enhance confidence level whilst on Aerial Runway (Individual encouragement) **25**	To encourage imaginative play by using building bricks & lego 1:1 **26**	Further development of play through using model cars & figures **27**	To allow opportunity for drawing with staff 1:1 **28**

Nov–Dec '88	November '88	November '88	October '88
Through interest in music allocate breathing space/time for himself **32**	Direct towards involvement in peer group, youth activity off-site **31**	Pursue interest of 'weather symbols' through painting 1:1 **30**	By use of simple art materials, encourage self expression **29**

Dec '88	Dec–Jan '89	Jan–Feb '89	February '89
To develop recognition of varying styles of music **33**	To improve understanding of one's own sexuality 1:1 discussion **34**	To develop understanding of personal circumstances home & school **35**	To begin joint weekly counselling sessions philip, RSW, field worker **36**

'The course has enabled me to understand just how simple objectives must be, even then they must often be broken down more'.

'What I initially saw as large was small'.

'He was motivated by being involved in a discussion about the aims of his programme with the housestaff. We do not see him sulking as much as before or saying he can't do it'.

'The programme has helped to determine areas of need and individual difficulties. Also, functions have been coordinated into a concise, easily read and understood form which can be operated by a team instead of being fragmented and spasmodic. In essence each child will have a programme of uniform nature'.

'The Grandparents have become involved in the programmes and seen progression. This has helped both with their relationships with the school and their relationship with Charlie'.

The same process also served to underline long-term deficiencies in our work. The quote 'Because of his vulnerability outside Crowthorn and the security of his own home it was thought that to do any work in independence might be taking too much risk', highlights this. Written about a twelve-and-a-half year old who had been a pupil at Crowthorn for five years it raised the question of when we began to take planned and calculated risks. It is often easy for the residential school to avoid real issues of preparing pupils for the reality of the world outside. Through staff group discussions/staff meetings and formal reviews the whole question of preparation for a return to a normal home from this less institutional base is undertaken.

Conclusions

The development of our 24-hour curriculum has been greatly enhanced by the standardization of practice across the various disciplines in the school. An objectives approach and the initial development of curricula documents by the teaching staff focused our work more clearly and precisely onto the needs of the individual. The aim of pitching academic work at a level that would provide pupils with progressive success raised the esteem of pupils and increased the job satisfaction of the class teacher. This same philosophy was then, through 'A Way Forward', translated into the working patterns of the residential staff with the following benefits.

1   It brought the status of the residential social worker equal to that of the teacher in Crowthorn School. The residential social workers have, through it, been given their own definite role within the Individual Treatment Programmes of our pupils. The Basic Skills Checklist has provided them the basis of a curriculum on which to work.

2 It has provided a common professional language between teachers and residential social workers.

3 The professional use of group meetings, assessment and recording skills, fundamentals of good social work skills, have been greatly increased. The confidence that using this system has given through the provision of success has also allowed the staff teams to seek out new techniques of intervention. This has underlined the need for the school as a whole to run staff in-service training programmes to teach and develop these. Such courses have been provided and will now be increased for all staff through the new appointment of a School Training Coordinator.

4 Increased skills developed by the residential social workers have resulted in them uncovering a greater complexity of problems within some of our pupils, particularly the discovery of abuse. Greater family involvement also brought to our attention the need for the vast amounts of planned intervention there also if successful reintegration of pupils to their home is to take place. This led us to identify where increased expertise and resources were necessary. NCH, our parent body, responded to this by providing enhanced staffing, encouraging the development of an off-site 52-week care provision, increasing specialist consultancy time and establishing the specialist field social work team referred to at the beginning of this chapter. Successful working practice then does sometimes mean that more, rather than less, work results, and more time and resources required as a consequence. It does, however, also mean that the cause as well as the effect is being addressed and that more satisfactory long-term conclusions are being reached through the increasingly sophisticated treatment plans offered.

5 The development of the model of each discipline, teaching, residential social work and lately field social work concentrating on their own area of expertise we feel is right. There is little confusion amongst the individual prefessionals as to what their job entails. Teachers teach and provide the highest possible quality educational service to our pupils. Social workers deal with the problems of social integration and reintegration. The children we serve are also much less confused by having a school apparently separate from where they live, very much like it would be in a normal home. From this less institutional base, with efficient channels of communication, careful planning, regular monitoring and mutual professional regard we can begin to deliver our 24-hour curriculum package.

Chapter 14

From Special Needs to Special Teaching:
A New Direction in Classroom Support

Andy Redpath and Brian Steedman

This chapter describes the work of a primary support service established by a senior member of staff from a local special school (1987–8). During its initial year of operation it was evaluated by the co-author, whilst on secondment at the Cambridge Institute of Education.

In his poem *On Ice*, Erich Fried describes a boy arriving late for school. When asked by his teacher for an explanation, he complains that the ice was so slippery that for every step he took forward, he slipped back two. 'In that case', asks the teacher, 'how did you get here at all?', 'I gave up and tried to go back home,' the boy replies. In certain respects, this story illustrates two themes of this chapter. Firstly, mainstream schools need to foster flexible and positive teaching styles amongst their own staff, instead of looking to special schools as a first option for release from difficulties posed by some children.

Secondly, special schools need to assist in the process, rather than use their energies exclusively to sustain a separate educational setting for a minority of children. By turning our attention away from the goal of special educational needs, towards the individual needs of all children, like Fried's schoolboy, we may similarly discover that we have arrived at a more appropriate destination.

This may seem a strange message from two teachers who for most of their careers have worked in special schools. However, after spending some years acquiring the necessary skills for teaching children experiencing learning and behavioural difficulties, the authors are convinced that some of these methods can be successfully employed by mainstream colleagues. Similarly, in the process, special schools have much to learn from the mainstream. Learning new skills may seem a daunting task for teachers, particularly at a time when there are so many other changes happening in education which make demands on staff time. This chapter is an example of how the work of one particular support service, operating in an urban borough, used special school expertise to help primary teachers develop their skills, thereby enhancing the performance of all children in the classroom.

Woodvale is widely regarded as a successful special school, providing an extensive range of part-time and full-time provision for children with emotional and behavioural difficulties between the ages of three and sixteen. Involvement in mainstream primary schools dates back to the early 1970s, when the concept of part-time provision was pioneered. Under this system, children normally attend Woodvale for five morning sessions, returning to their mainstream school for the afternoon. Teachers from Woodvale liaise with the mainstream school, monitoring progress, offering advice, and arranging a system of rewards which can be provided by Woodvale for achieving agreed behaviour targets. Whilst recognizing that this arrangement helped many children 'keep one foot in the door' of mainstream school, and produced individual cases of successful reintegration, this method of working concentrates on the child as the prime focus of concern. Pressure for a new form of primary support came from two directions.

Certain primary school headteachers recorded their interest in cooperating in some form of mainstream school support emanating from Woodvale. They were alert to the value of assistance that could improve the professional skills of their own staff in teaching children experiencing behavioural difficulties. Suggestions for discussion included working alongside classroom teachers, organizing an exchange to enable the mainstream teacher to work at Woodvale and the sharing of professional expertise to help maintain pupils in mainstream schools. One headteacher stated an interest in drawing up a school policy for rules, sanctions and rewards for children with the involvement of the educational psychologist and teaching staff. There is no mention of withdrawing children, instead the focus is upon adapting school policy and expertise to help meet the needs of the child in the ordinary school setting.

Another impetus for extending Woodvale involvement in mainstream schools came from the Urban Borough working party set up to consider provision for pupils with emotional and behavioural difficulties. The working party expressed support for the Warnock Report's notion of a continuum of provision. It was agreed to set up a pilot primary support service based at Woodvale. This would involve a teacher from Woodvale working in close partnership with educational psychologists and initially serving two schools. Thus the pilot primary support service was set up under circumstances favourable for its success.

At this point it is worth asking, what were the skills acquired over the years at Woodvale, and how could this special school expertise be harnessed for the benefit of mainstream colleagues? It is not only the pupils who can become cocooned in the safe haven of a segregated, special education. Staff also can become isolated from, and out of touch with, the demands of ordinary schools. They have little knowledge of organizing a large class, or expertise in delivering a broad curriculum.

Despite this isolation, however, there are many positive features of special schools which can offer mainstream colleagues fresh perspectives on teaching style. As a place of last refuge, rarely are 'problem' pupils ever excluded or referred on to other institutions. Teachers have to accept pupils as they come. Confrontational and critical approaches cannot be used as a response to pupil failure. Teachers become resourceful in seeking out and emphasizing positive qualities in children and building upon them. Praise and encouragement are salient features of the pupil teacher relationship, which can have a marked success in improving a child's self-esteem. At Woodvale, where behaviour modification programmes are used, pupil effort and achievement is often recognized by giving the child small rewards, this can range from sweets to spending time on enjoyable activities.

Also, special school teachers do not work alone, but necessarily become adept at sharing classrooms with other teachers and welfare assistants. They develop skills in assigning roles within the class, and deliberating about their own practice with others. Consequently, as a result of pooling ideas, there is often a lowering of the stress that isolation brings. Teachers develop a language appropriate for communicating this exchange, stressing positive, problem-solving approaches, which avoid attributing blame. Failures occur, but lead on to redefinition of problems and fresh attempts at success. In this way, teachers come to view themselves as change agents in the child's educational development. Seemingly intractable problems can become manageable when shared with fellow members of staff in this way.

Children who display emotional and behavioural difficulties have often experienced unreasonable and capricious demands in their dealings with adults. A consistent approach by all staff is an essential ingredient in effecting any change in a pupil's behaviour. This develops routinely at Woodavle through observation of colleagues' methods, collectively drawing up individual development plans for children, and working cooperatively with other staff. The formal programme of training received by all new staff is reinforced by informal advice and support from colleagues and contributes towards establishing a shared school ethos.

It must be emphasized that these skills represent no easy solution. In fact an abiding memory one of the authors has, is of the message he would have liked to have sent back from Woodvale to his former colleagues in a comprehensive: 'if only you knew!': if they only knew that recommending pupils for a special school education resulted in no magic cure. Quite the reverse, it was the beginning of a hard slog!

The Woodvale ethos pervades the aims of its primary support service whilst reflecting current thinking on pupil disaffection. This regards pupil performance as more likely to be influenced by such factors as teacher expectations, curriculum design, and school organization, rather than by some inherent child weakness or 'deficit' (Galloway, 1985; Dessent, 1987). Consequently, it is argued that teachers should be in the business of encouraging all children to succeed, rather than focusing on the special needs of a few (Ainscow and Tweddle, 1988). An important aim of the service is to reduce the need for withdrawal of students from mainstream classes and schools. This will be facilitated by offering techniques in classroom management to the teacher, and thereby increasing his or her confidence in their ability to handle disruptive behaviour in a positive and flexible way. At the wider school level the support service envisages being involved in an examination of the curriculum, setting up school-based in-service training, and the development of school policies on behaviour management.

Traditionally teachers are used to coping with problems on their own. The classroom is often regarded as a private domain where individual resourcefulness determines whether the initiate either sinks or swims! In supportive schools the constructive help of colleagues is at hand, but even here, including outsiders in this sharing process can provoke anxiety. Not least for the support teacher! Coulby (1986) has emphasized how teachers are often resentful of 'experts' who offer 'self evident or impractical help', and stresses the need for those involved in support work to develop 'collaborative contact' with classroom teachers.

After spending many years working in the safe haven of a special school, venturing into a local primary school to offer support, one is immediately struck by the hustle and bustle which accompanies large numbers of children actively engaged in the business of learning. There is little wonder that children who have received a prolonged special education, often find it very difficult to leave their protected environment and re-integrate into ordinary school. Also, given the volume of children experiencing problems in urban schools, it is apparent that the most needy child is not always the one selected for special school attendance — the continuum of provision does not always run smoothly!

Given current procedures, support in schools will inevitably start with the referral of individual children experiencing learning/behavioural difficulties. A constructive problem-solving method is employed, based upon the model of Coulby and Harper (1981), and Lane (1986). The first step is to establish the nature of the problem and agree its definition with the class teacher. Observation of the class follows, and perhaps redefinition. During this stage it is important to be alive to a repertoire of teaching styles and sensitive to the nuances of the interaction process. Support needs to build on the teacher's existing strengths, rather than transplant alien 'solutions' which may be inappropriate to the given setting. At this point it is also valuable to talk to the child, communicate the teacher's concerns and ascertain his or her perceptions of the situation.

Subsequently progress will be discussed with the class teacher regularly and routinely. An integral feature of this process is the notion of experimentation. Initiatives are seen as collaborative attempts at improvement, which are expected to be re-appraised and modified as developments require.

Support teachers can involve themselves in the class by working with groups of children, not necessarily restricting their attentions to the referred child. This has the advantage of not drawing attention to them and reducing the possibility of comment from peers. Modification of the pupils' learning materials may occur, enabling them to complete the tasks set and make a contribution to the lesson. Teachers can become exasperated with the lack of performance and move too quickly to punishment. The main concern is with providing access rather than setting up separate learning programmes.

This approach can be illustrated by reference to work with a second year junior class at one of the schools served by the support teacher. Children discussed a topic in groups, wrote down ideas, and then presented their views to the rest of the class. The support teacher moved freely between the groups, enabling children experiencing problems to participate. As well as providing help with written work and spelling, he encouraged the involvement of children at all levels of classroom activity. On one occasion, a boy who was reluctant to present his work, was jovially marched out to the front of the class. The pupil succeeded and was clearly pleased at having done so. The support teacher often sat near pupils who were having difficulty with concentration, jollying them along and maintaining their interest. In discussing methods of team teaching Thomas (1986) has described how it is beneficial for one teacher to maintain the flow of the lesson, while the second adult gives individual help to children experiencing difficulty. The support teacher performed the latter role, being alert to the aims of the class teacher, and reinforcing or explaining them to groups of children. Teachers who worked closely with the support teacher stressed that an important feature of the way he worked was that he did not take over the class but tuned into what they were doing and enhanced the process.

This work began to build relationships within classes which were of benefit to mainstream teachers. The support teacher demonstrated positive responses to pupil behaviour. When calm needed to be gained before an activity began, he would show approval of children who were behaving well. It was surprising how quickly the rest of the class responded, thus minimizing the need for teacher criticism of undesirable behaviour. Also, changes in classroom organization were suggested. In some cases, new classroom layouts were discussed in order to maximize teacher vision and reduce crowding. More effectively stored equipment, giving children greater responsibility, reduced confusion in class and increased the teacher's time for active work.

It cannot be overemphasized the extent to which this learning process was one of exchange which was enjoyable to both parties. The support teacher often felt he lacked practical expertise in curriculum development, but he could pose useful questions which led on to joint solutions. In most cases the major role in this kind of problem solving would be adopted by the class teacher. In one instance, the support teacher suggested that a more differentiated mathematics curriculum was needed in order to take account of individual performance. His own experience, however, was limited to small group work, and he felt he had little to offer. In the event, the class teacher was quick to develop this insight, and rapidly reorganized her classroom arrangements. As a consequence more effective learning began to take place, especially for children presently failing and beginning to get 'sucked in' to other, less desirable pastimes.

It was the support teacher's view that many of his own ideas needed to be modified in the light of mainstrean classroom experience. Behavioural objectives approaches were often too time consuming to be applied strictly, and there was a threshold beyond which most classroom teachers could not go with complicated responses to individual pupil difficulty. Recording had to be organized with this in mind, therefore, as did the use of material rewards for acceptable behaviour. It is also important to mention that much special school 'academic' work is narrow, overtly concerned with basic skills, of low status in student eyes and seen as boring and repetitive (c.f. Tomlinson, 1982). Since this was where the support teacher's recent experience had been, rapid adjustments had to be made in order to have a positive effect on mainstream classroom practice. Our view is that, without adequate preparation, this will be a recurring problem for a special school staff seeking to have an impact in ordinary schools. We are, however, encouraged by recent experience of the work of Johnson and Johnson (1986), in the area of cooperative groupwork. This promotes a constructive awareness based curriculum, which can be offered to children with widely varying attainment levels found in both special and mainstream sectors alike.

The extent to which many classroom problems began to be seen as extending beyond the individual child, emerged quite markedly from the pilot ptoject. Class teachers acknowledged with admirable candour areas of difficulty, and frequently pointed to lack of adequate training as students, especially in the area of classroom organization and management. Significantly, many problems extended beyond the individual classroom and required a whole school solution. What was required was the mobilization of the school's resources to more appropriately meet their own needs. It was important for the support service to be actively engaged in this process. Consequently the support teacher was soon participating in what became known as 'projects'.

Most commonly, projects began with concern about playground behaviour. Both pilot schools evolved guidelines on playground behaviour, which outlined acceptable conduct, and defined rewards and sanctions. Children, staff and parents were familiarized with the guidelines, which demonstrated how the consistent teamwork evident at Woodvale could flourish in the mainstream. The result was to give children clear messages about adult expectations, and remove from staff the stressful need to desperately devise responses to unpleasant incidents 'in the heat of battle'!

Subsequently other pressures evolved, ranging from guidelines for infant children to preparing juniors for secondary transfer. Hearteningly, many initiatives were instigated without necessarily involving the support teacher, clearly indicating that the pooling of ideas had become established practice. Hopefully, as the support service grows in experience, there will be opportunities to generalize successes to other schools; thereby minimizing the likelihood of individual establishments toiling in isolation to 'reinvent the wheel'. One of the support teacher's greatest feelings of achievement comes from listening to the change in tone of staffroom conversations, where frustration and anger have given way to calm deliberation. When schools begin to take responsibility for their own problem solving, they tend to do so with a great sense of exhilaration, a commodity understandably in short supply in many urban schools.

It remains to be said in this brief synopsis of the support service's pilot run, that enlightened school management played a vital role in any change. Where there is effective communication, where decisions once taken are carried through quickly, and where cooperative and generous relations between staff are perpetually liable to break out, there is a realistic prospect of success. That the support service was accomplishing many of its objectives was borne out by plans to extend it throughout the borough.

It must be emphasized that these conclusions are based upon one example of support work. We stress the importance of support teachers possessing the necessary skills and experience to be effective. Equally, staff going into schools must be flexible enough to adapt their special school experience to a new setting, and readily drop those practices which are inappropriate. Moves which turn away from categorizing children, and instead seek to extend the range of teaching skills and the quality of the learning environment, can benefit teachers in both special and mainstream schools. A corollary of this must be that as teachers and schools realize their own potential, the support teacher will ultimately withdraw.

Whilst holding to the conviction that many children need not arrive in special schools if they are effectively supported in the mainstream, it is not suggested that this is inevitably the case for all children. Where placement in special schools is necessary, by establishing close links with their mainstream colleagues, staff in special schools can enhance their own curriculum and teaching skills, hence making the special school more ordinary. Support teachers reaching out from special schools are in a unique position to effect this two way process of exchange. Through sharing ideas, we may turn away from concern with special needs, and instead concentrate on becoming special teachers. Steps taken to improve teaching must ultimately benefit all children, including those deemed to have special educational needs.

Chapter 15

The Sedgemoor Centre:
Striving to Be Special

John V. d'Abbro

The Sedgemoor Centre is the only day educational provision funded by Somerset Education Authority for youngsters deemed to have Emotional and Behavioural Difficulties (EBD). Typically students referred to the Centre whilst having rejected the mainstream experience and having failed in it, overwhelmingly have greatest difficulties not with academic attainment but rather with social and personal adjustment and inter-personal relationships.

The Centre opened in Spetember 1982 in response to the needs of four local comprehensive schools with the remit of working with twelve secondary age pupils and ultimately reintegrating them back into their mainstream feeder schools. In September 1984 due to the changing nature of referrals and the failure of this reinte-gration policy the criteria of admission was targeted specifically at twenty fourth and fifth year youngsters, but now with a non-integration policy. With this new brief the staff instigated an intense period of curriculum development in which the Centre's stated aims and objectives have been deliberated upon, specified and ultimately developed into a strident curriculum. The major thrust of which is to offer an alterna-tive and in some ways compensatory educational programme. There are two main themes within this paper. The first concerns issues surrounding the ideology behind the design of the Centre's curriculum. The second is an in-depth explanation of the means through which it is delivered.

Some writers still believe that maladjustment and disruption are one and the same phenomenon, with analysis falling along one continuum, which embraces a concept of excesses and deficiences. However within the Centre's curriculum is an acceptance that this is not the case. An interactionist perspective is taken which highlights a model in which many different causative agents are applicable. One of which is the school based aetiology which criticizes school systems be they pastoral, curricula, management, and highlights how such systems in themselves can become catalysts for deviant behaviour.

This perspective also demonstrates how descriptions of disruptive behaviour can be context bound and is diametrically opposed to the medical model with its insistence upon degrees of deviant behaviour which are owed as part of an individual pathology. Whilst it is beyond the scope of this article to analyze the differences between maladjustment and disruptive behaviour, in practice many of the strategies outlined will be more readily applicable in work with disruptive students in the mainstream setting as distinct to disturbed youngsters who in many cases will need to be educated outside of the mainstream provision.

Set against the well documented criticism of special schools curriculum (Booth, 1983; Tomlinson, 1982) and the students failure in mainstream schools, it should be apparent that any curricula designed to meet the needs of the Centre's students would need to be different from that experienced in their previous schools. In attempting to meet these needs of the students, a genuine commitment to curriculum innovation focused on two facets of design:- (1) The extent to which the curriculum is open to critical scrutiny to those other than the designers, and (2) who would be the designers. Whilst not losing sight of the fact that any school which makes attendance compulsory (such as the Centre) cannot be seen as democratic, we should not lose sight of the fact that the curriculum can be negotiated even if it is not negotiable. Within this statement is the implication that the teacher, whilst part of the learning process, is not the embodiment of all knowledge. The teacher needs to be a facilitator, a counsellor and a listener as opposed to a deliverer of packaged knowledge and ideas. In designing the curriculum, therefore, the staff had to be involved in a progressive shift away from teachers as authority towards teachers as co-partners in the enterprise of learning, from students being teacher dependent to being teacher independent. Gammage's (1982) social psychological perspective would appear to be the most closely allied in terms of policy action to that within the Centre. He suggests that:

> The curriculum as a whole is best perceived an an educationalist's blueprint for human development. This blueprint is not only bound up with questions of socializtion and a validity of certain sorts of knowledge, it is more directly interpreted by someone other than the designer. Furthermore, in passing it on, the transaction itself frequently overrides the content (p. 158).

The growth of special education over the last century is now well documented. Writers such as Tomlinson and Barton (1984), and Ford, *et al.* (1982) have highlighted the politics of special education and the powers of vested interests, and whether one views analyses such as these from a macro- or micro-sociological perspective one cannot ignore the effects of the hidden curriculum. An easily identifiable example of the effect of this unplanned learning is readily apparent in the way many of the students who are referred for interview present a very poor self-image. Many have suffered what Hargreaves calls the destruction of dignity (1982, p. 17). Within the planning of any curriculum attention to these effects needs to be catered for. Indeed Brennan (1985, p. 60) believes that some of these influences are so strong that strategies to combat their effect should be planned for. Within the Centre's curriculum various strategies have been designed to ameliorate some of these negative by-products of curriculum design. This introduction to some of the issues surrounding the design of the Centre's curriculum is offered in order that the reader may more readily understand the context in which the following objectives of the Centre are delivered.

1 A Counselling Approach to Education
2 An Appropriate Curriculum
3 The Orchestration of Success
4 The Introduction of Phased Privilege Systems
5 Systematic Discipline
6 Organizational Quality
7 Residential Experience
8 Home School Liaison
9 Quality of Staffing
10 The Use of Outside Agencies.

These objectives have been laid out in random order for whilst in practice they are all in operation within the milieu of the Centre different ones will act as 'prime movers' for different youngsters. Many are also interrelated and where appropriate will be illustrated as such.

The phrase 'A Counselling Approach to Education' hopefully conjures up notions of quality of interactions. Having carefully and appropriately planned work (Organizational Quality) its delivery will be of little value if the quality of relationships between students and teacher are not of a genuinely positive nature. I do not wish to imply that it is easy to work with EBD people and at times it is hard to separate the behaviour exhibited from the person underneath, but a degree of 'unconditional positive regard' is essential if the phrase is to be more than another rhetorical term. It may also be one of the hardest for mainstream schools to emulate. At the Centre the term implies high levels of student involvement in its day-to-day running. It says to them that they are accepted for what they are. To arrive at a position in which high levels of trust, sharing and honesty prevail, commitment from staff and students must be present. Illustrating this point Raffe (1986) has shown that young peoples' decisions are less influenced by the content of educational provision provided than by the context in which it takes place.

The commitment to this approach starts at interview, for when youngsters arrive they are told that they have been referred rather than sent. Whilst it may appear that the Centre is the last option open to some families, this is legally not the case. One of the hallmarks of the Centre's success is that it is not obliged to take youngsters which it considers inappropriate referrals and demonstrates the LEAs commitment to the Centre by refusing to allow it to become a dumping ground for problem pupils, as is the case in many other similar establishments as illustrated by HMI (1978), Lloyd-Smith (1984).

The interview process currently in use at the Centre is designed to give prospective entrants a balanced view of the Centre, its environment and facilities with youngsters being shown around initially by a student before a more formal interview with the whole family, etc. It is a policy that only the headteacher will read referral papers prior to interview in order to cut down what may become 'contaminated space' around an individual. If a youngster is accepted in time all staff will read background and case notes. Youngsters are told at interview that coming to the Centre will be a fresh start. This policy helps to ensure that this is the case. The emphasis behind this ideology is best summed up by the following quote:

> We have in store for you no 'easy steps to mastery', no moral uplift programme, no guaranteed rules for breaking bad habits which you are actually determined to keep. We undertake to do nothing to you. Instead we state some instructions by means of which, if you so desire, you may launch yourself on a progressive personal adventure wherein, by your own efforts, you may do something for yourself — namely discover it, organize it and put it to constructive use in the living of your life (Perls *et al.*, 1951, p. 4).

The pastoral system in operation facilitates youngsters receiving conselling support both on an individual and group basis. As part of the Centre's moral education programme students are counselled in a group basis. In these sessions encounter group and consensus morality rule the day, even though this approach is not without some controversy — Wilson (1967), McPhail (1978 and 1982). In practice many of the youngsters 'get it wrong' when it comes to awareness of what is normal practice. Individually youngsters are supported by their keyworkers on a daily/weekly basis in what is seen as counselling support and not just discussion, even though at times this dicotomy causes more problems than it solves. However, as a planned strategy counselling support must stand up on its own merits and not just become passive collusion. On birthdays and Christmas students receive presents from the staff. This is done to engender a more family like atmosphere within the Centre, as illustrated two years ago when one of the students became pregnant and later returned to continue her studies with her new baby. In time it is hoped that the effects of a counselling approach will enable mutually respectful and emphatic relationships to develop. It also shows a more human side to the job. This is indeed 'risky' but it is another example of how staff are prepared to desert from the traditional safeness of being a person in authority over young people. This is an alternative pedagogy, which on the one hand demands a high expectation of behaviour and effort, but on the other achieves it through cooperation and consensus rather than coertion. I believe it is important for all students, but especially those with emotional and behavioural difficulties, that high expectations of their performance is expected in order to maintain their self-esteem and to offer goals and challenges which stretch but not overwhelm.

The curriculum at the Centre offers youngsters a real alternative to that which is on offer in most mainstream schools. It is not exam driven and subject-based and, as mentioned earlier, not designed solely by the teachers. Both traditional and innovative elements are to be found within its makeup and delivery, and at all times is appropriate and relevant to the needs of the students.

Figure 1 shows examples of the current timetable on offer at the Sedgemoor Centre. The first innovative feature of the curriculum has been in the adoption of working a four term year. It is beyond the scope of this article to give an in-depth analysis of the four term year and how it works out in practice, but shorter and more regular terms have resulted in less student absenteeism (the Centre boasts a 94 per cent attendance rate at present), less stress on staff, a drop in crime-related activities during the summer holiday, greater harmony between parents and their children during the vacation time. Another feature of the four term year is that it has enabled the courses offered at the Centre to be dovetailed neatly into a 'spiralling curriculum', which has certain in-built features. An example of which is the increased amount of work experience that a student does as he or she is preparing to leave school. The day is split into two parts with the morning sessions consisting of all the core courses studies (see Figure 2). Attendance at these sessions is compulsory and the expectation of both staff and students is that this is very much 'heads down' time. Many youngsters on arrival at the centre have, through their disrupted schooling careers, learnt the habit of working below their potential. Many need to learn or relearn how to learn and overcome deeply ingrained behaviour which impedes learning. I believe the structure of the morning sessions affords this with emphasis placed on individual programmes for basic subjects (English and maths) augmented by various courses of life and social skills. Much of the design of these courses has been influenced by the AEB basic tests and many youngsters go on to take these exams in the Christmas prior to them leaving. There are slots within the timetable for students to carry on exams started at their previous schools or to pursue exams which they become interested in during supported self study sessions. Whilst the term may be relatively new (Waterhouse, 1983) the philosophies of the approach can be readily found in resource-based learning, open learning and distance learning, and whilst this approach fits neatly into the overall curriculum thrust of the Centre, there is, I believe, additional currency in adopting this way of working with EDB students, in that it implies that students are 100 per cent responsible for their behaviour and learning during this time. For some students this is by no means easy but it does help to develop an understanding of their locus of responsibility (Charlton, 1985). For in this type of learning both the affective and cognitive domains flow together. While thinking the learner is also feeling and vice versa. I believe this confluence encourages students to understand and be able to deal with their own and other

Terms 1 and 4	9.15–9.30	9.30–10.15	10.20–11.00	11.15–12.15	1.00–2.15	2.30–3.30
MONDAY	PREFECT TUTOR GROUP	5th Year: MATHS	ENGLISH	SOCIAL SKILLS	WOODWORK	SNOOKER
	JOINT TUTOR GROUP	4th Year: MATHS	ENGLISH	HOME MANAGEMENT	MOTORBIKES	
				SEDGEMOOR CENTRE LTD		
TUESDAY	TUTOR GROUP	5th Year: MATHS	HUMANITIES	LEAVERS PROGRAMME	DUKE OF EDINBURGH AWARDS	
		4th Year: CURRENT AFFAIRS	SUPPORTED SELF STUDY	SCIENCE PROJECTS	POP VIDEOS	
WEDNESDAY	TUTOR GROUP	5th Year: MATHS	PREPARATION FOR PARENTHOOD	HOME MANAGEMENT	SWIMMING	a) Weight Training b) Badminton c) Squash
		4th Year: ENGLISH	SUPPORTED SELF STUDY	MONEY MANAGEMT. AND INTRODUCTION TO WORK	ART / ENGINEERING	ROUND ROBIN / ENGINEERING
THURSDAY	TUTOR GROUP	4th Year: MATHS	INTEGRATED STUDIES	SOCIAL SKILLS	SKITTLES + UNIHOC ROUND ROBIN / DRUM WORKSHOP	COOKING
		5th Year: WORK EXPERIENCE PRACTICAL, WORK EXPERIENCE COURSEWORK, WORK EXPERIENCE CANVASSING		WORK EXPERIENCE	WORK EXPERIENCE CANVASSING	WORK EXPERIENCE CANVASSING
FRIDAY	JOINT TUTOR GROUP	5th Year: CURRENT AFFAIRS	SUPPORTED SELF STUDY	JOB PREPARATION	TUTOR GROUP	TUTOR GROUP
		4th Year:	PREPARATION FOR LIFESKILLS			

Terms 2 and 3		9.15–9.30	9.30–10.15	10.20–11.00	11.15–12.15	1.00–2.15	2.30–3.30
MONDAY	5th Year	PREFECT TUTOR GROUP	MATHS	ENGLISH	SOCIAL SKILLS	ENGINEERING	ENGINEERING
	4th Year	JOINT TUTOR GROUP	MATHS	ENGLISH	HOME MANAGEMENT	FOOTBALL	FOOTBALL
TUESDAY		TUTOR GROUP	4th Year: PREPARATION FOR PARENTHOOD	SUPPORTED SELF STUDY	SCIENCE PROJECTS	CANDID CAMERA / SWIMMING	CANDID CAMERA / SNOOKER
			5th Year: WORK EXPERIENCE PRACTICAL, WORK EXPERIENCE CANVASSING, JOB CANVASSING		WORK EXPERIENCE COURSEWORK, WORK		
WEDNESDAY		TUTOR GROUP	4th Year: HUMANITIES	ENGLISH	LIFE SKILLS	MOTORBIKES	
			5th Year: PREPARATION FOR PARENTHOOD	PROJECTS	JOB PREPARATION	ART/POTTERY / DRAMA	
THURSDAY		TUTOR GROUP	4th Year: MATHS	CURRENT AFFAIRS	SOCIAL SKILLS	WOODWORK / ORIENTEERING	SKITTLES
			5th Year: WORK EXPERIENCE PRACTICAL, WORK EXPERIENCE CANVASSING, JOB CANVASSING		WORK EXPERIENCE COURSEWORK, WORK		
FRIDAY	5th Year	JOINT TUTOR GROUP	MATHS	HOME MANAGEMENT	LEAVERS PROGRAMME	Week 1: Tutor Groups / Week 2: Options – Popmobility Cooking	
	4th Year		CURRENT AFFAIRS	INTEGRATED STUDIES	MONEY MANAGEMENT		

Figure 1: Sedgemoor Centre four term year timetable

MATHS

ENGLISH

HOME MANAGEMENT

LIFE SKILLS

SOCIAL SKILLS

MONEY MANAGEMENT AND INTRODUCTION TO WORK

LEAVERS PROGRAMME

PREPARATION FOR PARENTHOOD

SCIENCE PROJECTS

SUPPORTED SELF STUDY

JOB PREPARATION

Figure 2:   Core courses studied

people's feelings; feelings that come from the cognitive content of learning and are explored along with the emotions generated by social interactions.

The short modular courses studied, allow more flexibility in design and are therefore usually more dynamic in presentation. They also reduce the risk of boredom. Credence for this approach comes from the County's TVEI modular schemes and Hargreaves (1984) who in his report to ILEA recommended that schools replace their two year courses with short half term units. One characteristic of young people in general, but more specifically maladjusted youngsters, is their inability to perceive or achieve far off goals. By breaking down modules into ten week blocks the staff have been able to keep objectives within the grasp of even the least able students. The mornings therefore are very tightly organized and structured, and because of this at times we are able to be flexible. It would not be unusual for a highly motivated student to keep doing maths work through English. Youngsters often go out of the Centre to verify some hypothesis which they may have read. On one occasion on a cold winter's morning, we all downed tools and went sledging. The afternoon sessions are all option based with youngsters picking an activity for a term at a time. The range of options offered since the Centre has been open is vast — well over 150 to date. Some popular options are available all the time, for instance, the motorbike option and swimming, but sometimes very obscure options are designed, i.e., birdwatching. At times, to help run these options, what Topping (1983) calls 'para-professionals' are called in; these being parents, neighbours, friends and ex-pupils. By choice students can also opt into voluntary work and link courses with the local tertiary college.

As mentioned earlier, one of the hallmarks of the Centre's curriculum is the position that the staff take within its design. The curriculum within a school should not be seen as static and as the youngsters and staff grow, so should the curriculum. If the work that youngsters do at school is to be owned by them, it follows that they must have a say in its design. Unless schools make a mechanism by which this will happen, it simply will not. At the Centre students are given the facility to comment on the delivery of work and also to help design their own individual programmes. Three times a year students have detailed reviews in which targets are set for academic and behavioural progress. Through their own pro-formas they can comment on their perceptions of progress over the last four months, and also air complaints. The staff fill in their own pro-formas and send out specially designed ones to social workers, educational psychologists, the careers service, and doctors (if appropriate). This ensures that a multi-disciplinary approach actually happens and is not just paid lip service to. These reviews give teachers feedback which is used within the Centre's review and development scheme and further within the school's on-going whole school review.

One characteristic of all the youngsters at the Centre is that of failure. One strategy adopted is to plan for success in a youngster's school life and then openly build upon it. We call this the Orchestration of Success. Its aim is to bolster a youngster's flagging self-image and make him or her feel good about themselves. Lawrence (1973) pointed out that children often read better when they feel better about themselves and Robinson and Maines (1988) suggest that:

> The recent emphasis on parent involvement in children's reading probably owes its success to the sharing of the positive experiences by the parent, the child and the school (p. 8).

The focus of each morning's Tutor Group is usually some positive feedback to one youngster or another. As a condition of a work experience placement, employers must give an honest reference about how well or badly a placement has gone. In line with current practice the Centre encourages students to collate a personal portfolio and these references feature highly in students portfolios. As part of the fifth year leavers programme, students are taught how to use these portfolios when canvassing for jobs.

As cited earlier, youngsters are targeted for success in their school work. This at times means using many of the behaviourist strategies found in many special schools; for instance, precision teaching, task analysis, computer assisted learning etc. Students can also get commendations for twelve weeks continuous attendance and for prolonged periods of good behaviour. As part of the Centre's record of achievement scheme youngsters can achieve certificates for all core courses as well as the County's designated record of achievement scheme (OCEA).

All the decoration done at the Centre is done via the County's self-help scheme.

This gives us various spin-offs. The instructor who works at the Centre is able to take youngsters on a withdrawal basis and teach them how to decorate. Once an area is finished the youngster signs his or her name to the work, again demonstrating to students that they have some ownership of the Centre. The only grafitti on show at the Centre is the 'official' grafitti in the games room designed by the students. As is good practice in any school, examples of good work are openly displayed all around the Centre, and in one of the classrooms each youngster has their own piece of wall in which to display work. I believe that being positive about people generates positive results. We therefore constantly attempt to build on any success that a youngster achieves at the Centre as well as on the more appropriate sides to their nature. This coupled with a planned strategy means that success happens because it is planned for.

The use of a privilege system at the Centre may initially appear to be a contradiction to some of the other strategies used at the Centre. Whilst this privilege system has quasi behaviourist trappings, it is not a behaviour modification system. The system operates on several levels influencing both individuals and groups of students and is explained to youngsters in depth at interview. In essence the operation of the system is simple and reflects a large amount of development during the time that the Centre has been open. Its present design owes much to the ideas of the students themselves.

The system operates on a points basis with the more points earned translating into the more privileges earned. Students are marked at the end of each lesson or option and get a mark for behaviour during free time. This is intended to give students instant feedback on their behaviour and effort during the day. It also enables some youngsters to have a short achieveable goal; a good mark at the end of a lesson. At the end of each day and subsequently each week, all marks are added up and this decides which group the youngster will be in the following week. There are three privilege groups — red, amber and green (no prizes for guessing where the idea came from!). Privileges gained include being allowed out at break times, the use of the Centre's games room, access to the tuck shop, etc. There are certain sanctions for breaking the rules of the Centre which are few but essential ones only. For example, if a student took a day off without the consent of their parents/guardians, they would lose a set amount of points which will drop the youngster into a lower group the following week. If a student were to earn a really low score, they would incur heavier consequences, such as missing options, work experience, trips out, access to the games room, etc. However, youngsters do have the option of earning points back by doing voluntary detentions during breaktime or after school when a job will be set, i.e., cleaning the Centre's minibus, chopping firewood for old age pensioners, etc. This facet of the system gives the youngsters a way out and also the ability to make amends with dignity. After being in the top group for a consecutive period youngsters are taken off the privilege system and given prefect status. Prefects have all the privileges that are available at the Centre, some of which only they have. A prefect can lose this status by being given three warnings. I believe it is important to have this structure within the system for it allows youngsters to demonstrate that they can work around the framework of relationships. When they leave school, there are no privilege systems and we would view it as a partial failure if youngsters had not grown to a position in which they did not need the system by the time they left.

I believe that systems manage people and that it is people who make people grow. It is the quality of relationships between students and staff that bring about many changes in the youngsters at the Centre, but in a youngster's early days, before relationships are established, the privilege system helps manage and establish the ethos of the Centre. It also gives teachers a framework in which to operate where expectations are clear with set consequences for breaking rules and further gives the staff a framework in which they can sanction youngsters with the minimum amount of damage inflicted to relationships.

Whilst the privilege system stands up in its own right, it is also part of the systematic discipline and organizational structure of the Centre. Many of the numerous visitors to the Centre comment on the almost total lack of disruption, many saying that this is the consequence of small class sizes and good student staff ratios. This is, though, a shallow level of analysis. Traditionally many of the youngsters at the Centre have encountered problems and difficulties when confronted with matters to do with discipline, and yet disruptive behaviour is rare at the Centre.

The strategies adopted to bring about this climate operate on two levels simultaneously. Many of them are designed to actually prevent disruptive behaviour from occurring at all. Most of the bureaucratic quotedious activities of large secondary schools are not evident at the Centre. Uniform rules are less restrictive, there are no registration periods, and the timetable has been designed so that there is always one member of staff on non-contact time to pick up a potential problem. A condition of acceptance at the Centre is that students and their families agree to respect the rules. It is also emphasized that help does not equal punishment. Rules are few but essential. All rules are written up on the walls and copies of them as well as the procedures of the privilege system are sent to parents/guardians on completion of interview. Times of the day which are potentially disruptive are stage managed, break and dinner times are supervised, with youngsters not going out being actively engaged. Staff supervise youngsters into taxis at the end of the day. The whole rationale of this approach is that it is designed to offer a structured setting in which expectations are high, firm but fair. There are set consequences for dealing with the breaking of rules. It is interesting to note that many of the past students when asked say they found the structure of the Centre a calming influence which offered them security.

Twice during the school year students embark on a residential experience, the basic aim of which is to have a good time by sharing various experiences. On camp, staff and students cook, eat, work, play and sleep in the same dormitories/tents together. The intention from the staff's point of view is to consolidate the honest relationships engendered at the Centre. Some activities are planned; these depending on where the trip is. But the intention is that youngsters make their own fun and not rely on staff to act as some type of 'Redcoat'. For some youngsters this is very hard; it may be the first time that they have had to cope without television and arcades. We always go to one of the county's outdoor pursuits centres on Exmoor near Christmas time. Whilst very well furbished, the site is very remote and gives scope for extended student and staff interaction. Ex-students usually join us on these trips, again helping to maintain the family atmosphere. During the evening sessions encounter group type activities are taken part in; some of the most moving experiences I have had as a person have been on some of these trips. Whilst many mainstream schools participate in these residential experiences, what is less likely in my experience is the degree to which staff are prepared to take the emotional and personal risks involved and truely let down the barriers and show the other side of their personas which exist outside of the school setting. In the past parents have offered their expertise to these ventures; a few years ago when we went to Cornwall, one who was a lifeguard laid on a day's water activities, including surfing and canoeing.

> Where parents are encouraged to come into school and given positive —
> not necessarily ancillary — roles, where they are given the opportunity to
> use the facilities and expertise of the school, where, above all, they are
> involved in an equal and active dialogue on the education of their children,
> the results will be to reduce disruption (Coulby, 1984, p. 111).

This quotation aptly amplifies another one of the planned intervention strategies of the Centre that of home liaison. At interview it is explained in detail to parents/guardians that they are an integral part of the process that may ameliorate their child's difficulties, and that the thrust of the Centre's work is towards a sharing of the difficulties between themselves, the staff and the youngster. It is pointed out that attendance at parents' evenings is obligatory! I feel that parents should share the progress that their youngsters are making. For some it may be the first time that they have had positive feedback around school life. The expectation here is very much not one of crisis management with parents only coming in when there are problems at school. Parents are sent home weekly reports which give feedback on the privilege system and also bits of information which may be necessary. They also have to agree to teachers doing home visits. So in practice parents and staff get together on at least six times in a school year. At times when a youngster has been presenting difficulties at home or at the Centre, the privilege system has been modified so that each can support the other. So essential is this support viewed by the staff that on one occasion a youngster who was repeatedly breaking sanctions had his placement withdrawn because the parents reneged on their offer to support the Centre in carrying out of the agreed sanctions.

The quality of staff in any school is crucial to the delivery of the curriculum and at the Sedgemoor Centre staff appointed are interviewed in three separate sessions over two days. The interviews involve the whole staff team, the management committee and students. The interview process starts with an informal meeting on the night before the more formal interviews. Youngsters are invited to this session. Whilst it is pointed out to them that they will not have a final say in the matter, their views are respected and taken note of. The next day candidates are interviewed in a large group, then in pairs and finally individually. This may seem a rather arduous procedure but it is essential that 'we get it right', for as Brennan (1985) has pointed out when dealing with students with emotional and behavioural problems:

> The ethos of the group at any time will owe more to the adults involved than would be required or occur in a normal adult–child group. Consequently the pattern of adult relationships and behaviour will require close attention and analysis as part of the overall curriculum input. Identical adult behaviour is not the objective but adult consistency is (p. 60).

At the Centre there is a policy of continuity. This is done to pre-empt the classic 'wedging' that many disturbed and disruptive youngsters are so good at. Staff will openly support each other in public and redress any areas of concern in the appropriate place — the Staffroom! Detailed planning takes place to achieve cohesion amongst the staff via several mediums. The main one of which is the Centre's review and development scheme which is multi-directional. In essence staff appraise each other subjectively. Twice a year we sit in on each others lessons with a specific brief to look at the quality of classroom practice and to see if the correct parity exists when marking cards for the privilege system. We work out personal targets of development and whole school development policy action. These are appraised on-goingly as part of a whole school review. We also receive comments from youngsters as part of their own review scheme. The Centre receives many visitors who have to agree to fill in a visitors' proforma which is sent out prior to the visit and adds as another source of feedback. We have two staff meetings a day and an extended one at the end of the week. This helps to ensure that difficulties are sorted out quickly and helps to ensure that a mutually supportive environment is maintained.

The last planned intervention used as part of the Centre's ten point plan is the use of outside agencies. In special schools generally multi-disciplinary liaison features highly in the delivery of the curriculum. We use the spectrum of other professionals. Educational psychologists help design individual learning programmes and sit in on reviews. They have also run inset courses for staff. Once every four months we have a meeting with all the social workers who have clients at the Centre. Social workers drop in a lot to support youngsters and the Centre has a named social worker who is the co-ordinator for all students. The Social Services are prominent features in nearly all the families lives of youngsters at the Centre and it is essential that liaison between the two services is clear and consistent in order that an 'us and them' situation does not exist. The careers service will attend parents' evenings in the fifth year and have input into the students reviews. Community links exist with most of the large industries in the locality (most of whom participate in the Centre's work experience scheme). The Police help in running the motorbike option and also in some of the mornings' core sessions. Whilst this list is not exhaustive, it does offer an insight into the role of the external agencies within the Centre's curriculum.

Despite, and possibly because of, current legislation, mainstream schools face problems with disturbed and disruptive pupils. For teachers working with these youngsters the job can be both difficult and challenging, but ultimately it is still the responsibility of teachers to maintain discipline in schools if genuine educational activities are to take place. Disruption in schools is not going to go away and in order to combat this teachers must develop workable whole school policies on disruption in its own right and not, I would suggest, as part of a whole school approach to special educational needs. In these policies the systematic use of praise and positive reinforcement are two important strategies to be utilized. Schools need to be more aware of the antecedents of disruptive behaviour and have agreed procedures for dealing with incidents when they arise. Pastoral systems need not to operate solely in the punitive mode. The challenge of the National Curriculum will be in the purposeful curriculum design for these youngsters, with syllabuses that pay recognition to individual needs and achievements. Teachers by their own examples and expectations can show youngsters that they and their work is important. They need to see these youngsters for what they can be, not for how they are. For many of the youngsters at Sedgemoor Centre the experience is, I believe, special in the best sense of the word but is it so extraordinary that mainstream schools could not make it ordinary?

Chapter 16

Integration Through Physical Education

David Stewart

According to the *Oxford Dictionary* — and who are we to argue with that admirable compilation — 'special' refers to that which exceeds or excels in some particular fashion or which is marked by having a distinct or individual character. 'Special schools', therefore, are not the same as others. They are smaller than their large neighbouring comprehensives; they have smaller teaching groups; the children can thus receive more attention, and this in turn may lead to easier learning. All these are benefits: all these are in some way desirable: all help to make a school special. But what are the drawbacks? First, a child finds itself in a special school because he or she suffers from one or more disadvantages — poor literacy, poor numeracy, some physical disability, or any combination of the three. Secondly, human nature being what it is, those who allocate resources tend to apportion more to the able and less to the disadvantaged; lack of funds tends to produce inferior facilities; inferior facilities do not attract adequate funds; and so the slow downward spiral to inadequacy is maintained and unwittingly encouraged. Funds for PE equipment in a special school may be as low as £150 per annum; those in a comprehensive as high as £2,000. How special can you get?

But perhaps the single most frustrating aspect of this side of special schools is that their being special denies their pupils access to the full breadth of the curriculum. Put quite simply, lack of ability, either academic or physical, has resulted in these children's being subjected to an official view of what is appropriate for them. They are not to be put in a mainstream school but in a variety of special schools where specific needs can be met by specific attention.

This has its advantages, as we have seen; but it has its disadvantages, as we have also seen, and we must therefore ask ourselves whether the first outweigh the second, the pro the contra. Actually, the question has been answered for us by the 1981 Education Act. If one had to pick out the key principle of the Act it would be 'integration', for one of its most important points is that Local Education Authorities must, under certain given circumstances, make sure that children with special educational needs are given the opportunity to be mainstreamed.

So far so good, but unfortunately the Act contains a loophole, an escape-hatch for those who either do not wish to fulfil its enjoinment, or those who feel they cannot because they do not know how to go about integration. There are problems, of course. Can a mainstream school meet the needs of special children without negatively affecting the rest? How is one supposed to integrate children en masse at a stroke? Does the very physical structure of many mainsteam school buildings inhibit integration — of the blind, or of those in wheelchairs, for example? Yes, there are genuine problems. Often the spirit of administrators is willing but the flesh is weak, and it is to this particular set of symptoms that I should like to address myself in the rest of this chapter. Integration is possible, straightforward, relatively simple, and immensely desirable, and the test case of Physical Education illustrates all of these adjectives perfectly.

Let us start with basics, since physical ability or physical disability is common to all children, no matter what type of school they attend. The continuum of physical ability can be expressed thus:

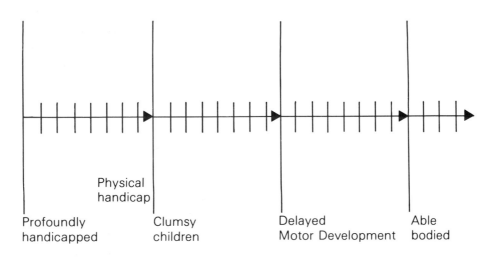

Figure 1: Continuum of physical ability

In this diagram we have a scale moving forward, beginning at 0 but remaining open ended. Some special schools are asked to cater for children towards the zero end of the scale, i.e., those with profound handicaps. Now the important point here is that although these children may be currently in possession of abilities operating at the far end of the continuum they still have the potential to move further up the scale. Next we come to the physically handicapped child, who is likely to be experiencing education in some form of special unit, although he or she may not be suffering from academic difficulties. Those children who are deemed to be either 'clumsy' or delayed in their motor development present a different problem, because they are independently mobile and exist in both mainstream and in the special school. Finally we have the able-bodied, largely to be found within the mainstream school. There is, however, one child who may find himself in a very peculiar and highly unsatisfying situation, and that is the child who is able-bodied, the child who may well be achieving standards of physical excellence, but has been placed, for whatever reason, in one of the special schools. This is the child who will be particularly disadvantaged by inferior facilities, although it must also be said, and stated as clearly as possible, that any child in a special school will be disadvantaged if he is faced by inferior facilities, whether he has good physical ability or not.

Here, then, we have the range of children who are to be integrated. How is integration to be achieved? First, by finding mutually beneficial physical activities for those concerned, and secondly by using the flexibility of the special school's timetable to support the inevitably more rigid mainstream timetable. It is here, in fact, in the special schools themselves that the process leading to integration starts. For it is they who begin by rationalizing their own PE programmes in terms of where their children exist on the continuum of physical ability, and of what can be done internally both to meet those particular needs and to identify what can be done to pursue integration.

I can best explain and illustrate all this by recounting my own experience. The Lady Adrian School in Cambridge is a school for children with moderate learning difficulties and they are aged between 5 and 16 years old. Here, the most readily identifiable of those children who were going to require a rationalization of their PE programme were those being withdrawn from my PE lesson to be treated individually by the physiotherapists. These children had been diagnosed by the medical profession as severely delayed in their motor development ('clumsy' children, as registered on the continuum). After consultation with the school physiotherapist, it was agreed that provided the activities on offer were suited to that child's needs, it would be preferable to work him or her in a group rather than in individual situations. Organizing and selecting activities for one child was an easy task. More difficult was including several such children in a lesson where many more capable children were present; and the only effective answer to this problem was to work the DMD children as an autonomous group away from their more able peers.

The major worry for all the adults concerned was stigmatization. Would the DMDs be perceived as *disabled* children inside their own school? To counter this, I decided not to withdraw the group from any of its normal PE lessons. It was important that the children enjoy, and be seen to enjoy, the usual quota of physical education alongside everyone else. So the extra time for them to work as a special group had to be negotiated with other members of staff who were understandably apprehensive. Why was it important, they asked, to give up academic time to physical activity, especially when one remembers that a child has been referred to a special school because of a basic learning difficulty?

The answer, of course, is simple. *Mens sana in corpore sano,* as Juvenal put it: a healthy mind flourishes with a healthy body. Improvement in physical skills allows the mind to feel confident. A child who is ill at ease with and within his body fidgets and scratches, and drops things and finds it difficult to draw or write; this difficulty engenders boredom and self-mistrust, which in turn destroys concentration; this lack of concentration is betrayed by more fidgeting, more scratching, more dropping, and so on and so forth. 'Look after the pennies and the pounds will look after themselves', runs the old proverb. Look after basic physical skills and academic rewards may follow. It seemed to make sense, and so I got the time I wanted.

Once agreement on this was reached, we set about the task of organizing the activities, based upon the components of efficient motor function, which were *within the abilities of all the children and would ensure a high degree of success for each child.* The results were gratifying, indeed remarkable. First and foremost, perhaps, was the reduction in anxiety, the increase in activity, and the sheer enjoyment which the children began to exhibit. Within a term, for example, boys and girls who previously were desperate to hide their inabilities became more than keen to show off their newly awakened physical abilities.

This success, however, brought a whole new set of problems. The children involved were all between the ages of 5 and 10 years and thoroughly enjoyed activities based upon infant-type development games and play. Now the Lady Adrian School caters for children between 5 and 16 years old. So once we had rationalized the programme for children at the younger end of our range and opened up the group to children with minor developmental delays, *including children from other schools in the group,* we were still left with a large group of Lady Adrian children between the ages of 11 and 16 years who were suffering to varying extents from delays in their motor development. Had I pursued the same approach with these older children, who are involved in more sophisticated peer groups, then I feel certain the stigmatization I spoke of earlier would have taken place. What we needed was a different reason for their being given extra time to work on their physical development.

A resolution of this difficulty occurred to me when I attended an in-service day run by Veronica Sherbourne. The topic was 'Relationship Play'. Now, the basis of this activity is partner work and its tool the human body. Its aim is to bring to life bodies which seem to be lifeless, no matter where they be on the continuum of physical ability. The whole process requires that people turn away from the notion of the body's *inability* and look on it in terms of what it *can* do. Conceived so that the able-bodied can work with the profoundly handicapped in a meaningful physical context, relationship play lends itself readily to combinations of children along the whole range of the continuum of physical ability. Its strength as a form of physical activity lies not only in the calibre of physical exercise it provides but also in the emotional impact (with regard to improved self-image, self-esteem and self-confidence) it imparts to its participants.

To make each relationship work best one needs to make sure that there is a significant difference between the partners — adolescents working with infants/juniors, for example, or a DMD with a profoundly handicapped child. In fact, the wider the gap, the greater the emotional impact; and those involved soon come to feel a need for each other's presence and thus a bond is created from the physical dependence of one upon the other.

This, then, seemed to be a way forward for Lady Adrian, and for my unresolved teenage group in particular. I started by working a number of 13-, 14- and 15-year-olds alongside a group of ambulant children from a nearby SLD school, the Rees Thomas. Several results flowed from this. Although the age gap between the two groups was narrow, the Lady Adrian children were more capable physically and this, in itself, gave their self-esteem a boost. Then they were able genuinely to assist the others with their physical improvement — another psychological boost, this time for both parties. Anyone who finds physical activity extremely hard work all the time, and who has become used to the notion of constant failure, blossoms under the sunshine of even small success; and this pleasure, this improvement encourages the partner who has contributed to it. Thirdly, I now had a good reason for running an extra PE session. Those taking part would not find it demeaning. On the contrary they soon started to look forward to it as one of the highlights of their week.

This combination of two schools, then, was most encouraging. After only two terms we were left with a group of children who were less fraught at the notion of physical activity, were making marked progress in terms of strength, stamina and coordination, and — just as important — enjoying their PE lessons to the full; while bringing the two schools together in a mutually beneficial way, thereby reducing the feeling of isolation which all too readily attaches itself to special schools, was an additional, and not unimportant, bonus.

Even for young children, however, constant attack upon improvement of skills will lose its emotional impact unless variety of approach is maintained. So when it came to dealing with a group younger than these teenagers, relationship play also provided an answer to boosting interest and cementing those achievements which had been made already. The easiest way of providing this would have been to combine them with the Sherbourne group. A bigger challenge, however, was to raid the comprehensive across the road and hijack some of their fifth years, because it seems that the children in comprehensives most obtainable when one is forging community links are those who, despite their special needs, are still being educated in a mainstream comprehensive. They probably already operate within a flexible timetable and one more option eases the pressure on the staff who are attempting to maintain them in school.

Negotiations with the special needs teacher produced a group of ten fifth year pupils who came along for one term, their final term, to work with the young DMD group through relationship play. The physical qualities the older children brought to the younger children meant that it was not necessary for the youngsters to wait for the adult to swing them higher, chase them faster, challenge their strength. Each child now had its own teacher.[1]

Again the group was a success for all concerned, but an even more important breakthrough had been made here. Mainstream and special school children were integrating, and the benefits of the integration were not all flowing one way. Suddenly these educationally reluctant fifth years were being given real responsibility for another person, and their response was to be committed, caring, reasonable, compassionate and, above all, reliable — qualities which had been all but submerged during the past few years. They felt good about themselves and they took a real interest in the younger children. The whole exercise scored high in emotional impact.

Hoping, then, that the Lady Adrian/Rees Thomas Sherbourne group would benefit from a similar experience, I set about the task of finding a suitable group of mainstream infant/junior children with possible delays in their motor development, who would benefit from experiencing relationship play with the adolescent DMDs. Using the headteacher grapevine, I made contact with such a school close to our own, St Luke's C of E infant and junior school.

This school had recently acquired a new community sports hall, which seemed to provide an excellent space in which to work a large Sherbourne-style group. The appropriate information was given to the headteacher of St Luke's and he undertook the task of informing staff and compiling a group of children who might suitably be withdrawn from lessons to joins us for one 45 minute session per week. The group composition was as follows: ten children from Lady Adrian, six from Rees Thomas and sixteen from St Luke's, staffed by two teachers, one welfare assistant and one PE-trained volunteer. The activity base was to be relationship play and there was a clear chronological age gap. The sports hall was twice the size of our own school hall and everything seemed to be perfect. Within a matter of weeks, however, the group was falling apart. Why?

The answer is quite simple. During the initial transfer of information, I had mentioned that one of the side-effects of relationship play was an improvement in children's behaviour, and this had been seized upon with alacrity by the adults who were not familiar with this type of work. About 30 per cent of the St Luke's children turned out to be nuisances whom any teacher would be glad to lose for a while. By 'nuisance' I mean 'badly behaved'. These children had problems, to be sure, but their problems were not based on deficiencies in motor development. So they came into the group with good physical capabilities, able to intimidate the older children and command an inordinate amount of negative attention from the adults. Add to this poor facilities — cold, hard floor, very poor acoustics and shelves all around the room, so tempting to climb upon — and in retrospect, it is hardly surprising we had so many initial problems.

How does one deal with such a situation? Improving facilities takes time although now, six terms later, the acoustics have been rectified, and mats on the floor ease the discomfort of crawling, sitting and lying exercises. As for the shelves, we actually used their existence as a starting point for 'negotiations' over behaviour problems. By negotiation I do not mean we bargained with the nuisances on equal terms. What happened was that we would alternate between leading the session and working privately on the most difficult individuals so that the flow of the lesson would not be affected. After all, the majority was working hard and having fun. So ours was a clear policy of accentuating the positive and minimizing the negative, and it simply wore the negative children down. Within the third half term the objectives with which we had set out were beginning to be realized and the benefits for all children who are given such an opportunity were beginning to materialize.

Thus far, then, we had experience of linking groups from four schools, all within a two mile radius, involving children between the ages of 5 and 16 with varying academic and physical abilities. However, when I looked again at the continuum of physical ability I saw that there was a group of youngsters who were still isolated, the profoundly physically handicapped. It was at this point that the physiotherapy grapevine came into play. Another SLD school, known as the Windmill, had actually staged an in-service day, headed by Veronica Sherbourne, on relationship play. The need for this type of activity in their school was self-evident, but there is one obstacle which always has to be overcome when one attempts to set up Sherbourne-type groups — finding enough able bodies to accommodate the needs of the handicapped. Inspired by the results achieved by the links that were operating up till now, the Lady Adrian established contacts with the Windmill with a view to giving some of our more able seniors the opportunity to benefit not only physically but also psychologically from working in such a meaningful way with special care children. Distance, however, provided another example of a problem which often faces such links. The two schools are eight miles apart and so school minibuses are essential. Now, travel takes time and colleagues had to be asked to allow this time to be taken out of their lessons. Actually this is not as much of a difficulty as you may think because — and I should like to stress this part — once the staff have grasped how meaningful this activity is for all concerned, you will receive their full support.

What we can see falling into place now is a network of schools within a community which are integrating and linking not simply or bureaucratically in response to an Act of Parliament, but in order to meet, in a mutually beneficial way, specific physical needs of some of their children. 'A master-passion is the love of news', said George Crabbe and, as in any community, news spreads fast. In no time at all, therefore, good news about what had been achieved reached other schools in the network, like Topsy grew. Indeed, it continues to grow. Figure 2 illustrates the number of schools which have made or received input from other schools in that network which exists around the Lady Adrian School — all of these links being based

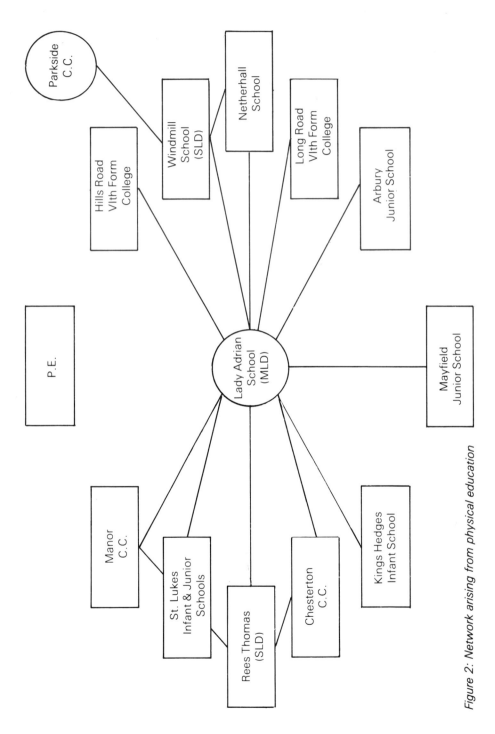

Figure 2: Network arising from physical education

upon shared physical activity, (i) motor development skills, (ii) relationship play or Halliwick swimming groups whose methods, for those who may not be familiar with them, might be described as a 'watered down' version of relationship play.

The most recent innovation within the network involves children from Chesterton Community College, who are studying for GCSE community studies. They complete one of their six modular requirements by working with special care children. One such group worked in the Rees Thomas School alongside Rees Thomas children and taught by Lady Adrian staff. Another worked in Chesterton's swimming pool with children from the Windmill, using the Halliwick swimming method: and the subsequent written work presented by the Chesterton children, many of whom have learning difficulties themselves, was in many cases the best work they were producing within school and indeed some of the best work they had produced for some time.

As each term progresses — and it is now some three years since the process began — the network takes even deeper root. This was illustrated recently by the creation of a links group wherein teachers from the varying institutions meet to discuss current links, future links and any in-service requirements which may be needed to achieve those ends.

In conclusion, then, what I have been seeking to explain is that a group of schools which between them cover an enormous range of both physical and emotional needs has realized, in a practical fashion, the idea that if we truly wish to better the lot of every individual under our care, we do so best by mutual dependence, by cooperation rather than isolation. Many excuses can be made to avoid the problems of integration — some real, others only apparent — but if schools are serious about a community approach to their role in society and their duty to the educative process, they must be prepared to make some sacrifice to ensure that each child has access to the facility or expertise which best meets his or her needs, no matter where that facility or expertise is based. And we must all be ready to alter our perception of the 'special' child, and learn to view him, not as a patient passively waiting for treatment, but as a participant actively concerned in both his and others' improvement.

---

[1] When integrating these older children it is vital that they be fully informed about their role in relationship play. Only then can they feel responsible for their partner, and only then will a real relationship start to be formed.

Chapter 17

Bridging the Gap in Cheshire

Norman Butt

Introduction

Integration means many things to many people. To some it means the full functional integration of all children with special needs into mainstream schools regardless of difficulty. To others it may mean simply locational integration by putting, say, a special school on the same campus as a mainstream school. To yet others it means the functional integration of pupils with mild special needs into 'normal' lessons instead of the 'remedial' class. Hopefully in any LEA a variety of integration schemes are in place, the variety resulting from the particular needs of the children, their age, the types and severity of their disabilities, and the resources of the LEA.

For many years Cheshire has espoused the principle of integration. It has encouraged its special needs provision in mainstream schools to adopt whole school policies; throughout the 1970s and currently it has established 'unit' provision attached to mainstream schools and encouraged at least social integration of the pupils attending these; and it encourages its special schools to develop programmes of integration with neighbouring schools and outreach and support schemes. In 'A Review of Special Education', completed in the county in 1987, it was stated, 'Where children need to be educated in a special school there should be a plan to give them every possible opportunity to join their peers in "mainstream" classes in primary and secondary schools' (p.7). In some schools this policy has been effected with tangible success.

It is of course too easy to talk about integration. It can be said to be happening when a child is simply attending a 'normal' class. One must ask what is the educational benefit if a child is simply sitting at the back of the class with perhaps a classroom assistant sitting alongside. Take the assistant away and is one any further ahead than in the nineteenth century when special education was barely in existence? Integration can become interpreted in locational terms only, that is, where a child with special needs spends varying amounts of time in a mainstream school, regardless of the educational value. Integration has meant in some LEAs a move toward closing down special schools, sometimes as a part of a plan restructuring educational provision. At risk in all this educational and often political debate is the child.

It is therefore insufficient to talk in terms of bricks and mortar provision; real integrational practice is where functional and curricular integration actually takes place. That is, in the quality of the educational experiences received by the pupil, the relationships and atmosphere in which the experiences are delivered, and the self-respect, dignity and competences achieved by the pupil. However, as we shall see shortly, where a facility is located is an important first step towards encouraging deeper forms of integration.

Cheshire provides a range of provision intended to match the range of needs. This means that as well as the units mentioned above, the county has off-site units, day schools, residential schools, and the use of specialist out-county schools. In addition mainstream schools are encouraged to adopt whole school special needs policies. Arguably then, pupils attending residential schools, should have the more severe or at least the more complex difficulties, making integration rather more difficult than from the units. The schemes to be described, which are case studies of two such residential schools, should therefore be seen in this context.

The Hebden Green — Woodford Lodge Link

Hebden Green is a residential and day school for pupils with physical handicaps. It caters for the 2 to 19 years age range. It takes boys and girls and encounters the full range of disabilities, with the preponderance being pupils with cerebral palsy or neuro-muscular disorders such as muscular dystrophy. It has capacity for 130 pupils, and has physiotherapy on site. It is situated in the middle of the county on the same campus as a large comprehensive school. It is the only residential school for pupils with physical disabilities in the county, although there are two more day schools.

The comprehensive school has a remarkable record on special needs issues. The school is known as Woodford Lodge County High School. It has a special needs department which practices support strategies and is located in what the school knows as the Learning Centre. The school houses a county resource for EBD pupils, accepting twenty-one such pupils in a unit on site. A recent HMI visitor commented on the unusually high level of acceptance of these pupils in mainstream lessons. In addition this school has forged links with a nearby school for MLD pupils, accepting these pupils into certain mainstream lessons. The LEA has put some additional resources into the scheme about to be described, in the form of installing a lift in the comprehensive school, allocating one additional teacher and one extra classroom assistant. This school has itself allocated one teacher to the job of liaising with the special school over the integration.

At present some thirty-three physically handicapped pupils — all of secondary level — spend varying amounts of time at the comprehensive school. The amount of time spent in each school is determined by individual needs, and not by a rigid philosophical belief. Children who require a heavy input of physiotherapy need to spend more time at the special school, thus utilizing its specialist resources. This is particularly the case with muscular dystrophy cases. Some children only require access being made available to the ordinary classroom. They are quite able to cope with the curriculum, and as long as the teacher is accepting and sensitive they require no additional support. Others of course require mobility assistance during lesson change-overs, and in reaching the lessons in the first place. These pupils with need of intensive medical and educational help must remain in the special school. Therefore the integration allows little saving in the way of staff time in the special school. Such savings as there are are offset by the disruption caused by having to get the pupils ready for their mainstream lessons, putting coats on, arranging the teaching groups and materials, and so on, and doing the whole thing in reverse when the pupils are taken back into lessons when the mainstream session is over. This is one reason why the LEA has to provide additional resources.

With some pupils attending mainstream for just a couple of lessons per week, varying up to some pupils attending mainstream for a considerable part of the week, a great deal of flexibility and goodwill is required from the staffs of both schools. Commitment and enthusiasm from all involved in the scheme are vitally necessary. The overall ethos and creative climates of the schools are essential factors in developing and maintaining the quality of the provision. Both schools have continually to evaluate their effectiveness. Key management issues here are the aims and objectives to be achieved by the pupils, analysis of those structural barriers to making the scheme work better, including communication, distribution of authority, use of resources, morale, innovation, management styles and pattern of decision-making.

The special school really behaves as a resources centre, offering specialist knowledge and acting as a service delivery agent. The children remain on the roll of the special school so it is actually in part contracting out its own function of educating the pupils to the comprehensive school. As implied earlier, the special school has little in the way of resources it can hand over to the mainstream school, and the LEA's help is modest. The mainstream school has also been going through a period of rapidly falling roles, so what could have been acute stumbling blocks have been overcome by goodwill and cooperation, especially on the part of the two headteachers.

Accepting that the process could be managed largely using existing resources, when the scheme was initiated other important factors remained to be tackled. They were:

1   Assessment and evaluation of the scheme. Basic questions such as, where do we want to arrive at? Where are we now? What routes are available? What

problems can be anticipated? Have the objectives been reached? How can the process be improved?

2   Social interaction. In this area great sensitivity, delicacy and caution are essential. Social experiences are vital but virtually impossible to manufacture. An incidental approach following very careful planning was regarded as essential. It is not possible to apply a given formula to this area. Flexibility, open-mindedness and freedom from rhetoric are important attributes for all concerned, especially for staff.

3   Staff. A multi-professional, multi-disciplinary approach that incorporated dedication, enthusiasm and professional application were vital. Both headteachers were 'champions' of the cause, a deputy head in each school was given overall responsibility for the project, and each school created a coordinator/liaison role for a teacher. Although the management structure was important, equally important was recognition of the key role of everyone. Important staff qualities were, the ability to solve problems and to apply balanced judgment, organizational ability, decisiveness, sensitivity, motivation, creativity, and the ability to cooperate.

Access to a wider, more enriching curriculum is often cited as one of the main reasons for integration into mainstream, but providing an individual educational programme which was broad, balanced, and relevant, relied once again on flexibility and adaptability. One could not naively assume that just because the special pupils had no cognitive difficulties they could simply fit in with the mainstream curriculum. Once again liaison and cooperation was necessary over the learning programmes. There had to be a match of the curricula in both schools if the pupils were to move easily across. Individual programmes had to be devised in the special school which prepared each pupil for the mainstream experience. The need here for staff flexibility and a willingness to change is plain.

This innovation has required very wide vision. It has moved from 'mere' invention to development, diffusion and adaption as part of a dynamic change process. Over time, the commitment and enthusiasm on everyone's part has overcome problems such as staff defensiveness and protectiveness of the pupils, and problems with bureaucracy, hierarchies, poor financial rewards and passivity.

Unfortunately the future of this project is in doubt at the time of writing simply because of the financial constraints imposed upon the LEA. The additional resources, modest as they are, have to be accounted for. The effects of local financial management are as yet unknown. It looks increasingly likely that the LEA might not be able to maintain its input, while LFM (Local Financial Management) will almost certainly mean that the schools involved will not be able to afford to resource it. Needless to say, the scheme is very popular with parents. What their response will be to any proposal to end the scheme remains to be seen.

The Cloughwood Campus Scheme

It is frequently said that the more obvious the disability the greater is the sympathy of the public's response. The two most difficult disabilities to get folk to understand are uncomplicated moderate learning difficulties and emotional and behavioural disturbance, especially the latter. One is reminded of the two headteachers engaged in fund-raising activities. The head of the severe learning difficulties school raised £2000 on one Saturday afternoon; the head of the EBD school raised £600 in four years! His telling comment was 'No-one loves our youngsters'.

Cloughwood School is a residential school for EBD youngsters aged from 9 to 16 years. Since it is residential it is at the severe end of the continuum of provision, as far as complexity of difficulty is concerned. The school has a role of approximately fifty boys. It too is situated on a campus. This campus contains two comprehensive secondary schools — one denominational, the other not — two primary schools, another residential special school, catering for a mix of MLD and SLD pupils, and a college of further education. Quite nearby is a sixth form college. In locational terms some form of integration is easy. Barriers to the social and functional integration of these youngsters, though, are attitudinal and not so easy to overcome.

Excellent relationships have been developed with the non-denominational comprehensive school. About 10 per cent of pupils have full-time education in mainstream. In addition, approximately 4 per cent are integrated for specific subjects only. These figures vary over time, of course, but the average number receiving full-time integration over the last five years varies from 6 per cent to 14 per cent. Since all of Cloughwood's pupils at some time have attended mainstream schools, its aim is *re*-integration rather than integration. This does give initiatives a slightly different slant. These youngsters have experienced mainstream schooling before, and the experience for some will not have been any too pleasant. This means that a degree of disaffection may be present in the pupils, as well as the emotional liability per se.

One of the strengths of Cloughwood school is its curriculum focus. The headteacher is adamant that the most successful way through to these troubled youngsters is through success in school. He has no time for therapeutic approaches which are seen by some as a substitute for a sound curriculum. Neither does he believe in taking the youngsters on adventure trips and 'running the legs off them' so that they don't have the energy left to cause trouble, a sentiment heard in some corners of EBD provision. Instead he provides what he calls a 'turbo-charged curriculum'.

Other terms the head uses to describe the school are, 'a comprehensive school with beds', and a 'mini high-school'. Great use is made of the twenty-four hour day enjoyed by residential schools, so that as well as having as near as possible a day-time subject-based curriculum, the school is proud of its extended day curriculum. Not only does this provide further opportunities for success, but since many of the activities are conducted in the community, many social contacts are created. The school is keen to look beyond its own walls. The extended curriculum contains among its impressive list of activities, cadets, scouts, sporting experiences such as athletics and especially trampolining, where the pupils set national standards. Other activities such as karting involve positive interaction with other children. An integrated ski trip with some mainstream schools in Crewe, provided a wealth of opportunities for social interaction. All fourth and fifth year pupils have attended the local colleges and a number also enjoy residential courses in a local agricultural college. Work experience has long been a feature of the personal and social development programme.

The local high school reintegration programmes offer certain pupils the opportunity of co-educational schooling within a wider social setting. The choice of subjects available then is much broader than can be offered in a small school, giving the pupils the options of following their preferred subjects. The school's philosophy acknowledges that there is little value in just locating a child within a mainstream setting. There must be a carefully laid out and carried through plan of full functional integration for those pupils who are thus educated alongside their peers. The school tries by all these means to ensure that the pupils do not become too reliant upon the facilities, in terms of staffing, emotional support and physical care they enjoy at Cloughwood.

Although the scheme has been running now for several years, the head of Cloughwood remains very much in touch with the programme. This gives it its proper importance. A deputy head oversees the day-to-day running and is 'group tutor' for the campus-based pupils. The integration is not one way, and this deputy actually teaches in the mainstream school for a number of sessions, as does the Cloughwood's literacy specialist. The CDT specialist also assists in the college. The school offers to the mainstream school coaching in trampolining and other sports areas. In addition Cloughwood offers advice to the mainstream school on behavioural or specific learning problems. Programmes are planned by the particular specialist from Cloughwood. Since the integration works two ways it is rare for there to be any negative reactions from mainstream pupils. They recognize the 'centre of excellence' status Cloughwood school has in certain activities, and this reflects on the pupils. This shows that the stigma of living in a residential special school is not indelible. Its erasure is a vital factor because any reintegration scheme is not likely to succeed if the pupils have negative self-images before they even start.

Attitudinal problems are not the sole province of mainstream teachers. Quite often there are adjustment difficulties experienced by special school teachers. They look upon the youngsters as 'their' pupils, and resent the 'interference' of others. They may also in some instances become very defensive about their own skills, assuming they do not exist in the repertoire of mainstream teachers. Also it is often true that mainstream teachers look upon special school teachers as having a 'soft option' by having such small classes. Misunderstandings can occur with each accusing the other of not living in the real world. The 'real world' of the special school teacher is coping with severely disturbed youngsters all day long. The real world of the mainstream teacher often being having to cope with a class four times the size of the special class, containing pupils themselves not too distant, in terms of disaffection and disturbance, from those in the special school. Developing relationships between such staffs can therefore be seen as difficult, and at the same time essential. Mutual appreciation of one another's daily task and a desire to offer help to one another must be the key. Achieving this supportive atmosphere can only occur if staff are personally acquainted and trust one another's professionality and judgment. Such mutual respect is important if the reintegration is to succeed. The EBD child requires a large amount of self-motivation and Cloughwood acknowledges the appropriate kudos mainstream education gives a child. This can be a very positive factor for some pupils within the peer group hierarchy of the school.

Cloughwood does not run a modified curriculum as this would make reintegration into mainstream impossible for the children. This is one feature of the National Curriculum which is bound to have a very far-reaching effect on those schools which have concentrated more upon adjustment than curriculum. Teacher methodology and style, pupil relationships, and the extended day are features which can be used to promote functional integration rather than impede it. TVEI(E) involvement is another aspect of education which will help bring the special school nearer to mainstream.

In future Cloughwood intends to develop further its role as a support facility, offering short-stay facilities, as well as perhaps part-time attendance. It also wishes to extend its role as an outreach support agency, from the immediate vicinity of the campus to a much wider area. The LEA's intention is to explore varieties of support for behaviour problems in mainstream schools, and Cloughwood's aspirations could well fit in with county plans.

Conclusions

Describing two schemes allows one to draw out certain features which are common to both and then to suggest that these factors may be contributing to the success of the schemes.

Common sense dictates that unless headteachers are committed to the scheme, integration initiatives are unlikely to succeed. Doubtless, pressure coming from all members of staff in an institution could result in change, but unless the power-holders and resources managers are committed, the change is not likely to have any permanency. As described, all the headteachers in these two schemes have been committed to at least attempting functional integration.

Both special schools have seen it important that they looked out from their small, but intense world to the wider community. It is unfortunately too easy to see the world begin and end at the doors of the special school, especially a residential one. As Cole (1986, p.14) says, '— teachers — may have been sucked into the vortex of emotions, conflicts, stressful relationships, and tiring duties which can characterize some boarding schools and which leave them with little energy or desire to find out what is happening in the world outside'. It takes a deliberate, planned decision to ensure this perception does not develop. Residential schools in old buildings in delightful but remote areas run special risks of insularity, so the value of locational integration can again be seen as something which should not be underestimated, since it makes insularity more difficult, and the community more easily accessible, which itself may be more enquiring and supportive.

Campuses, locating special and ordinary schools within yards of one-another, can therefore be very advantageous in achieving integration. However one should not think that integration will be that easy even on a campus. One is reminded of an experience where an LEA wanted to convert a redundant primary school within yards of a mainstream primary and mainstream secondary school into an EBD school. There was a public outcry. Public meetings were held, the schools' governors were extremely combative, and it was clear that this particular community would not have an EBD school on that campus at any price. The outcry was sufficient to block the proposal completely. So in developing a campus incorporating an EBD school, probably the special school should be placed there first, or at least at the same time as the mainstream schools. Arriving late could mean difficulties.

One very evident common factor in both the schemes described is staff readiness. Of course not every teacher leaped with equal enthusiasm into the scheme. But sufficient were behind the idea to enable them to get started. Careful planning, foresight, and support was forthcoming from the senior management of the schools, which allowed the more cautious teachers to see the merits of the schemes and come to change their minds. There was a considerable degree of open-mindedness and flexibility amongst all the teachers to begin with, though, because in the same way that it is necessary to have headteacher support for a scheme, sooner or later the 'chalk-face' workers must believe in it or it will become such a chore to them that it will eventually run out of steam.

Finally, concern with the curriculum was something common to both special schools. The 1980s have been the decade of the curriculum and there is no evidence that it will become less important. The National Curriculum, in whatever form it ultimately takes, looks here to stay. TVEI(E) is a central curriculum feature and has already served to pull special and mainstream schools closer together. Virtually all pupils with special needs will be expected to follow the National Curriculum, especially where there are no cognitive difficulties. It seems, then, unavoidable that special schools will have to develop their curricula in ways which accommodate the National Curriculum criteria and at the same time meet the special curricula needs of their pupils. For some types of special need this will not be easy, but the problem is already with us.

The solution will almost certainly mean a closer match between mainstream and special school curricula. Mainstream schools will have to develop support systems and specialist teachers will need to learn how to teach in a more differentiated way. If they manage this they will in fact be able to cater for a wider variety of pupil needs. When the special schools develop their curricula more towards mainstream, then with appropriate support, both within the mainstream school from its resources, and emanating from the special school acting as a support system, we should see more meaningful integration than we have hitherto. In all these changes, the schools described in these schemes seem to be well placed to cope with them.

Acknowledgments

Warm thanks are extended to Kim Jones of Hebden Green School, and Dave Smith, headteacher of Cloughwood School, for their assistance in writing this paper.

SECTION 4

Comparative

Chapter 18

Special Education:
A View from the United States

Helen King with assistance from Dr Murray Morrow Jr

As varied as the colours of the rainbow are the children we find before us each day in our classrooms. Some youngsters come to us bright and eager to learn all we can put before them — others come to us seemingly unable, yet desperately in need of learning 'the basics'.

A basic philosophy for any educator or administrator in special education is the belief in the ability of all students to learn and their entitlement to assistance on an individual basis. In many cases, this means a programme tailored to meet the student's specific needs. This assistance may include cognitive, psychomotor and affective skill areas, each designed so the student can attain the highest personal, vocational and academic adjustment skills.

Such educational training takes place both in traditional school buildings and in 'real-life' situational settings, so that it may be transferred into practical skills.

The Law of the Land

In the United States, Public Law 94–142 is the dominant legislation in the field of special education. The law became effective on October 1, 1977 and includes mandates in seven major areas.

1 Schools must take the appropriate measures to both identify and locate every qualified handicapped individual who is not receiving appropriate public education.

2 Handicapped children must be provided a free and appropriate public education regardless of severity of their handicap.

3 Programmes and services in special education must be designed to meet individual needs of handicapped persons.

4   Handicapped students must be educated with non-handicapped students to the maximum extent appropriate considering the needs of the handicapped student.

5   Placement and evaluation procedures must be adopted to insure that the appropriate identification and placement are made.

6   Procedural safeguards must be established to allow parents and guardians to influence and/or contest decisions regarding their children's placement and evaluations.

7   Schools must provide supplementary aids and services to enable a student in benefitting from his or her public education.

In addition, many of the fifty states have passed legislation governing a number of facets of special education within their unique school districts.

Delivery of Services

Special education departments typically deliver their services in a variety of settings. These include: mainstreaming, self-contained classrooms, consultation and/or contracted services usually offered within small group settings.

A child, 2–5 years of age, may be serviced by the Pre-Primary Impaired (PPI) programme. However, in most cases, services are delivered to students within their neighbourhood school. This includes three levels (elementary, middle and high schools). At the elementary level, special education staff service students from their first days of school at age five to grade eight. At the high school level, students are serviced from grade nine to grade twelve (usually age 17). Many school districts use middle schools (or junior high schools) to teach students in the sixth, seventh, eighth and, in some cases, the ninth grade.

In many communities, centre programmes have been established. In these programmes, several school districts pool their efforts to send students to a single self-contained school usually in a centralized location. Students enter the centre programmes via a referral from their local school district and, if appropriate, are formally entered into the programme through the findings of the Individual Education Planning Committee (IEPC). In most areas, the programme cost is 100 per cent reimburseable unless all county, state and federal funds are exhausted. In that case, the charges go to the local school district. Students attending centre programmes are usually not graded and receive cognitive, psychomotor and affective area skill training. At approximately 14-years-old, most of the student's curriculum is vocationally/affectively based. Support may include: services of the psychologist, orientation/mobility training, on-site speech therapy, occupational/physical therapy, a nurse or other support as may be needed.

In addition, some states mandate that a special education department service private schools as well. This assistance may be in the form of direct service, consultation and testing and is done 'on-site' within the parochial school building.

Service Philosophy

Some states mandate a free, appropriate public education to all eligible handicapped individuals from birth to 26 years of age. For this handicap eligibility to apply, a student must have a handicapping impairment that results in a need for special education and related services. In many school districts, the impairment is defined only as a handicapping condition which interferes with the student's success in a 'general education' classroom.

In many locales, a special education department will develop its own curriculum and/or modify and adapt the general education curriculum to meet the needs of the student in the special education programme.

General education classroom teachers are asked to consider the special problems and programmes in which the student may be involved. Classroom activities assigned to the student are, at times, adjusted to allow grading to reflect progress that is appropriate to the student's intellectual and physical abilities. For example, an oral test may be administered rather than a written test. The concept presents challenges not only for the special education staff but for the general education teacher as well. Naturally, this means that special education staffs have worked closely with general education teachers to provide ideas on how a teacher might effectively work with the lower-functioning student and to monitor the student's progress.

Dr John P. Mathey of the Wayne County Intermediate School District and Dr Matthew Trippe of the University of Michigan have reported in a paper:

> This shift from exclusion to inclusion is indeed a radical change. Having been socialized to believe that the special child has needs which the regular teacher cannot accommodate, teachers are now being asked to foster the growth of these very same children in their classes. It should come as no surprise then that many teachers view this development with great apprehension. In addition, the lack of experience with persons with disabilities generates anxieties and concerns. Our segregated schooling practices have had questionable or limited success with handicapped children and have resulted in generations of children and adults who have had only the most limited of contact with persons with disabilities. Viewing the problem from this perspective, the futures of handicapped children are too important to risk placing these children with teachers whose attitudes could result in more harm than good for the child.
>
> The assignment of handicapped children to regular classrooms is a very complicated process, particularly in a society that is riddled with subtle

handicappist thinking and feeling. It requires close cooperation between regular and special educators, opportunities for teachers to explore their feelings, and opportunities for teachers to be involved in the decisions that affect their lives.

In some states, it is the policy of the boards of education that handicapped students should receive their educational training in an age-appropriate, regular education environment (unless this assignment is considered inappropriate). It has been the belief that regular education programmes maximize the potential of handicapped students. It is also believed that these programmes assist both the handicapped and non-handicapped individuals for integrated community living.

This concept of 'least restrictive environment' ties into the idea that students should be allowed to attempt to function within the mainstream while receiving the minimum amount of support needed from a special education programme.

Mainstreaming is a concept related to least restrictive environment. Mainstreaming is based on a principle that students receive major benefit by being educated in the same classrooms as general education students. In most cases, support services (provided by the special education staff) are based on the IEPC.

Clearly, some students do not benefit as much as others. However, the IEPC is the tool that assists a special education administrator and his or her staff to determine appropriate placement as well as the amount of time the student spends in a particular classroom.

Mainstreaming proponents argue that integrating handicapped children into a regular, general education classroom will result in at least three positive outcomes:

1 An increased social interaction time will result between handicapped and non-handicapped students;
2 There will be a better acceptance of handicapped children by their non-handicapped peers; and
3 Handicapped children will imitate or model the behaviour of their non-handicapped peers as a result of the increased exposure between the two groups.

School districts across the United States strive to provide 'functional activities'. This is a fairly general term referring to any activity at school, in the community or in the home that must be done as part of surviving in life. This activity may be as simple as making change for a dollar.

Sample Staff Organization

Some districts have found it practical to divide their special education staff members who hold the title of 'teacher' into two groups. The groups may be categorical resource room teachers as well as cross-categorical resource room teachers.

In general though, a special education teacher assists in the development and coordinates the implementation of the curriculum for the individual student in his or her charge. The teacher:

— assures that the IEP goals for each student are appropriate and lead to a measurable final objective;
— records data and keeps records on IEP goals;
— keeps the parents updated on the student's goals and the progress toward reaching those goals;
— reports to the building principal and to the director of the special education programme.

The categorical or cross-categorical classroom teachers work with youngsters on a daily basis. A categorical classroom serves only one special education certified population whereas a cross-categorical room will house youngsters of varying certifications. Typically these settings are reserved for those students who require in excess of one-half of the school day in special education to meet their educational needs. The students receive the majority of their academic instruction from and are graded by the special education teacher. Mainstreaming is minimal and occurs in age-appropriate general education rooms. The cross-categorical classroom teacher is responsible for no more than a total of fifteen students, teaching a maximum of ten in the classroom at a time. Teachers assigned to categorical rooms have varying caseload numbers depending upon the certification of the youngsters in the class.

A resource room teacher usually provides student instruction and works with both the general education teacher and the building teacher consultant. The subject of instruction usually varies with individual students and the resource room teacher frequently teaches only one or two content areas. The resource room teacher usually sees the student no more than 50 per cent of the student's day. Instruction may be for as little as one-half hour per day.

The resource room teacher's caseload may be made up of eighteen students encompassing learning disabled, emotionally impaired, physically impaired, and educable mentally impaired. Class size is limited to ten students at any one time. In many school districts, this is the teacher who develops the IEP.

At the elementary school level, the resource room teacher may provide pre-referral consultation. Students enrolled in the resource room programme may not be instructed solely by the resource room teacher in any more than two of these instructional content areas: mathematics, written expression, basic reading skills, and language arts.

In Michigan, the elementary resource room teacher is accountable for the evaluation of no more than two students at one time. Time is allocated to the elementary resource room teacher to carry out this responsibility.

At the secondary level, the resource room programme is designed for students who need three periods or less of their instructional day in special education. Secondary schools servicing students through more than one resource programme may departmentalize. Special education teachers at the secondary level teach either education courses which have been approved for graduation by the local school board or special education courses within an approved special education curriculum.

On the other hand, teacher consultants provide instructional services which are supportive of both the special education and the resource room teacher. Teacher consultants do not award grades, teach a regular education or special education class or subject. The teacher consultant's role is to provide consultation to general education personnel on behalf of the handicapped students on the teacher consultant's caseload. Working as a member of the multi-disciplinary evaluation team, the teacher consultant assists in the evaluation of the educational needs of students suspected of being handicapped. Teacher consultant caseloads are limited to twenty-five students. In establishing the caseloads, school administration considers the allocation of time to each of the following: instructional services, evaluation, consultation with both special and general education personnel, report writing and travel between schools. Teacher consultants usually do not serve in a supervisory or administrative role. In many districts, they are considered part of the teaching staff.

Specialists who may also work with the child include the following:

- The speech language therapist, a speech pathologist who is certified to test and work with students who show discrepancies in speech and/or language which interferes with classroom learning.
- The school psychologist, who provides psychoeducational testing and, later, consultation. The school psychologist also does classroom observations and makes recommendations for student service both to professional staff and to parents.
- The social worker, who explores and sometimes offers support services (either from the school district or the local government) to the student and/or the student's family. The social worker may encourage parents to take advantage of mental health programmes as needed and forward referrals to agencies in the mental health areas. He or she also attempts to improve the interaction between the home/school/community environments to enhance a positive self-concept and educational success for the student.
- The occupational therapist or physical therapist, who offers assistance in the medical or orthopedic areas. The OT or PT may work directly with students in gross/fine motor areas to help remediate certain psychomotor handicaps. Therapists may be called upon to conduct student evaluations in the psychomotor area and to develop appropriate IEP goals.

Procedural Example

The process of bringing the handicapped student into the programme, servicing the student, and exiting the student is outlined here. The procedures are those used in the Wyandotte School District in Wyandotte, Michigan USA.

The pre-referral is a request for instructional assistance by the general education staff. This procedure may lead to a referral for a psychological evaluation and consideration for special education placement or services.

Before submitting a pre-referral communication memo, the general education teacher should have considered the following criteria:

- Parent contact. The parent should be made aware of the behaviours (either academic or social) that are of concern to the teacher. This contact should be made by the classroom teacher and recorded for later use/reference.
- Documentation of the behaviour. The classroom teacher should be recording all relevant information in regards to the behaviour in question. (Work samples, charting of behaviour/frequency, strategies/interventions attempted to alleviate the behaviour and the subsequent outcomes.)
- A review of the student's CA-60 (cumulative school records); if the youngster's test scores are commensurate with grade placement, there is no reason to suspect a learning handicap. Therefore, a pre-referral for an academic reason would not be justified.
- Enrollment in the school's compensatory education programme. Compensatory education is a federal programme which works with youngsters who are working approximately one year below their current grade level in either the reading or math areas. If the student does not qualify for compensatory education services, it is more than likely that he or she would not qualify for special education services either.
- Attendance. A student who is receiving failing grades due to poor attendance should not be considered to be a valid special education pre-referral.
- Frequent moves. The student who has been enrolled in a number of school districts probably will have difficulty adjusting to the expectations of his or her current situation. This may be the reason for a 'set-back' in performance and should be investigated by the classroom teacher before putting in a pre-referral.
- Review of previous testing. The student's file should be checked for earlier psychological test results. Most test results summarize recommendations for the classroom reacher; these should be reviewed and attempted before submitting a pre-referral. In addition, if the most recent test results are within the three-year limitations, careful consideration should be given as to the validity of the pre-referral.

During the special education referral process, teachers of students encountering continuing difficulty in any general education classroom within the Wyandotte School District will follow this process in order to have the student(s) evaluated by the special education personnel.

1 Teacher contacts building principal.
2 Principal determines the disposition of the problem and when appropriate, contacts the teacher consultant (using the pre-referral communication memo) to begin intervention strategies.
3 Pre-referral communication memo given to teacher consultant for distribution. (Copies given to principal and classroom teacher and teacher consultant and/or teacher of the speech and language impaired and/or the school social worker.)
4 Pre-referral forms(s) will be distributed to the classroom teacher by the special education personnel originally assigned by the principal.
5 A child study team meeting will be held to determine if the formal referral process should be initiated.
6 The special education principal will contact the child's parent or guardian with the evaluation consent notice.

Evaluation

Documentation by the general education teacher is critical in pointing out the specific behaviour of concern, its frequency of occurrence and the intensity of that behaviour. Credibility is established with further information in regards to attempted interventions and subsequent outcomes.

Classroom observations are conducted to augment teacher perceptions of continuing difficulties interfering with progress in the general education classroom.

Learning/achievement skill levels are compared with grade placement and age standard scores. To be considered for special education services, there must be a severe discrepancy between the child's performance and his or her ability levels.

A formal psychological test battery is administered to those youngsters who have been identified through a child-study team as being suspected of having a handicapping condition which is directly related to their difficulty in reaching success within the general education programme. This evaluation takes place generally not more than once in any three-year period and will include the following:

a review of child-study team information;
psychoeducational test observations and results;
learning/achievement test results;
diagnostic impressions and summary;

recommendations to be considered for use within the classroom setting as well as ideas for consideration by the parent for use outside of the school situation.

Upon the completion of the formal psychological evaluation, a multi-disciplinary evaluation team meeting (MET) is held. At this time, all professional staff who have personal knowledge of the youngster and his or her problem(s) are invited to attend to express their professional opinions as to the child's present level of performance versus his or her expected level of achievement and how this information directly relates to the current educational placement of the child. After the review of all available information, the 'team' then decides the youngster's eligibility for special education services in accordance with the State special education rules and the guidelines of the Intermediate School District.

Certification is based solely on the handicapping condition and its interference with expected performance. Prior to the IEPC, the members of the MET sign a release stating that their findings do not relate the impairment solely to environmental, cultural or economic differences.

An Individual Education Planning Committee meeting is conducted after the multi-disciplinary team meeting; it is here that programme placement and type of services are defined.

Programme services available are determined on an individual basis and must provide for the youngster within the least restrictive environment. Important: certification does not necessarily reflect consistent programme or services across-the-boards.

Range and frequency of services depends on the severity of the handicapping condition and its interference with the youngster's performance in the general education setting. It is here that the specific services offered are enumerated along with a 'schedule' for number and length of sessions.

Special components of the student's programme may become part of the IEPC. This section may include educational opportunities for the child within the general education classroom such as oral tests, taped texts, reduced daily assignments, modified grading system, etc. Duration of service states the time between the initial IEPC and the post-initial meeting where the IEPC is reviewed and if appropriate, revised in accordance with observed progress toward the goals and objectives written for the child. The IEPC services cannot be continued without a review being held at least annually.

District assignment of responsibility states the location (by building) of the programme and the immediate supervisor who insures the implementation of the IEPC as written.

The parent commitment section allows for one of these three responses: agreement with the IEP as written; disagreement with the IEP and a request for a meeting within seven days with the parties involved at the building (district) level; or disagreement with the IEP and a request for due process procedures to be implemented with the possibility of a hearing conducted at the Intermediate School District level.

The post-initial is a review of the original IEPC and generally involves those people directly involved with the youngster on a day-to-day basis. This review is conducted at the end of each school year and its recommendations for continuation of the goals and objectives are implemented in September of the following school year. Once a youngster has demonstrated the ability to be successful in the general education programme with only minimal adjustments being necessary, he or she may be considered eligible for 'exit' from special education. A one year follow-up period is provided in order to assess the student's ability to maintain the necessary skill levels to meet the criterion within his classroom programme. Exit from special education does not disallow involvement in programmes serving youngsters who have deficits in their learning, for if those needs can be met on a continuum with lesser services, support programmes are available (and are strongly suggested) before consideration is given to special education placement or service.

Identification

As we see patterns begin to develop within families, attempts are being made to identify those youngsters who may be considered 'at risk' or 'high risk' individuals. It is becoming clear that a definite need exists to seek out those who due to environment, culture or economic differences may enter the academic arena predisposed to learning difficulties. If these youngsters can be identified early, appropriate interventions can be implemented in an attempt to increase their skills to a close-to-expected entry level criterion.

It is in the area of needs versus eligibility that one finds the most sensitive of professional dilemmas. Altruistically, we as educators understand our moral obligation to undertake the necessary steps in order to satisfy the unique needs of our individual students. Realistically, we are bound by the governing rules and regulations to work with the populations identified as meeting the eligibility requirements of the Special Education Code. The intent of Public Law 94–142 is to service those youngsters who are unable to succeed in general education without supplementary services from special education staff or programmes.

Fortunately, we have available to us government-funded programmes which serve the 'gray area' student, albeit on a less-intense, perhaps less-direct level. There are times however, when we question viability of the available services because periodically we run across a youngster needing more support than one programme is able to offer yet dictates do not allow enrollment with the (seemingly) next available programme on the continuum of services.

The pre-referral process specifically identifies the youngster's weaknesses as perceived by the classroom teacher. It is seen as an essential step in diagnosing a true learning difficulty as opposed to a problem with teaching and learning style incompatibility.

Reporting Progress

In addition to the regular report card, there is a minimum of one parent contact per semester. This documented contact may be either written or verbal.

With regard to card marking for special education students in general education buildings, the responsibility for determining the appropriate 'remark code' or 'scholarship code' rests with either the special education teacher or the general education teacher. Building procedures for entering the marks on the card are directed by the building principal.

In keeping with the mainstreaming philosophy, general education teachers and resource room teachers are encouraged to issues letter grades (A,B,C,D,E) as well as comments using the general education report cards and associated procedures. However, a special education student is usually evaluated in relation to his or her handicap and capabilities. Certain considerations should be included in an evaluation. These considerations are regardless of the student's handicap and include:

1   Attendance. Students in the special education programme are expected to attend school regularly and are expected to adhere to attendance policies (including tardiness).
2   Behaviour. School behaviour standards are expected to be followed.
3   Effort. An honest effort is expected from every student in the programme. Students should attempt to complete all class activities and homework assignments.

If a student meets this criteria but because of a severe handicap cannot meet the most adjusted academic standards, then an alternative grade can be issued ('H' for credit, 'CP' for continuing progress toward IEP goals).

Day-To-Day Operations

'Ownership' — all students should be considered general education students with special education acting as a support service not as a uniquely separate placement.

Meeting individual needs of students is demanding, yet critical to skill development. It does not preclude groups of youngsters; it does require careful selection of groups within a classroom.

Learning centres are quickly becoming more and more popular in the classroom as we see a need for allowing for independent skill development. Following instruction and guided practice, this concept allows for independent student practice and gives the student greater freedom to increase his or her level of expertise.

'Tracking' resurfaces periodically as a way to develop groups of similarly performing youngsters and can be a useful tool in the design of a curriculum as opposed to slotting students in homogenous groupings.

In order to build skills, one first needs to know the youngster's present level of performance ('prior knowledge') which then determines the usefulness of learned and to-be-learned concepts and activities. The transfer of a learned skill to a variety of settings is critical in demonstrating true mastery.

In the area of curriculum modifications, one method that is being implemented in general education classrooms is the cassette taping of highlighted student texts (removing extraneous information from the student text page which has been cross-referenced with the teacher manual) and thus allowing for multi-sensory application (aural-visual).

Team-teaching is also being successfully implemented at all levels and in varying degrees. The team-teaching experience should have a positive evaluation of positive outcome for all involved — the general education and special education students as well as the teaching staff. The term 'team-teaching' precludes joint and shared responsibility for all levels of instruction including planning, preparation of materials, and evaluation. A key role of special education personnel in this venture is to be a support/resource to the presenter — identify through task analysis the critical information to be addressed, assist with the development of multi-sensory methods of instruction, reinforce study skills like note-taking, outlining, test-taking, and devise alternative methods of evaluation of materials presented.

It is vital to teach student responsibility to self. Mainstreaming attempts to break down the barriers that have for so long shielded youngsters in our schools from situations where they were not perceived as able to 'quite belong' — sometimes from even their neighbourhood school! We need to teach the basic academic skills but also among them, socialization, to prepare our students to deal with the world as it is outside of the school environment.

Finally, a word about organization. To insure consistent practices within the department throughout the district, we have found it beneficial to establish a handbook of administrative policies and procedures for special education. As the policies are put into practice, revisions are made accordingly. Sample pages of this handbook are included as Figures 1 and 2. Figure 1 shows the steps to receiving special education services. Figure 2 shows the flow chart for the special education staff.

Figure 1:   Steps to receiving special education services

REFERRAL
Student is suspected of having a handicap

within 10 calendar days

SCHOOL REQUESTS CONSENT TO EVALUATE STUDENT
Principal for Special Education sends notice to parent(s) explaining
parent(s)' rights and requesting consent to evaluate the student.

within 7 calendar days

PARENTAL CONSENT GIVEN TO HAVE STUDENT EVALUATED
(If no response from parent(s) within 7
calendar days, schools may request
a hearing or terminate special
education process).

EVALUATION
School psychologist and other professionals have 30 school days
during which to observe and test the student and to prepare a written report.

PARENTS INVITED TO IEPC MEETING
An IEPC must be held at a mutually agreed upon time and place, not
more than 30 school days from date of parental consent.

INDIVIDUALIZED EDUCATIONAL PLANNING COMMITTEE MEETING
School staff and parent(s) determine student's eligibility and
recommend a programme of services, then write annual goals and short-
term instructional objectives for the student.

immediately

SUPERINTENDENT RECEIVES IEPC REPORT ———┐

within 7 calendar days

PARENT(S) NOTIFIED   SUPERINTENDENT
Superintendent (or his designee) REQUESTS HEARING
informs parent(s) in writing of the Superintendent disagrees
school's intent to begin services. with IEPC recommendation
                                 and asks that a hearing be held.

within 7 calendar days
or receipt of notification

PARENTAL CONSENT GIVEN   HEARING REQUESTED BY PARENT(S)
Parental consent required if   Parent(s) not in agreement with
special education services   school's decision may ask for a
are being provided for the   hearing on the matter.
first time.

within 15 school days   no less than 15, nor more
of parent notification   than 30 calendar days

SPECIAL EDUCATION PROGRAMME   HEARING HELD ┘
OR SERVICES BEGIN   Hearing officer holds pro-
                                 ceedings and reaches decision.

Continued overleaf

215

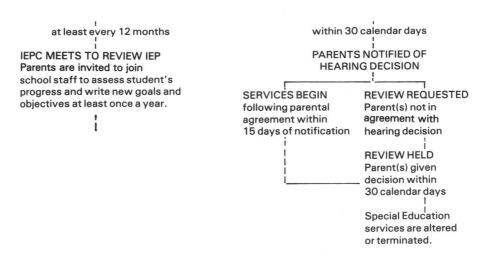

at least every 12 months

IEPC MEETS TO REVIEW IEP
Parents are invited to join
school staff to assess student's
progress and write new goals and
objectives at least once a year.

within 30 calendar days

**PARENTS NOTIFIED OF
HEARING DECISION**

SERVICES BEGIN
following parental
agreement within
15 days of notification

REVIEW REQUESTED
Parent(s) not in
agreement with
hearing decision

REVIEW HELD
Parent(s) given
decision within
30 calendar days

Special Education
services are altered
or terminated.

Figure 2: Flow chart for special education staff

WYANDOTTE BOARD OF EDUCATION

SUPERINTENDENT

PRINCIPAL FOR SPECIAL EDUCATION

TEACHERS OF:	SUPPORT STAFF:	CENTRE
EDUCABLE MENTALLY IMPAIRED	SPEECH	PROGRAMME ADMINISTRATORS
LEARNING DISABLED	SOCIAL WORKER	OF:
EMOTIONALLY IMPAIRED	PSYCHOLOGISTS	TRAINABLE MENTALLY IMPAIRED
PRE-PRIMARY IMPAIRED	PSYCHIATRIST	COUNSELLORS
RESOURCE ROOM	CONSULTANTS	EVALUATORS
WORK STUDY	SECRETARIES	OCCUPATIONAL THERAPISTS/
PHYSICAL VISUALLY IMPAIRED	DEPARTMENT HEAD	PHYSICAL THERAPISTS
HEARING IMPAIRED		SPEECH
OTHERS AS NEEDED		PHYSICAL EDUCATION
		SECRETARIES
		PSYCHOLOGISTS

Chapter 19

Teaching Special Needs Children —
A Comparison of Two Systems

Sharon Crean

Teaching children with special needs is a challenging and continually changing task. Policies and priorities alter from year to year. Many of these changes are completely out of the teacher's control, but some happen due to input and pressure from teachers. Having taught special needs children in the United States (Oregon) and in Britain (Humberside), allows me to see these changes from a different angle. Many of the concepts and terms just recently introduced into the British education system were actually in practice in the United States some ten to fifteen years ago. In this chapter I will discuss the concepts of mainstreaming and least restrictive environment, integration of special needs children in the school situation and into the community, the individual education programme, parental involvement, teaching to objectives and the use of continual assessment procedures. I will also share with you the strengths and weaknesses of these ideas and concepts based on my experiences both in Britain and in the United States.

Mainstreaming: The 'Least Restrictive Environment'?

In Oregon, the policy for mainstreaming followed a concept called the 'least restrictive environment'. Children with special needs were each individually assessed with regard to their ability to cope within the mainstream school. As part of the child's individual educational programme, a 'least restrictive environment' plan was stated. The pupil's strengths and weaknesses were listed in the areas of social skills, academic, mobility, self help, and communication skills. The authority provided checklists and assessments to aid the teacher in this task. Then the pupil's skills were matched to the appropriate activities that were available in the school. This 'least restrictive environment' plan was monitored closely by the teacher, or teachers, involved. There was no point in having a pupil in a classroom situation in which more stress was created for either the pupil or the teacher. The important factor was finding the environment where the child with special needs could fit in, within his or her own limitations. The amount of time each special needs children would spend in the mainstream classes could vary tremendously, since each child and each activity was evaluated separately for its appropriateness.

It is important for local education authorities to inform their teachers about the concept of mainstreaming and to clearly explain their mainstreaming policy. These policies can vary a great deal from one authority to another. Oregon's mainstreaming policy was a cautious one and therefore grew gradually. Many schools initially had one special education teacher in a self-contained special unit on the school grounds. This teacher played a major role in changing the policy into reality.

One of the vital factors that helped the mainstream teachers to accept our special needs children was the willingness to communicate with them. Most of these mainstream teachers had seen the special needs children on the school grounds but could not imagine what or how they were being taught. We invited teachers into our classrooms to see exactly what was going on. In the past the special education teachers had been quite separate from the mainstream school, even though they have had a classroom at the school. We were also employed by a separate section of the authority, not by the head of the school where the special unit was based. In order for our children to be accepted as part of the mainstream school, we, as teachers, had to work hard to become part of the school. Attending staff meetings and sharing in school extra-curricular activities was part of this step towards being accepted into the school 'family'. At times it was difficult since we had our special unit meetings and related commitments to make as well. The slow, gentle approach worked. Gradually more and more teachers made room for our special needs children and were willing to accept our support in the classroom. The policy was not to force mainstreaming on any teacher. This policy of gradual change did work, especially when mainstream teachers knew that the special needs child in their classroom would be given the level of support needed for the child to cope in his or her least restrictive environment. If this level of support is not given, both the children and the teacher will suffer.

The policy of mainstreaming special needs children is bound to be affected by the current trend of financial cuts in local education budgets. This is a concern of many teachers. Some authorities are being challenged by teachers who are asking 'Why are we mainstreaming children?'. 'Is it a way to save money, or is it for the good of the children's education?' One hopes the answer is that it is in the best interest of all children. But the high level of support for these special needs children must continue to exist, even once they join the mainstream school. The needs of children may change but they will not disappear. Mainstreaming of special needs children can be successful but it must be supported with the full backing of the education authority — politically and financially.

Integration: School and Community

Once a policy for mainstreaming special needs children into schools has been decided upon, then the work really begins. Careful planning on how to integrate these children into the school and the community must be done. From what I have experienced in the USA I feel that when special needs children are placed in mainstream schools alongside their peers, they are eventually accepted as part of society. As a child in California, I attended school alongside blind and mentally handicapped children. They attended a special 'room' during part of the day for their special needs. The mainstream children knew these children were 'different' but they were accepted totally as part of the class. Several of our teachers were blind so this just reinforced the fact that handicapped people were just as much a part of society as anyone else. Unfortunately, in Britain there has been a history of keeping these children apart from their peers and society. Too often the special schools are at the edge of the town or in a village. This decreases the number of people in the community that even realize special needs children exist.

Since mainstreaming policies differ from authority to authority I will describe one followed in Oregon and how integration of special needs children takes place. These ideas and the way the problem of integration is approached could be applied in most mainstreaming policies. I will describe ways of planning integration and suggest some activities that could prove successful in starting integration. I will also discuss how volunteers can be used in the school to make integrated activities a success.

The special education policy in Oregon is simply that every child is entitled to an education in their least restrictive environment. This also means that children should be educated in their local school whenever possible. To remove them from their local school is, in a way, restricting the environment since they would (1) have to travel for longer periods in the day, and (2) not be attending school with children from their neighbourhood. Within this framework, provisions are made for most children who are visually impaired, physically impaired and hearing impaired to attend the local neighbourhood schools. These children receive extra input from peripatetic specialists who work either directly with a child or give support to the education teacher to assist in the education of that child. The level of support could vary depending on the needs of that child. If these children cannot cope with the mainstream approach, there are units at certain mainstream schools. These are used for mainly hearing impaired children and deaf-blind children.

The largest group of children with special needs is the one with moderate learning difficulties. In each neighbourhood school there is a unit called the Learning Resource Centre (LRC). This is where the children with moderate learning difficulties receive extra assistance with maths, reading and writing skills. These children are enrolled with a mainstream teacher who is responsible for their education. The Learning Resource Centre teacher assists the mainstream teacher in that he or she designs individual programmes for these children. Some of these programmes are worked on in the mainstream classroom and some in the Centre. The amount of time each child spends in the LRC depends on his or her level of skills, both academically and socially. Some children may spend a few minutes each week in the LRC working on specific skills while others may spend the majority of their time in the LRC working on all skills. All children that attend this Centre go back to their own classes for the less academic subjects; such as physical education, art and social studies.

The group of children who have the most difficulty being accepted as part of the school and the community are the severely mentally handicapped children. In England these children will be the last ones to leave the safety net of the special school. In Oregon, even the most profoundly mentally handicapped children are based in classrooms at a mainstream school. These classrooms, actually self-contained units, are spread around each county. In some counties these units are age-range classrooms but in other counties the units are based on catchment areas. Needless to say, the variety of special needs within each unit is very diverse.

One of the problems of having these children so widely dispersed is that the resources must be spread thinly. In a special school in England that has been purpose built, there may be a hydrotherapy pool, adaptive physical education equipment or other specialized teaching equipment. With the special units spread around the county it is difficult to share equipment such as this. Also, peripatetic staff, such as, physiotherapists and speech therapists must travel more to meet the needs of pupils. Either more resources are needed or one does without.

The other problem of having special units for severely handicapped children in mainstream schools is the isolation that teachers may feel. The teachers of special needs children have teaching problems unique to the mainstream teachers. The special unit teacher may be working out a complex feeding skills programme while his or her colleague is debating which unit of physics to teach. The teachers who work in these special units need to meet with other teachers who are teaching similar children. When I taught severely handicapped children in a special unit, I met twice a month with other teachers working in similar units. We shared teaching programmes, equipment and gave each other necessary support. Also there was one person who supervised these special units giving support and ideas to the unit teachers.

Planning integration activities for severely handicapped children can be quite a challenge. Gaining access for the special needs child into classrooms can be as difficult as climbing Mount Everest. This is where all your hard work of becoming an active member of the school staff should pay off. Hopefully, the education authority will have helped the special needs children to be more easily accepted by providing in-service training for mainstream teachers. The teacher experienced with special needs children should make herself, or himself, available to mainstream teachers to answer questions or concerns they may have. Information shared at an informal level is usually the most revealing. It is during these discussions with colleagues that you will find out which teachers are willing to accept your special needs children into their classrooms. This is the first hurdle in integration — finding the classrooms and activities that are available to severely handicapped special needs children. Once this has been done, the planning of integration can begin, using the following points as a guide:

1   Match each pupil's skills to appropriate activities that are available in the school. Avoid integrating too many pupils into the same activity at the same time.

2   Write an integration plan for each pupil which contains long-term goals for each child and objectives to meet these goals. This will inform everyone involved why the child is being integrated into the specific activity.

3   Plan for assistance from a teacher's aide, a volunteer or an older pupil, where necessary to make the integrated activity a success.

4   Teach the pupils specific skills if they are lacking in skills which are preventing them from involvement in integrated activities.

For special needs children, especially severely handicapped children, it is sometimes difficult finding appropriate activities that will facilitate integration. The following list (Couse, 1977) may give you a few ideas to get some social interactions going between the mainstream and special needs children.

1   Arrange for the special needs pupil to have lunch at the same time as the mainstream pupils. If possible, arrange this so the pupils go at the same time as their own age group.

2   During dinner, sit one or two special needs pupils at tables with other mainstream pupils. (Select children with adequate self-feeding skills to join this activity!)

3   Plan physical education activities with a mainstream classroom. Games such as volleyball can be played with mixed ability children.

4   Integrate individual pupils into physical education classes, once they have acquired skills sufficiently to be actively involved in lessons. Activities such as, swimming, football or badminton could be appropriate.

5   Plan games or activities during breaks and invite other children to participate with the special needs children.

6   Share library time with a mainstream classroom, if your school has the facilities.

7   Arrange for each of the special needs pupils to be 'adopted' by a mainstream classroom and join in that class on non-academic activities such as films, assemblies, school outings, etc.

8   Assign the more capable special needs pupils to a 'homeroom' where they report each morning for attendance, bulletin, etc. They may also be able to go to assemblies and lunch with the class.

9   Invite mainstream pupils into the special needs unit to participate in group activities such as art, music or listening skills.

10   Train mainstream pupils to act as aides in the unit. Arrange specific times and specific programmes in which for them to be involved. These aides can also be used to go with special needs pupils into other classrooms to assist them in integrated activities.

11   Invite teachers to send you a few of their pupils who may need special tutoring in exchange for sending some of your pupils to them for group activities.

When trying to integrate special needs children into the mainstream school activities or lessons, it is important to know which behaviours or skills a child would need in order to be successful in that specific activity. Following an 'integration sequence' can be most helpful in finding out (a) what skills the child will need and (b) if the child's integration activity is a success. A possible integration sequence is listed below.

1   The special needs teacher visits the mainstream classroom to see what type of behaviours and skills are needed for that specific class. One way of doing this is to isolate three pupils and monitor the performance of these pupils during the chosen activity or lesson. The teacher can then make a list of all the skills that are required of pupils in that activity.

2   The special needs teacher and special needs child return together to this mainstream class. The teacher observes the child in the class, using her list of required skills to see how many of these skills the child exhibits.

3   If the child has any major skills deficits, the special needs teacher then designs a teaching programme to teach these skills.

4   After learning these new skills necessary to the mainstream activity, the special needs child can be integrated into the activity. The child may need maximum support at this time. That is, a teacher or aide may need to stay with the child in the classroom throughout the activity.

5   The process towards independence can now begin. The level of support for this special needs child should gradually change. This support could change from full-time support, to periodic checks during this activity, to occasional observations from the doorway, to leaving the child completely unattended.

6   When the child is capable of attending the mainstream activity independently, the teacher then only needs to make random visits to the classroom to observe the child. These visits are to ensure that the child is managing to cope with the activity and to see if there are any new skills that may be needed to continue his successful integration. The list of skills needed for this activity can now be used to show the progress made by the special needs pupil.

Integration of children who were, at one time, kept separate from their peers may take a long time to occur fully. These special needs children have been kept away from their local school, so it will take time for them to be accepted as part of it. In Oregon, special needs children have been attending local schools for many years now. Because of this, they are now accepted as part of the community. They go to the same school as their neighbours. The children interact socially in their natural environment and learn that not everyone is the same. Unfortunately, in England most of the special needs children still attend special schools. This must change for the benefit of the community. Once special needs children attend school alongside their peers they will begin to become accepted as part of the community. Children need to grow up being exposed to all types of people — which would naturally include all types of handicapped people. These more aware children will, in turn, become adults who will be more understanding members of the community.

I will never forget an episode that happened years ago while I was teaching in Oregon. Two schools had merged to form a middle school of which my special needs unit for severely mentally handicapped children became a part. Therefore, half of the children at this new school were not used to being with children as handicapped as mine. There was one boy, a large boy for his age, who was the school 'bully'. I noticed him teasing several of the special needs children at break time. So I decided to have some 'chats' with all the children in the mainstream classes. I talked to them about what we did in our classroom and the different needs these children had. I invited these children, in small groups, to come into my classroom to play games with the special needs children. After this, the bully became very involved with my class and made sure that no one ever bothered them again. Many of the mainstream children became so interested in what we were doing that we had a very busy classroom, full of children from all over the school

Many of the suggestions for the integration of special needs pupils involve the use of mainstream pupils as aides or helpers in the classroom. If handled correctly, the use of these pupils can be a real advantage to the classroom teacher and to the children involved. It is important to spend time training mainstream pupils who wish to 'help' with the special needs children. This is especially important if they will be working with severely handicapped children or children with sensory handicaps. Spending time explaining various types of handicapping conditions that the children in the special unit have, helps the pupils to understand their needs better. It is also important to explain clearly what you want your pupil helpers to do. This should be written down in a teaching programme so the pupil knows what he or she is expected to do and also what is expected of the special needs child. Each teaching programme should be explained, and demonstrated if possible, to the pupil helpers. Their ability to run individual programmes needs to be monitored closely as well. This can be done by observation and by using simple forms for recording individual programmes. It may be helpful to give each pupil helper a handout to remind them of their role and explain what is expected of them as helpers with special needs children. The table below gives some ideas for the handout (Proulx, 1979). It could be appropriate for either pupil helpers or volunteers from the community.

Sometimes the use of pupil helpers can create problems. This is why it is important to train them and monitor what they are doing closely. In several schools in which I have worked, the pupil helpers are themselves pupils who have learning difficulties. Using these low achievers can be very successful. For once in their lives they are better at a skill than someone else. Older children who are having reading difficulties can help younger special needs children by listening to them read. The older pupils get additional

Table 1. *General Information for pupil 'helpers' or volunteers working with special needs children*

Do	DON'T
1 Ask questions about anything you want to know or need to know in order to do the teaching programme successfully.	1 Don't let the pupil run the programme by what he will, or will not do. You are running the programme.
2 Be enthusiastic and show interest in the special needs pupil with whom you are working. Be a friend.	2 Don't forget to read the directions before working with the pupil.
3 Keep your recording sheets and equipment organized and put them away when finished.	3 Don't interrupt a teacher who is in the middle of running a programme with another pupil except in an emergency. Ask your questions later.
4 Read thoroughly the directions in each programme you run and collect equipment needed. These directions and equipment will change as the pupil improves in the skill.	4 Don't forget that the purpose of a teaching programme is to teach the pupil new skills which can allow him more independence. Don't foster dependence by doing things for him that he is capable of trying for himself. It may be quicker or more convenient to do it yourself, but we are not here for convenience.
5 Be consistent in what you do... following the programme 100 per cent even if you are tired or rushed. Ask for help if you need it.	
6 Be objective when you work with a pupil. We need to know what he *does*, not what anyone thinks he can do or might do under different circumstances. Record *exactly* what the pupil does during the programme time.	5 Don't mother the pupils. Give them as much freedom as they can handle. They need your patience and objectivity. They all have loving parents.
7 Give suggestions for changing programmes or starting new ones.	
8 Get help immediately if the pupil has a seizure or becomes unmanageable. If this is a possibility you will be informed beforehand so you will know what to expect.	

practice in reading by assisting the less able child. In the past I have often been asked by a teacher to take pupils with social problems and train them as helpers in the special needs class or unit. These pupils come with many problems of their own. Many of them see no reason to be at school and have serious home-based problems. Generally, I have found that even these disaffected pupils will respond well to becoming trained helpers. This may be because they have a different role as helper or that they feel they are needed. Of course, there will be failures in using pupils as helpers but I feel it is worth giving any pupil who shows an interest, or willingness, a chance to try.

Assessing and Stating Special Educational Needs of Children

The education of special needs children has been strongly affected by laws that have recently been passed. This is the case both in Britain and in the USA. All teachers in Britain are aware of the 1981 Education Act and the procedures it lays down to assess children with special needs. The 1981 Act states that education authorities must find out what help is needed by children who are having difficulty in school. When the needs are known, the right help must be given. Once this statement of needs is made for a child, and the child is getting the help stated, a review is written each year. This annual review will describe the child's progress over the past year and confirm whether or not the extra help the child is receiving is appropriate. Parents are also asked for their views as part of the review.

The procedures for assessing and stating the special educational needs of children in the USA are similar yet different. The law, Public Law 94–142, has four basic principles. The first principle is that schools must actively seek out handicapped or special needs children. They also must provide free multi-disciplinary testing and evaluation procedures to identify the special needs of each child. No one test or single procedure will suffice. The second principle of the law is that the special needs child must be placed in the least restrictive environment that suits his or her special needs. When appropriate services are not available, the local education authority must create them or pay for the child to attend school elsewhere. The third principle of Public Law 94–142 is that an individualized educational programme must be written for each child. The parents are requested to take an active part in the preparation of this plan, along with the mainstream teacher or special education teacher or both. Often other professionals are asked to contribute as well. As in the UK this programme is reviewed annually. The fourth principle of this law is that parents have the right to appeal if they disagree with the diagnosis, placement or instruction given to their child. Procedures vary from state to state but the usual appeal procedure is an informal hearing, then a formal hearing at the local authority level, then a formal hearing at the state level.

As you can see the procedures for stating the needs of these special children is very similar in both countries. The major difference is in the development and the monitoring of the individualized programme for the child. In Britain the annual review is written by the teacher or the professional most closely involved with the child. It is written as a report of what the child has attained over the past year. This is then shown to the parents and progress made by the child over the past year is discussed. In the US, the review is written using behavioural objective terms to state what the child will be working on in the coming year. Long-term goals and short-term objectives to meet those goals are written out clearly in behavioural terms. Each one of the long-term goals is discussed with the parents and agreed on before it can be included in the child's individualized programme. Then when this programme is reviewed in one years time, it is easy to ascertain if progress has been made. An important point to make here is that the individualized programme is not considered to be a contract so the teacher is not legally responsible if the child does not meet all of his or her long-term goals.

Individualized educational programme (IEP) formats vary from state to state but all must list the child's current skills, set out specific goals for the year and detail the services that will be provided. Because the IEP states the long-term goals and short-term objectives for each child, the IEP is the actual day-to-day working document used by the teacher. It is not filed away and brought out once a year. The IEP is referred to frequently and updated when skills are learned and amended, with parental approval, if new objectives or goals need to be added. In this way, it serves as an evaluation device to show progress as well as a form of communication between parents and teachers.

Parental involvement is an important factor in the education of special needs children in the US. As was stated previously, the parents are encouraged to actively participate in the development of the IEP. Each objective set out for their child for the year is discussed with them. Obviously, the classroom teacher has objectives in mind, or even written out, before the IEP meetings but parents must agree with these objectives before they can be accepted as part of that child's individualized programme. If parents feel strongly about a specific skill they wish their child to attain, this will be included, if it is a realistic goal.

Another significant difference between the annual review and the IEP used in the US is the inclusion of a section titled 'Parent Involvement/Training'. Written out on the IEP form is a space for an objective or activity required of the parent. Each parent is asked to become involved in some way with their child's education. Depending on the child's needs and the parents themselves, these objectives vary greatly. Some parents choose to work on specific skills for a certain amount of time each week. Other parents might be encouraged to spend five minutes each day playing with their child. If parents are not very interested in their child's education, they might be encouraged to visit the classroom one time each term. As a teacher, I found this parental involvement section most helpful. It gave me a lever to get certain unwilling parents actively involved with the special needs of their child. Since this objective or activity was reviewed along with the child's progress at school most parents felt obliged to carry it out. The parents behaviour was being monitored as well as that of their child.

Teaching Special Needs Children

Once the child's special needs have been assessed and stated, then the task of how to teach that child begins. The teacher who has written out the child's needs in behavioural objective terms will be at an advantage at this point. A programme to teach to these objectives can be easily set up. In Oregon, where I worked, all teachers are required to write an individualized programme for each objective included in the child's IEP. These programmes are written in small sequenced steps towards each teaching objective and show day-to-day progress made by the child.

Information on the child's progress with each programme is collected daily or weekly, depending on the task or activity. This information shows the teacher if the child is progressing or not. If the child is not making progress, then the programme must be changed to meet the needs of that child. Often teachers become frustrated when a child fails to learn a specified skill. The teacher asks 'How can I get through to this child? Am I a failure as a teacher?' However, if changes in the teaching programme are made — a step added, the amount of prompting changed, or the reinforcement strengthened — the child will make progress. The following flow chart for individual instruction (Anon, 1977) is helpful to follow when trying to decide whether changes need to be made in the teaching programme.

When writing individualized programmes it is easier if a specific format has been designed for teachers to follow. In Britain the National Portage Association has a specific format for its home visitors to follow when writing objectives and teaching programmes. Most schools are now tackling this problem as well. When I began teaching in Britain the schools where I worked had no such format. I had become so used to teaching using sequential teaching programmes that I began writing my programmes in a format very different from the other teachers at this school. The headteacher was supportive of my 'new' approach so I was given the freedom to do this.

There are specific components that each individualized programme needs to have. First and most important is a clearly stated long-term objective. This must be stated in observable and measurable actions. It is helpful to ask questions when writing objectives: Who is doing what, under what conditions, and to what degree of success. Once the objective is stated then comes the task of breaking this down into a sequence of easy-to-learn steps, or short-term objectives. For each sequential step towards the long-term objective it is important to include specific instructions on how to teach each step. After deciding on a long-term objective I generally include the following components for each step of the individualized teaching programme:

1	Procedures	— This includes what you are going to do to teach this skill. It will include what materials you need to use and where the instruction will take place.
2	Prompts	— This includes any prompts used by you, the teacher, in teaching the specific skill to the child. Prompts can be verbal requests, imitation, or physical assistance.
3	Correct response	— This is the behaviour or skill that you are expecting of the child. It can also be called the short-term objective.
4	Consequences	— This is what happens when the child responds to the task, either correctly or incorrectly. If correct, the child would receive some form of reinforcement (praise, tickle, star). If the child is incorrect, procedures need to be followed to help that child learn the skill. This might be the teacher giving the correct response and repeating the step with the child. It also could be giving complete physical assistance through that step.
5	Criteria	— This includes how many times the child is to do the task and what degree of success is expected. This can be stated as a percentage, or over a period of time, or out of a certain number of attempts.

By breaking each step into these components you can clearly see the sequence of what you are teaching. It is important not to change too many of the components in one step at one time as this can confuse the child.

The advantage of teaching using individualized programmes which include the above components is that you are keeping a close eye on the child's progress. You are continually monitoring this progress every time you run the programme. If for some reason, the child stops showing progress, you can change the components of that step one at a time, until the child is successful. The disadvantages of using detailed individualized programmes is that it can be very time consuming. It does create paperwork. One solution to this problem is that teachers can pool their ideas and the programmes they write. We did this where I worked in Oregon. Teachers were able to draw ideas from one another. Once a programme had been written to teach a specified skill, all teachers received a copy. Often, with minor changes, this programme could be used with another child who was trying to achieve the same objective. I feel that the advantages of using individualized programmes for specific objectives outweigh the disadvantages. The benefit of being able to continually monitor and assess the progress of each child is important if you are to meet the special needs of that child.

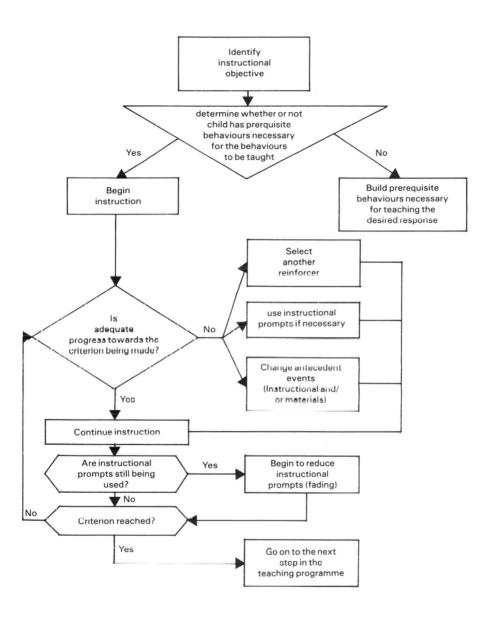

Figure 1: A flow chart for individual instruction

Conclusion

Special education is a constantly changing field. It is important for teachers to be aware of what is happening outside of their own school. In these tight financial times it is often impossible for teachers to visit other schools with similar problems to their own. With increasing demands on teachers, it is also difficult to find time outside of school hours to share with other teachers. So, we must resort to books and articles in newspapers or magazines to keep abreast of what is happening in the field of special needs. Through resources as these, teachers can gain new ideas, or gain the confidence to try something different in their approach to teaching. I hope you have found this chapter useful and that it has played a part in the process of teachers sharing thoughts and ideas.

Notes on Contributors

Derek Baker is a former teacher of Moselle School (MLD) in the London Borough of Haringey. He is currently Manager, Education Support with responsibility for special needs at Apple Computer UK. His teaching experience includes comprehensive schools, a residential special school (EBD), and day special schools (PhH). He also taught in Canada at an elementary school and on undergraduate education courses. Following teacher training at St Luke's College, Exeter, he read for his MEd (Educational Administration) at the University of Alberta, and has the Advanced Diploma (Special Needs) of the University of London.

His interests include the management of change, and the use of microcomputers in special education as both a learning and administrative tool. He has contributed to a number of conferences and special needs courses and for two years has been a tutor at the Cambridge Special Education Summer School. In recent years he has visited Sweden and the United States to give presentations and to observe their 'special provision' in action.

Keith Bovair is currently headteacher of the Lady Adrian School, Cambridge, for children with moderate learning difficulties; born Detroit, Michigan, 1949; Graduate of the University of Michigan, BSc in Special Education, Distinction, 1975; taught children with emotional and behavioural difficulties Ferndale High School, Ferndale, Michigan (received a Community Mental Health Award for programme); moved to England in 1977; teacher in charge, Intermediate Treatment Unit, Sheffield, 1977–1980; headteacher, residential school for emotionally impaired, Tyne and Wear, 1980–1984; Visiting Schoolteacher Fellow, Department of Education, University of Cambridge, 1989. The Lady Adrian School received the Schools Curriculum Award for 1987.

John V. d'Abbro is presently head of the Sedgemoor Centre for children experiencing emotional and behavioural difficulties. He has previously taught in a residential school for emotionally behaved/disturbed boys, in schools for children with moderate learning difficulties and initially taught in mainstream schools. He has recently completed an honours degree in special education.

Robert Ashdown PhD (Wales), has worked as a teacher of pupils with severe learning difficulties in this country and for two years in British Columbia, Canada as a teacher of children with language disorders. He is headteacher of St Luke's School, Scunthorpe and at the time of writing he was headteacher of the Rees Thomas School, Cambridge. Both schools cater for pupils with severe learning difficulties.

Dr Peter Avis is Director of Resource Organization, Doncaster, Director of the Micro-Electronics Project, Doncaster and an active member of CET. He was previously a head of department in a secondary school in Derbyshire. Apart from his national reputation in the Information Technology field in Great Britain, he has lectured internationally on IT.

Norman Butt is presently Principle Adviser — Special, Cheshire; previously he was an adviser to mainstream secondary schools. He was a lecturer at the West London Institute and taught in secondary and primary schools, running a MLD unit. He was an adviser remedial teacher in Staffordshire and head of a large remedial department in Cyprus for the Service Children Education Authority. He has written several articles on behaviour modification, specific reading difficulties, sequential reading, Doman Delacato, whole school approaches and in-service training for special needs.

Mike Conquest was previously deputy head of Beverley Grammar School and currently seconded to the Humberside LEA to develop pupil assessment procedures.

Jim Crawley has taught in secondary modern, comprehensive, EBD residential, PH, MLD and SLD schools. He has been deputy head in three residential schools and is currently a deputy headteacher in a day MLD school in a London borough. He is completing his MSc in Psychology of Education.

Sharon Crean is presently supervisor to the Humberside Portage Service. She was born and educated in the United States. She received her Masters degree from Portland State University, Oregon in the field of the education of the mentally handicapped. She taught in Multnomah and Jackson County, Oregon for over six years in special units for severely mentally handicapped children. Moving to England, she has been teaching severely mentally handicapped children in Humberside since 1982.

Kathleen Devereux has an MA — Child Psychology (Leeds), and has been closely involved with children with special needs over the course of many years — as teacher, senior educational psychologist and tutor at the Cambridge Institute of Education. She is now continuing her commitment to this field in retirement and is an active member of the National Council for Special Education.

Stan Forster has been head of Crowthorn School, Edgworth, Lancashire which is a non-maintained residential special school catering for up to a hundred children who are experiencing learning, social and emotional problems. It is funded by NCH, a national child care charity. Prior to this, he was head of Dartmouth, a secondary EBD school. He was a member of the working party responsible for the compilation of Problem Behaviour in Primary Schools, and Coventry Education Committee SNAP training course. He has had extensive experience teaching children with special needs since 1969, teaching in assessment centres, residential social work in a community home and as a principal of Stoke House, a mixed assessment centre which incorporated a regional secure unit. Under his leadership, peripatetic assessment in the child's own home and community was pioneered.

Patricia Keogh since 1985 has been coordinator of the Heltwate School Mainstream Support Service. She has been a teacher at Heltwate School, Peterborough, a school for children with moderate learning difficulties, since 1978. Previously she has been a psychiatric nurse and is currently studying for an MA in Applied Research at the Cambridge Institute of Education.

Helen King born Wyandotte, Michigan; attended Eastern Michigan University obtaining BSc — Special Education; received MEd at Marygrove College, Detroit, Michigan. She is certified to teach learning disabled and emotionally impaired children; taught one year in Detroit Public Schools, in Wayne County Intermediate School District. Since 1974 she has taught for Wyandotte Public Schools, first with the trainable mentally retarded (1974–1979), then learning disabled and emotionally impaired (1979–1987) and since 1987 she has been a teacher consultant.

Deirdre Leach since 1982 has been head of Forteviot In-patient Unit of the Department of Child and Family Psychiatry, Edinburgh. She obtained an Open University honours degree in Psychology during this time. She was originally trained in Primary Education and taught an infant class for several years in Edinburgh. Her professional interests are cognitive therapy, family therapy and social skills training.

Sean McCavera left school at 16, went to Mid Herts College of Music — understudy of John Railton, Choral Conductor; attended Trinity and All Saints College, University of Leeds, BEd — History. He has taught in inner city comprehensives before moving into special schools and now is at Moselle School, MLD, Haringey, London.

Dr Murray Morrow Jr is presently director of special education, Wyandotte Public Schools, Wyandotte, Michigan; he began as a teacher in special education for Wayne County Intermediate School District and prior to his present position, he was programme administrator for Wyandotte Public Schools.

Graham Pirt is headteacher at Riverside School in Humberside. Most of his teaching career has been spent in special schools; both day and residential. Having completed a BA in Psychology and an MEd researching self-concept in pupils in special education he has spent the last few years attempting to widen the use of micro-electronics in schools for the benefit of both pupils and staff but particularly in relation to curriculum development and recordkeeping.

Andy Redpath has taught in comprehensives and a special school for children experiencing emotional and behavioural difficulties. He is currently headteacher of the Moselle special school in Haringey for children with moderate learning difficulties.

Leslie J. Rowsell is presently headteacher of Critchill School, Frome in the county of Somerset. The work of the school includes developing a Special Needs Support Centre, offering material and training support to the local educational community. Critchill school is one of six such support centres within Somerset. After eleven years working in Secondary Comprehensive schools in the North of England, he moved into the special sector in 1981. During his career as a teacher he has studied and undertaken research at both Leeds and Bristol Universities leading to an Advanced Diploma in the education of children with learning difficulties and a Masters Degree in Educational Management.

David R. Smith since 1984 has been head of Heltwate School, Peterborough, a school for children with moderate learning difficulties. Previously he has been a deputy head of Marshfields School (MLD) and has taught in primary and secondary sectors. He has worked for a total of twenty years in the field of special education. He has also been actively involved in Youth Work and the Duke of Edinburgh Awards Scheme.

Brian Steedman has recently established a support service for primary schools in Waltham Forest. He has taught in special schools for both children experiencing emotional and behavioural difficulties, and moderate learning difficulties.

David Stewart is presently responsible for the physical education programme at the Lady Adrian School, Cambridge, a school for children experiencing moderate learning difficulties. Previously he was a teacher and assistant teacher of boys PE at an 11–16 community college in Cambridge. He has written several articles on delayed motor development and is currently completing a book on this subject for Falmer Press.

Mike Swift has had eighteen years experience of teaching special needs children. After six years in mainstream education as a specialist remedial teacher he has worked in special schools for both moderate and severe learning difficulties. At present he is deputy head of Southall School, Telford.

Aileen Webber is presently in charge of the Physically Disabled Pupils Unit at Impington Village College, Impington, Cambridgeshire. Previously she was a teacher at the Roger Ascham School, Cambridge, working with children who were physically disabled. She has experience running a Remedial Department at a junior school in Essex, as a volunteer at Midfield Assessment Centre, Cambridge and is currently completing a four year therapy training course.

Diane Wilson is head of John Watson School, Wheatley, Oxford. Since 1967 the school has developed from a Junior Training Centre for Mentally Handicapped Children into a school which houses the local integrated nursery and which provides some time in local schools for almost all of the children. She was educated at Bacup and Rawtenstall Grammar School and began her work with children at Brockhall Hospital near Blackburn.

Mike Wright Cert Ed, Dip Ed, MED, is currently Senior Special Needs Adviser in Humberside. Previously after some twenty years experience as a teacher and headteacher in a variety of day and residential schools he was seconded to Sheffield Polytechnic as Lecturer to the SEN Diploma course. He has worked as SEN adviser in two local education authorities and held honorary positions as Lecturer or Lecturer Fellow at Sheffield Polytechnic, Bretton Hall College and St John's College, York. He has been involved in the organization and delivery of a variety of local, regional, international and DES courses and conferences. He has had a number of articles published over recent years.

Bibliography

ADAMS, M. (1987) 'Measurement Problems in Applied Music Therapy Research' *British Journal of Music Therapy*, 1, 2.

AGROTOU, A. (1988) 'A Case Study: Laura' *British Journal of Music Therapy*, 2, 1.

AINSCOW, M. and MUNCEY, J. (1981) *Small Steps*, Coventry LEA, Drake Educational Associates.

AINSCOW, M., MUNCEY, J. and FORSTER, S. 'A Way Forward', unpublished.

AINSCOW, M. and TWEDDLE, D. (1979) *Preventing Classroom Failure: An Objectives Approach*, Chichester, Wiley and Sons.

AINSCOW, M. and TWEDDLE, D. (1984) *Early Learning Skills Analysis*, Chichester, Wiley and Sons.

AINSCOW, M. and TWEDDLE, D. (1988) *Encouraging Classroom Success*, London, Fulton Press.

ANON (1977) 'A Flow Chart for Individual Instruction', STEPS Jackson County Education Service District.

ASHDOWN, R. W. (1985) 'Teaching receptive vocabulary to children with severe learning difficulties' *Special Education: Forward Trends*, Vol. 11, No. 1, Research supplement, pp. 23–26.

ASHDOWN, R. W. (1988) 'Teaching basic concepts to pupils with severe learning difficulties' unpublished manuscript.

BAKER, D. and BOVAIR, K. (1989) *Making the Special School Ordinary?*, Models for the Developing Special School, Volume One, Lewes, Falmer Press.

BECK, A. T. (1976) *Cognitive Therapy and the Educational Disorders*, New York, International Universities Press.

BOOTH, T. (1983) *Integrating Special Education*, Blackwell, Oxford.

BRENNAN, W. (1982) *Changing Special Education*, OUP Milton Keynes.

BRENNAN, W. (1985) *Curriculum for Special Needs*, Open University Press, Milton Keynes.

Central Advisory Council for Education (Newsom Report) (1963) *Half our Future*, HMSO.

CHARLTON, T. (1985) 'Locus of control as a therapeutic strategy for helping children with behaviour and learning problems'. *Maladjustment and Therapeutic Education*, Vol. 3, No. 1.

CHESELDINE, S. E. and JEFFREE, D. M. (1982) 'Mentally handicapped adolescents: A survey of ability' *Special Education: Forward Trends*, Vol. 9, No. 1, Research Supplement, pp. 19–23.

Circular Number 5, (1989) National Curriculum Council.

Circular 6/89, Department of Education and Science.

CLEMENTS, J. (1987) *Severe Learning Disability and Psychological Handicap*, John Wiley and Sons, Chichester.

COLE, T. (1986) *Residential Special Education*, Open University Press, Milton Keynes.

COULBY, D. (1984) 'The creation of the disruptive pupil' in LLOYD-SMITH, M. (Ed.) *Disruptive Schooling, the Growth of the Special Unit*, John Murphy Publishers Ltd, London.

COULBY, D. (1986) 'Intervention in Classrooms' *Association for Child Psychology and Psychiatry*, Vol. 8, No. 12.

COULBY, D. and HARPER, T. (1981) *DO5: Schools Support Unit Evaluation*, London, ILEA.

COUSE, P. (1977) *Integration Techniques*, Douglas County Education Service District and Oregon Mental Health Division.

CRUICKSHANK, W. (1986) *Disputable Decisions in Special Education*, University of Michigan Press.

DENO, E. (1970) 'Special Education as Development Capital', *Exceptional Children*, November, pp. 229–37.

DES, (1978) *Special Educational Needs* (The Warnock Report), Cmnd 7212.

DES (1981) Education Act 1981, HMSO, London.

DES (1987) *Special Education Needs: Implementation of the Education Act (1981)* HMSO, London.

DES (1988) Education Reform Act 1988, HMSO, London.

DES and Welsh Office (1988) *Mathematics for ages 5 to 16: Proposals of the Secretary of State for Education and Science and the Secretary of State for Wales*, HMSO, London.

DESSENT, T. (1984) 'The Resource Stretch', in BOWERS, T. (Ed.) *Management and the Special School*, London, Croom and Helm.

DESSENT, T. (1985) 'Supporting the mainstream. Do we know how?' *Educational and Child Psychology*, 2, 3, pp. 52–60.

DESSENT, T. (1987) *Making the Ordinary School Special*, Lewes, Falmer Press.

DEVEREUX, K. and VAN OOSTEROM, J. (1984) *Learning with Rebuses: Read, Think and Do*, National Council for Special Education, Straford-upon-Avon.

DUNCAN, A. (1978) *Teaching Mathematics to Slow Learners*, Ward Lock Educational, London.

FISH, J. *Equal Opportunities For All*, HMSO, London.

FITZWILLIAM, A. (1988) 'An Assessment of the Benefits of Micro Technology in Music Therapy' *British Journal of Music Therapy*, 2, 1.

FORD, J. MUNGON, D. and WHELAN, M., (1982) *Special Education and Social Control. Invisible Disasters*, Routledge and Kegan Paul, London.

FRIED, E. (1978) *100 Poems Without a Country*, London, John Calder Press.

FULLAN, M. (1982) *The Meaning of Educational Change* OISE Press, Ontario.

GALLOWAY, D. (1985) *Schools, Pupils and Special Educational Needs*, Croom Helm, London.

GAMMAGE, P. (1982) *Children and Schooling, Issues in Childhood Socialization*, Allen and Unwin, London.

GEARHEART, B. R. (1980) *Special Education for the 80's*, St Louis, London.

GETZEL, L., and GUBA, E. G., (1957) 'Social Behaviour and Administrative process' *School Review* No. 65, Winter, pp. 423–41.

GILLHAM, B. (1987) *A Basic Attainments Programme for Young, Mentally Handicapped Children*, Croom Helm, London.

GOULD, S. J. (1981) *The Mismeasure of Man*, W. W. Norton and Company Inc.

GREEN, R. T. and LAXTON, V. J. (1978) *Entering the World of Number*, Tames and Hudson, London.

GUBA, E. G. and STUFFLEBEAM, D. (1968) *Evaluation: The Process of Stimulating, Aiding and Abetting*, Columbus Ohio, Ohio State Evaluation Center.

GUNZBERG, H. C. (1963) *Progress Assessment Charts*, London, National Association for Mental Health.

HALLMARK, N. (1983) 'A Support Service to Primary Schools', in BOOTH, T. and POTTS, P. *Integrating Special Education*, Blackwell, Oxford.

HALLMARK, N. and DESSENT, T. (1982) 'A Special Education Service Centre: Special Education', *Forward Trends*, 9, 1, pp. 6–8.

HARGREAVES, D. (1982) *The Challenge for the Comprehensive School: Culture, Curriculum and Community*, Routledge and Kegan Paul, London.

HARGREAVES, D. (1984) *Improving Secondary Schools*, Inner London Education Authority, London.

HEGARTY, S., POCKLINGTON, K. and LUCAS, D. (1981) *Educating Children with Special Needs in the Ordinary School*, NFER - Nelson, Windsor.

HITCHCOCK, D. H. (1987) 'The Influence of Jung's Psychology on the Therapeutic Use of Music' *British Journal of Music Therapy*, 1, 2.

HODGSON, A., CLUNES-ROSS, L. and HEGARTY, S. (1984) *Learning Together — Teaching Pupils With Special Educational Needs in Ordinary Schools*, NFER-Nelson, Windsor.

HMI (1978) *Behavioural Units*, Department of Education and Science, London.

ILEA (1985) Educational Opportunities for All? Report of the Committee Reviewing Provision to Meet Special Needs (The Fish Report), ILEA, London.

JACKSON, B. and MARSDEN, D. (1986) *Education and the Working Class*, Cy Institute of Communities Studies Ark Paperbacks, Routledge and Kegan Paul.

JACKSON, S. (1983) *The Education of Children in Care*, SSRC, London.

JAMIESON, J. D. (1984) 'Attitudes of educators toward the handicapped', in JONES, R. L. (Ed.) *Attitudes and Attitude Change in Special Education: Theory and Practice* (pp. 206–22) Reston, Va, Council for Exceptional Children.

JENSEN, F. (Ed.) (1982) *C. G. Jung and Toni Wolff*, San Francisco, The Analytical Psychology Club.

JOHNSON, D. W. and JOHNSON, R. T. (1986) 'Mainstreaming and Cooperative Learning Strategies' *Exceptional Children* No. 52 (6) pp. 553–61.

JONES, A. and ROBSON, C. (1977) 'Language training the severely mentally handicapped' in ELLIS, N. R. (Ed.) *Handbook of Mental Deficiency: Psychological Theory and Research*, Lawrence Erlebaum, Hills Dale, New Jersey.

JONES, A. and ROBSON, C. (1979) 'Do we ask the right questions?' *Special Education: Forward Trends*, Vol. 6, No. 1, pp. 11–13.

KIERNAN, C., REID, B. and GOLDBART, J. (1987) *Foundations of Communication and Langauge: Course Manual*, Manchester University Press and the British Institute of Mental Handicap, Manchester.

KIRK, S. (1972) *Educating Exceptional Children*, Second Edition, Houghton, Mifflin.

KNOFF, H. M. (1985) 'Attitudes toward mainstreaming: A status report and comparison of regular and special educators in New York and Massachusettes', *Psychology in the Schools*, 22, pp. 411–18.

KOVACS, M. and PAULAUSKAS, S. (1986) 'The Traditional Psychotherapies', in QUAY, H. C. and WERRY, J. S. (Eds), *Psychopathological Disorders of Childhood, 3rd Edition*, Wiley and Sons, New York.

LANE, D. (1986) 'Promoting Positive Behaviour in the Classroom' in TATTUM, D. *Management of the Disruptive Pupil*, Wiley, London.

LAWRENCE, D. (1973) *Improved Reading through Counselling*, Ward Lock, London.

LEEMING, K., SWANN, W., COUPE, J. and MITTLET, P. (1979) *Teaching Language and Communication to the Mentally Handicapped*, Schools Council Curriculum Bulletin No. 8, Evans/Methuen Educational, London.

LEVITT, E. E. (1957) 'The results of psychotherapy with children: an evaluation' *Journal of Consulting Psychology*, 21, pp. 89–96.

LIEBECK, P. (1984) *How Children Learn Mathematics*, Penguin Books, Harmondsworth.

LIEBERMAN, L. M. (1984) *Preventing Special Education for Those who Don't Need it*, Gloworm Publications, London.

LLOYD-SMITH, M. (1984) *Disrupted Schooling: The growth of the Special Unit*, John Murphy Publishing Ltd, London.

MATHEY, P. and TRIPPE, M. (1977) *Professional Staff Development Needs of Classroom Teachers for Maintreaming — Some Frequently Overlooked Issues*, a paper presented at Downriver/Dearborn Learning Center, Michigan.

MERCER, J. R. (1973) *Labelling the Retarded*, Berkley, University of California Press.

McCONKEY, R. and McEVOY, J. (1986) *Count Me In*, Video course produced by St Michael's House, Dublin.

McPHAIL, P. (1978) *Moral Education in the Middle Years*, Longman, Harlow.

McPHAIL, P. (1982) *Social and Moral Education*, Blackwell, Oxford.

MITTLER, P. (1985) 'Integration: The Shadow and the Subbstance', in *Educational and Child Psychology*, Vol. 2, 3.

MYLES, B. S. and SIMPSON, R. L. (1989) 'Regular educators' modification preferences for mainstreaming mildly handicapped children, *The Journal of Special Education*, Vol. 22, No. 4/89.

NOLAN, C. (1988) *Under the Eye of the Clock*, Pan Books Ltd., London.

NORDOFF, P, and ROBBINS, C. (1975) *Music Therapy in Special Education*, MacDonald and Evans, London.

OCEA (1988) Oxford Certificate in Educational Achievement, University of Oxford.

O'HANLON, C. (1988) 'Alienation Within the Profession: special needs or watered down teachers? Insight into the tension between the ideal and the real through action research', *Cambridge Journal of Education*, Vol. 18, No. 3.

PERLS, F. GOODMAN, P. and HEFFERLINE, R. (1951) *Gestalt Therapy: Excitement and Growth in Human Personality*, Dell Publishing Compant, New York.

PETERSON, R. F. (1973) *Teaching Functional Mathematics to the Mentally Retarded*, Charles E. Merrill Publishing Company, Columbus, Ohio.

PROULX, B. (1979) 'Volunteer Training', STEPS, Jackson County Education Service District.

RAFFE, D. (1986) 'The content and context of Educational Reform', in RAGGART, P. and WIENER, G. (Eds) *Curriculum Assessment some Policy Issues*, Pergamon Press, Oxford.

Rectory Paddock School Staff (1983) *In Search of a Curriculum*, (2nd Edition), Robin Wren Publications.

RICHER, J. (1979) *Human ethology and mental handicap'* in JAMES, F. E. and SNAITH, R. P. (Eds) *Psychiatric Illness and Mental Handicap*, Gaskell, London.

RIDER, C. and KEOGH, P. (1982) 'Extending the Portage Model' in CAMERON, R. J. (Ed.) *Working Together*, NFER, Windsor.

ROBBINS, B. (1988) *MATHSTEPS: Learning Development Aids*, Wisbech, Cambs.

ROBINSON, G. and MAINES, B. (1988) 'They Can Because . . .', *Workshop Perspectives no. 3*, Association of Workers for Maladjusted Children.

ROBSON, C. JONES, A. and STOREY, M. (1982) *Language Development through Structured Teaching: ' Minicourse for Teachers of the Mentally Handicapped*, Video-course produced by Drake Educational Associates, Cardiff.

ROGERS, R. (1986) *Guiding the Professionals*, CSIE Publications, London.

RUSSELL, P. 'Special Action', 28-10-88, *Times Educational Supplement*.

SARASON, T. and DORIS, J. (1979) *Educational Handicap, Public Policy and Social History*. Collier Macmillan, London.

SCHOSTOK, J. F. (1983) *Maladjusted Schooling*, Falmer Press, Lewes.

SCHULZ, M. (1987) 'Stereotypic Movements and Music Therapy', *British Journal of Music Therapy'*, 1, 2.

SIMON, H. A. (1944) *Decision Making and Administrative Organization*, reproduced in MERTON, R. K., GRAY, A. P., HOCKEY, B. and SELVIN, H. C. (1952) *Reader in Bureaucracy*, The Free Press, New York.

SNELL, M. E. (1983) (Ed.) *Systematic Instruction of the Moderately and Severely Handicapped*, (2nd Edition), Charles E. Merrill Publishing Company, Columbus, Ohio.

STRANGE, J. (1987) 'The Role of the Music Therapist in Special Education', *British Journal of Music Therapy*, 1, 2.

SWANN, W. and MITTLER, P. (1976) 'Language Abilities of ESN(S) Children' *Special Education: Forward Trends*, Vol. 14, No. 4, pp. 273–285.

THOMAS, G. (1986) 'Integrating Personnel in Order to Integrate Children' *Support for Learning*, Vol. 1, No. 1, Feb.

TOMLINSON, S. (1982) *A Sociology of Special Education*, Routledge and Kegan Paul, London.

TOMLINSON, S. and BARTON, L. (1984) *Special Education and Social Issues*, Croom Helm, Beckenham, Kent.

TOPPING, K. (1983) *Educational Systems for Disruptive Adolescents*, Croom Helm, London.

WATERHOUSE, P. (1983) *Supported Self Study — A Handbook for Teachers*, Council for Educational Technology, McGraw-Hill, Maidenhead.

WHELAN, E. and SPEAKE, B. (1978) *Learning to Cope*, Souvenir Press, London.

WIIG, E. H. and SEMEL, E. M. (1980) *Language Assessment and Intervention for the Learning Disabled*, Charles E.Merrill Publishing Company, Columbus, Phio.

WILSON, J. (1967) *Introduction to Moral Education*, Penguin, Harmondsworth.

Wizard of Oz (1939), MGM.

Wyandotte Special Education, (1988) 'Administrative Policies and Procedures', Wyandotte Public School District, Wyandotte, Michigan, USA.

Index